*The French Revolution and
Enlightenment in England*

The French Revolution and Enlightenment in England
1789–1832

Seamus Deane

Harvard University Press
Cambridge, Massachusetts
London, England

1988

10   9   8   7   6   5   4   3   2   1

This book is printed on pH-neutral paper, and its binding
materials have been chosen for strength and durability.

Library of Congress Cataloging in Publication Data

Deane, Seamus, 1940–
    The French Revolution and Enlightenment in England, 1789–1832 /
Seamus Deane.
       p.   cm.
    Bibliography: p.
    Includes index.
    ISBN 0-674-32240-1 (alk. paper)
    1. English literature—French influences.   2. English
literature—19th century—History and criticism.   3. English
literature—18th century—History and criticism.   4. France—
History—Revolution, 1789–1799—Literature and the revolution.
5. Enlightenment.   6. England—Intellectual life—19th century.
7. England—Intellectual life—18th century.   8. Philosophy in
literature.   I. Title.
PR129.F8D4   1988   88-1243
820'.9'358—dc19   CIP

For Marion

Acknowledgments

This book could not have been written without the help and encouragement of many people. In particular I would like to thank Ian Jack of Pembroke College, Cambridge, and Charles Parkin of Clare College, Cambridge, for their advice and generosity in the early stages of my research. Paul Rees, now of Manchester University, was of more help than he could have realized. I simply listened and learned from his conversation. Many other friends have wittingly or unwittingly helped me in a variety of ways, particularly Roy Park of University College, Oxford, Donald Low of Stirling University, Carl Dawson of the University of New Hampshire, and Robert Shackleton of Brasenose College, Oxford. Helen Vendler of Harvard University kindly read the finished manuscript; her help and encouragement were invaluable. Of the many friends upon whose time and patience I drew, I would like particularly to thank Thomas Kilroy of University College, Galway, and Seamus Heaney of Harvard University. It is difficult to specify in what ways they helped but impossible to exaggerate the value of their friendship and support. Most of all I have to thank my children, Conor, Ciaran, Emer, and Cormac, who lived with this for so long, and my wife, Marion, who must have wondered at times at her own patience. As a token of my own wonder and gratitude I dedicate this book to her.

Contents

The French Revolution and Enlightenment in England

Introduction

The French Revolution profoundly affected the reception and interpretation of the French Enlightenment in England. The aim of this book is to demonstrate how that happened. There are two main narratives. One concerns the various intellectual relationships which a range of English writers developed with their French predecessors or counterparts: the debt owed by Godwin to Holbach and Helvétius or by Shelley to La Mettrie and the nature of Coleridge's confrontation with Rousseau are examples. The other narrative concentrates on the English reaction to both the Enlightenment and the Revolution, showing to what extent that reaction was governed by Edmund Burke and ultimately how it led to an enhanced definition of English national consciousness in this period. The narratives interconnect at many points, for the question of what the Revolution meant was bound up with the question of what specifically French characteristics had made it what it was. To see the Revolution as an essentially French phenomenon allowed it to be understood as alien to English circumstances and inclinations. Seeing it thus also helped to deny it the universal claims which it repeatedly made for its basic doctrines.

Thus what the English thought of the French was a reflection of what the English thought of the English. That was true before the French Revolution; it remained true after it, but in a different sense. The definition of the English and of the French national character became an integral part of the contemporary analysis of both the Revolution and the Enlightenment. Before 1801 it was routine to claim that the Enlightenment had directly caused the Revolution, either as the result of a deliberate conspiracy or as the consequence of the subversive effects of radical thought on the political system. A good deal of the comment provoked by the French Revolution was governed by the fear that its effects on the English political system would be cataclysmic. Much of it was based on a very scant knowledge of what was actually happening in France and on an even scanter knowledge of the relationship between these events and the writings of the great French intellectuals. The relative poverty of information was not in itself as damaging to the counter-Revolutionary case as it might seem, for the positive purpose of the anti-French reviews, books, and pamphlets was to describe the specific virtues of the English way of life and to demonstrate that it was the natural product of the English national character and English history. France therefore provided a useful contrast in highlighting what was distinctive about England's experience and its constitutional and cultural forms. In the early years of the Revolution it was tempting to compare the relatively peaceful English revolution of 1688 with the increasingly sanguinary character of 1789 and to derive from that a detailed account of the essentially stable and traditional features of the English system.

The consolidation of a national consciousness inevitably involved a discussion of the great questions of political liberty, ideological commitment, and betrayal. For the most part these questions were dealt with in concrete terms. Since part of the hostility to France had its source in a dislike of the abstract and doctrinaire quality of French thought, English commentators were obliged to refer their arguments to particular circumstances in order to avoid the errors for which they criticized the French. Burke was the great exemplar in this regard, although even he was willing to embark on sententious descriptions and definitions of liberty, despotism, and the foundations of a humane political and social system. It was he who taught a whole generation that support for or opposition to the Revolution was much more than a political choice; it was in effect a choice for or against humanity itself. Those who supported it betrayed the primary affections which the Revolution, in Burke's view, was determined to destroy. Correspondingly, William Hazlitt saw the repudiation of the Revolution and support for the Holy Alliance as a betrayal of the greatest cause that mankind had ever faced. Those who—like Sir James Mackintosh, Wordsworth, Coleridge, and Southey—had changed their allegiance were particularly vulnerable to the charge of betrayal, not only from others but from themselves. The remorse which was often a consequence of this conflict was understood as a punishment for the initial "crime," a strange transference of a concept which had once been central to the arguments of the early penal reformers, who argued that a criminal would be more effectively punished by remorse than by being broken on the wheel.

The division between those who supported and those who opposed the Revolution was predictably sharp; but the arguments they deployed are dictated by questions raised in the 1790s, and they share that common ground. The Burkean group, which includes Mackintosh, Croker, Southey, Wordsworth, Carlyle, and many others, envisaged the Revolution as the culmination of a great conspiracy, led by intellectuals who had gained control of the press, to overthrow all that was sacred and traditional. English society had to be mobilized to confront that challenge by demonstrating the superior advantages of the older, less doctrinaire, and more humane political and moral structures which had evolved from the distant past. The radical group, dominated by Godwin, Shelley, and Hazlitt, welcomed the Revolution but wondered where it had gone wrong, why it had been so bloody, what lessons its failure represented for the future. They dismissed the straightforward version of the conspiracy theory, but they did query the ways in which ideas could become political realities. For Hazlitt, the whole of the Revolution in its benign aspects was contained in the writings of Rousseau. Those who admired the thinkers of the Enlightenment were more able and willing to discriminate between their various contributions, whereas the antirevolutionaries tended to lump them all together in one condemned group, ignoring completely the various disputes that had driven them, and very often ignoring the generations that separated them.

The material for investigation in this field is so vast that I have had to be selective in organizing it. Blake is omitted because he has already received ample treatment. Byron's relation to the questions raised is too slight; Bentham, by contrast, would deserve an entire separate study. The central emphasis here is on literary figures. Other emphases would reveal new aspects, but the reception of the French Enlightenment and Revolution in England is essentially a literary and cultural story. It continued throughout the nineteenth century but had its origins deep in the eighteenth century. In the decades surveyed here, it passed through a critical transformation. England created a series of images of France which then produced countervailing images of England. It was a complex but singular process, part of the half-known, half-ignored literary history of the time.

1 Burke and the Enlightenment

The publication of Edmund Burke's *Reflections on the Revolution in France* in 1790 compelled those who took part in the subsequent political debate to declare, in however elementary a fashion, the principles of their political beliefs.[1] The kaleidoscopic changes taking place in France did not make their task any easier. Under such conditions there was inevitably a great deal of confusion and contradiction; positions were taken only to be later abandoned, and the charge of political apostasy was leveled at some of the most eminent men of the time.[2] The Whigs, who had initially greeted the Revolution with pleasure and condescension as the belated counterpart of 1688, visibly wavered in their support as the Revolution took its astonishing course. Many were repelled by the extremism and unfamiliar language of men like Thomas Paine. The glee and increased boldness with which other radicals greeted French successes irritated some and worried others.[3] The position of a man like Sir Brooke Boothby, who disagreed with Burke and yet also regarded many of Burke's opponents with distaste, is typical of the position in which moderate reformers of the period found themselves.[4]

The Revolution polarized British politics to an unprecedented extent. In a country where party lines had by no means run deep, profound ideological differences suddenly appeared. Yet the overwhelming support for the government in the country at large[5] ensured that this division would not seriously affect the political structure itself or, later, the administration of the war. The radical pamphleteers were defeated in the political debate because their arguments conflicted with the established sympathies of the population, especially when these had been awakened by the shock of a national war with France.[6] The more moderate reformers of the period managed to survive the hysteria and repressive legislation of the decade and transmitted to the next

century the rudiments of bourgeois liberalism—but they escaped political annihilation by an uncomfortably narrow margin.

More than anyone else, Burke was responsible for the incorporation
into the public debate of the names and reputations of the chief thinkers of the French Enlightenment. By picturing them as a band of atheistic conspirators who deliberately plotted revolution against throne
and altar, or as a group of impious and shallow authors who unwittingly cleared the way for it and were therefore at least morally responsible for its excesses, he created a climate of hostility toward them
which persisted in extreme form until 1802. His opposition to the
French intellectuals was of long standing, but it was in the anti-Revolutionary writings of his last seven years that he finally formulated
the grounds of his hostility toward the philosophes and Rousseau.[7]

The strategy of the attack Burke launched in the *Reflections* is simple
but effective. Voltaire, Helvétius, and others are singled out as rep-
resentatives of a dessicated and impersonal form of rationalism, while
Rousseau is represented as the standard-bearer of a new and diseased
subjectiviy and emotionalism, expressing itself in the thirst for novelty
and the endless display of Vanity. These mentalities, although different, are in alliance, according to Burke, in a double conspiracy. The
first—not taken seriously now but then passionately believed in by
many—is the conspiracy against Christianity and civil order in Europe.
The second, less of a chimera, is the union of professional authors
and the urban bourgeoisie against the landed aristocracy and the
peasant culture. Burke saw correctly that the victory of this combine
would lead to the surrender of the theistic, hierarchical order to the
secular democratic state. It is not surprising therefore that the only
thinker of the French Enlightenment whom Burke praises is Montesquieu. His panegyric to Montesquieu, the admirer of the British Constitution, is part of Burke's long, involved argument against the radical
spirit of the French Enlightenment. Voltaire, Helvétius, Condorcet,
and, less frequently, D'Alembert and Diderot are characterized as superficial, frivolous, shallow, given to scandalous levity, and entirely
bereft of that dignity and seriousness, that depth of learning and moral
gravity, which Burke associated with the classical historians and such
contemporaries as Montesquieu. The thought of such modern sciolists
lacks any moral dimension; it is concerned with symmetry, not with
men. Its object is not truth but originality and novelty, features irrelevant to the art of politics, the material of which, human nature,
is unchanging.[8] When political solutions which have nothing to do
with political circumstances are being proffered, then the system which
breeds such speculation must be in disrepair. People are not interested

in political theory when they are happy: "The bulk of mankind, on their part, are not excessively curious concerning any theories whilst they are really happy; and one sure symptom of an ill-conducted state is the propensity of people to resort to them."[9]

The connection between the prevalence of abstract speculation about political matters and the onset of social dissolution was made by Burke as early as 1756 in his *Vindication of Natural Society*, where he blames the innate frailty of human nature, which refuses "to compound with our condition,"[10] for its love of perfect theory. Thirty-four years later he intensifies the attack, finding that the application of a closed system, pure and complete in itself, to the illogical complexity of human affairs is an appropriate analogy for the French revolutionaries' attempts to construct a government on a priori grounds. The constant repetition of words such as *system, abstract, cold,* or *formal* in close relation to one another enables Burke to attribute to both philosophes and revolutionaries a common mentality, thereby insinuating a natural link between them. This would of course extend to their followers in England. The radical factions in England and France "are always considering the formal distributions of power in a constitution: the moral basis they consider as nothing. Very different is my opinion: I consider the moral basis as everything."[11]

The Family and the Cabal

The question of "the moral basis" of Burke's political thought has long been pursued.[12] In the context of his reaction to the French Enlightenment and Revolution, it is helpful to view this issue in the light of the conspiracy thesis by which he condemned them both. For in doing so he was compelled to define, or at least describe, the specific virtues of the civilization threatened by the French, to enhance its attractions, and to provide an explanation for its superior grace and durability.

A great deal of the power of the *Reflections* and the subsequent anti-Revolutionary writings derives from the designedly elaborate structure and texture of a style which declares the virtues of complexity in the brilliant formality of its own maneuverings as well as in the substance of its arguments. This is the high style of the ancien régime, gloriously intricate, Ciceronian and Senecan by turns, a display of the riches of an inherited tradition, and a remarkably effective contrast to the bluntness of the democratic style of Paine or Priestley.[13] The bare bones of their theoretical writings are nakedly exposed in comparison to the pleated quotations, references, imagery, subsidiary modifications, and periodic deferments of Burke. His consistent invocation of *King Lear* as a tragedy dominated by the themes of unnatural cruelty and subverted authority and by the imagery of man stripped of both his clothes and his dignity is only one of the best-known instances of Burke's precision in the accumulation of powerful traditional references.[14] Similarly, the association of images drawn from arithmetic, geometry, gambling, alchemy, and chemistry is exploited to emphasize the common theme of degradation and to link that with the metaphysicians, closet philosophers, sophisters, economists, speculators—all the insulting synonyms for revolutionaries and philosophes.[15] But these and other rhetorical strategies are themselves governed by a sovereign antithesis—that between the family, represented by the French Royal Family of Louis XVI, Marie Antoinette, and their son, the Dauphin, and the cabal, represented by the philosophes and their terrorist descendants, the Revolutionary mob. Cabal, mob, and family are the social and political constellations in the turbulent sky of contemporary France. It is Burke's purpose to demonstrate to England the disaster presaged by the first two and the order symbolized by the last.

It would be possible within the *Reflections* alone to show how the famous apostrophe to Marie Antoinette, with its liturgical and historical undertones, gathers within it all the grieving innuendoes of spoliation, rape, degradation, and stripping which thereafter haunt the whole work.[16] In the larger context, however, it is the idea of a general conspiracy to undermine established institutions which gives Burke's late writings their contemporary appeal and force, and enables him to establish a link between the influence of the philosophes and that of Rousseau. Despite the well-publicized differences between them, they have in Burke's portrayal a common interest: the destruction of traditional affections as a prelude to political revolution.

It was impossible to ignore Rousseau's influence but difficult to associate it with that of Voltaire and the Encyclopedists. The dispute between Rousseau and Voltaire, however, gave Burke the opportunity he needed. He cites David Hume as saying that Rousseau, perceiving that the conventional ways of arousing wonder had been exhausted, decided to produce new effects in his audience with the extravagance of his theories about politics and morals.[17] There is in consequence a readily identifiable difference between his speculations and those of the philosophes, who consciously strove to have their symmetrical, geometric schemes put into effect. Rousseau invented his to make a stir in the world; outlandishness, not practicability, was their chief feature. Thus he is the last person in the world to be taken seriously as a political thinker or mentor. Yet it is precisely because Rousseau was not a member of an organized group that Burke regards him as an ominous and dangerous figure. In his solitude, brooding on his individual self and experience, Rousseau created a new theory of sentiment, or, more accurately, found a novel way of corrupting normal human feeling. That corruption Burke christens Vanity: Vanity refers only to the self; normal feeling refers also to others. Vanity makes a fetish of eccentricity, valuing it to the degree that it differs from received wisdom and thereby gains attention for itself. It gives personal impulse priority over common sentiment and gives the notion of individuality the prestige which the philosophes, in their more directly political manner, would give to individualism. The extremism of feeling which Burke believes to be at the heart of Rousseau's conception of individuality is even more dangerous than the extremism of reason, which is the characteristic of Voltairean individualism. Vanity is the worse form of decay because it attacks affection:

> In a small degree, and conversant in little things, vanity is of little moment. When full grown, it is the worst of vices, and the occasional mimic of them all. It makes the whole man false. It leaves nothing sincere or trustworthy about him. His best qualities are poisoned and perverted by it, and operate exactly as the worst. When your lords had many writers as immoral as the object of their statue (such as Voltaire and others) they chose Rousseau; because in him that peculiar vice, which they wished to erect into a ruling virtue, was by far the most conspicuous.[18]

Vanity, raised to the dignity of a theory by Rousseau, becomes benevolence. In a passage which is the counterpart to the apotheosis of Marie Antoinette and the French Royal Family, Burke mounts a savage *ad hominem* argument against Rousseau. The apostle of universal benevolence abandoned his illegitimate children on the steps of a Parisian orphanage. This is the plainest proof, in Burke's eyes, of the intimacy between selfishness, licentiousness, and cruelty, especially when they have been disguised in the form of a seductive theory.

> Benevolence to the whole species, and want of feeling for every individual with whom the professors come in contact, form the character of the new philosophy. Setting up for an unsocial independence, this their hero of vanity refuses the just price of common labour, as well as the tribute which opulence owes to genius . . . and then he pleads his beggary as an excuse for his crimes. He melts with tenderness for those only who touch him by the remotest relation, and then, without one natural pang, casts away, as a sort of offal and excrement, the spawn of his disgustful amours, and sends his children to the hospital of foundlings.[19]

The vehemence of Burke's attack on Rousseau's corruption of feeling

indicates how important he believed true affection to be for the preservation of traditional society. Once the Rousseauistic contagion has
entered into family life, it spreads to teachers and children;[20] the ped-
agogues of "sound antiquity" are supplanted by the "gallants" of
Paris, who corrupt "a set of pert, petulant literators" and are supported
in their betrayal of "awful family trusts," perpetrated by the sexual
seduction of their female pupils. Under the influence of such teachers,
"debauchers of virgins," taste and elegance decay. Above all the passion of love, hitherto central to the old European code of chivalric
honor, is debased into lust and sensuality. Denied all its historic and
affective appeal, love becomes nothing more than the expression of
physical desire; the tender and complex sexual relationship is reduced
to eroticism and becomes finally obscene.[21]

The betrayal of the affections which bind both family and society
together, manifested in Rousseau's abandonment of his bastard children, in Louis XVI's degraded and precarious existence, in the corruption of the Dauphin by his tutor Condorcet,[22] is the most telling
feature of the new order inaugurated in France. The family of Marie
Antoinette, travestied by the Voltairean cabals, by Rousseau's
wretched treatment of his own children, and by the Revolutionary
mobs led by women,[23] is the central image which binds the *Reflections*,
Letter to a Member of the National Assembly, and *Thoughts on French Affairs*
into a composite account of Burke's defense of affection against the
subversions of the Enlightenment and the attacks of the Revolution.

Rousseau's corruption of natural affection was matched by the philosophes' denial of religion. After his visit to France in 1773 Burke
returned to denounce atheism in a speech in the House of Commons.[24]
Atheists, he claimed, are never to be tolerated because their creed
denies the existence of the divine foundation on which human society
rests. To choose atheism is to choose to leave society. A group of
atheists has, therefore, no civil existence. Its members are outcasts.
The weakness which makes men atheistic is the traditional sin of pride,
the belief that the world and human existence are amenable to the
force of reason. The individual will, forgetful of common wisdom,
demands that society conform to the theories it has generated and
which it comes to regard as objectively true. It stifles all feelings for
what actually exists in its eagerness to demonstrate what it believes
should exist.[25] Affection diminishes as respect for theory increases.
The revolutionaries are right only "if the constitution of a kingdom
be a problem of arithmetic."[26] Atheists are thus as naturally inclined
to unfeeling behavior as are practitioners of benevolence; the difference
is that the atheist regards feeling for others as a threat to the exercise
of objective reason, while the benevolist feels for others on principle

but not in fact. One preaches the virtues of reason, the other of feeling as a system. It is their reverence for system which disqualifies them as political thinkers.

Little of this is unique to Burke, although the application of his attack on self-styled experts and connoisseurs of feeling is fiercer than anything since Swift. Burke believed too that the contagion of the doctrine of false feeling, which could be explained by its superficial attractiveness and by the seductive power of Rousseau's writings, was accompanied by the spread of atheistic ideas, for which the only explanation seemed to be the existence of a successful conspiracy. Both the solitary outsider, Rousseau, and the outcast band of atheists were winning followers throughout Europe. The proselytizing activities of the writers who supported these positions were so effective that Burke believed Europe had been destroyed by a "literary cabal."[27]

Burke confirms his view of the Revolution as the successful achievement of alienated groups bonded together in a conspiracy when he compares the Revolution to the Reformation. The point of similarity between them is that each imported into the various countries of Europe interests *"other than those which arose from their locality and natural circumstances."* The atheist, who belongs to no state, is beyond loyalties and affections. He is the first cosmopolitan. All Burke's historical parallels for the Revolution are examples "of that species of faction which broke the locality of public affections, and united descriptions of citizens more with strangers, than with their countrymen of different opinions."[28] Here we see the convergence of the atheistic cosmopolitan with the Rousseauist disciple of benevolence. Their natural alliance is not with those close to them but with strangers. Atheism and benevolence are forms of ideological solidarity, identical in their rejection of local and traditional affections; they are the characteristic beliefs of alienated people. That is why such people are prone to prefer alien to home-bred connections.

The *Reflections* contain all the elements of the conspiracy theory which was to have such a vogue several years later. The elements are clearly specified: the existence of an atheistic cabal, fired by a proselytizing spirit and in command of the press, is the necessary prelude to the attack on established authority and its central symbol, the Royal Family: "The literary cabal had some years ago formed something like a regular plan for the destruction of the Christian religion. This object they pursued with a degree of zeal which hitherto had been discovered only in the propagators of some system of piety. They were possessed with the spirit of proselytism in the most fanatical degree; and from thence, by an easy progress, with the spirit of prosecution according to their means."[29] No single source can have given Burke the idea of such a widespread conspiracy. He could have heard much of it at his home in Beaconsfield, where he later received so many émigrés, including the Abbé Barruel.[30] It is also likely that Pitt manipulated the Treasury newspapers to exploit the panic about a conspiracy.[31] Furthermore, the appearance in 1790 of Thomas Holcroft's translation of the posthumous works of Frederick the Great, containing within its thirteen volumes his correspondence with Voltaire and D'Alembert, emblazoned by the iterated war cry "Ecrasez l'infame," helped to convince the public of the reality of the charge. Burke seems to have read the Abbé Barruel's *History of the Clergy during the French Revolution* in the original French about 1794,[32] thereby anticipating the Abbé's greatest fame, which came with the translation in 1797–98 of his *Memoirs Illustrating the History of Jacobinism* in four turgid, widely read volumes. Barruel gives Voltaire the central role in organizing a conspiracy of philosophes, Freemasons, and southern German Illuminati with the frequently avowed aim of overthrowing Christianity in Europe.[33] The first volume of these *Memoirs* contains a quotation from a letter Burke had sent Barruel;[34] another part of the same letter was used in the preface to an abridged version of the *Memoirs* by Robert Clifford, Barruel's translator, in which Burke remembers his visit of 1773 to Paris: "I have known myself, personally, five of your principal conspirators; and I can undertake to say from my own certain knowledge, that so far back as the year 1773, they were busy with the plot you have so well described, and in the manner and on the principle you have so truly represented.—To this I can speak as a witness."[35]

In 1797, the last year of his life, Burke thus publicly associated himself with the most ferocious and absurd of all the versions of the conspiracy thesis. In the same year there was further support from an Edinburgh professor, John Robison, who dedicated his treatise on the great conspiracy to Burke's close friend William Windham.[36] All of this coincided with the nadir of England's fortunes in the war. The effect on the public consciousness was deep and lasting. Burke was the dominant figure in impressing upon the general public the belief that the philosophes were impious, conspiratorial, and guilty, at least by proxy, of the crimes of the Revolution. It was not until 1802, when Francis Jeffrey reviewed Jean-Joseph Mounier's refutation of the conspiracy thesis in the first article in the first number of the *Edinburgh Review*, that popular belief in it was challenged.[37] Until then it was difficult to find any description of English or British society which did not emphasize the privileged position of family life and affections and contrast this with the spurious feeling or inhuman want of any feeling characteristic of the factions and cabals which had caused or controlled the society of Revolutionary France.[38]

The Counterrevolutionary Response

An essential element in Burke's defense of the English system was the claim that the English had remained and would remain loyal to their ancient traditions because these were in conformity with the requirements of human nature. From there it was a short step—quickly taken—to the further claim that the English, unlike the French, had a national propensity toward the natural. Native common sense gave the English an advantage over the vain, fickle, brilliant, frivolous French.[39] It did not trouble him unduly to decide whether the English tradition of liberty had formed the national character or whether the national character had formed the tradition of liberty. The interrelationship between the two mattered more than the priority of one over the other. English history illustrated the national character; national character was an embodiment of English history. Therefore the contrast between 1688 and 1789 was as telling as the contrast between the English and the French treatment of dissenting intellectuals.[40] Reverence for religion, respect for tradition, affection for the places and people of one's locality, sexual fidelity, reluctance to change, contempt for fashion, suspicion of brilliance, a sober dullness—these were the well-known English virtues, for every one of which the French had a corresponding vice. Even here there was a sexual differentiation: the French character was at root effeminate, the English manly. Much of this was traditional fare in the eighteenth century. In fact Burke gives as one of his sources John "Estimate" Brown's *Estimate of the Manners and Principles of the Time*, written to chastise the English for their debility and effeminacy under the Pelham administration during the Seven Years' War.[41] Burke's adaptation of this stereotype in the anti-Revolutionary writings of the 1790s was so effective that it amounted to little less than the canonization of the figure of John Bull, the quintessence of English steadfastness and xenophobia. The potential of such a figure for counterrevolutionary propaganda was fully realized in, for instance, the pamphlets of John Reeves's Association for Preserving Liberty and Property against Republicans and Levellers.[42]

Although he was willing to stress the beneficent sluggishness of the national character, Burke was also eager to galvanize it out of its customary sloth in the defense of "the old cause."[43] He included other traditional distinctions in his crusade against the Revolution. The standard contrast between the energy and instability of town life and the slow peace and security of rural existence was transformed into a battle between the enterprising vigor of urban Jacobinism and the staid calm of rural "property." Jacobinism is, after all, "the revolt of the enterprising talents of a country against its property."[44] Many variations are played on this theme. The "vanity" of the urban intelligentsia is opposed to the dutiful anonymity of the rural peasant;[45] the volatile fury of the urban mob is contrasted with the steady permanence of the rural community;[46] Paris, the great city, drains rural France of its vigor and then proceeds to dismember it on geometric principles which take no account of traditional divisions or natural features of the landscape.[47] Therefore the old system, if it is to survive, must be stimulated by an energy and conviction comparable to that of the Jacobins.[48] The natural sluggishness and timid inertia of property must be overcome.[49] Men must act out of a sense of the glory of the cause they are defending rather than from mere "melancholy duty."[50] Burke is demanding that the traditional society become conscious of its own nature in order to defend itself more effectively. His writings are conceived as an attempt to realize in articulate form what had until then been inarticulately at peace and unthreatened. This is his version of the other conspiracy—that of enterprise against property. He gives to property the voice which the philosophes had given to bourgeois enterprise.

The British Constitution was of course a standing rebuke to the symmetrical models of the French constitutional experiments and an expression of the national character.[51] In defining its indefinable fitness within the general providential order of things, Burke was glad to call on Montesquieu's support, even though it might be felt that, being French, Montesquieu would have been incapable of appreciating an institution so British. (In fact his appreciation was based on a misreading of the separation of powers he believed to see in it.)[52] Montesquieu was not French in the new sense. He was a member of that European civilization to which the old France had been central, and in the attempted destruction of which the new France was the missionary power. Burke's reading of the French national character is in effect a reading of modern French history. The country of Bossuet and Montesquieu belonged to the old European order; that of Voltaire and Rousseau, deriving from the decadence of the French Regency period, belonged to the modern world. Although this view of France is only lightly sketched by Burke, it initiated the fashion, adopted by later writers such as Coleridge, Cobbett, and Hazlitt, of explaining the rupture made by the Revolution as the culmination of a process begun long before, whereby an integrated culture had been broken down by the pressure of intellectual traditions which emphasized selfish individualism and the supremacy of reason over communal values and the preservation of traditional affections. Although Burke only adumbrated this view in relation to France, he was more detailed in his description of the beginnings of this process of degradation in England, led by the radical Dissenters Price, Paine, Priestley, and others. Jacobinism had formed itself into a nucleus in England dominated, as it had been in France, by a cabal of gifted intellectuals and propagandists whose disaffection had been universalized into a theoretical attack on the existing state of things. The conspiracy theory of the French Revolution was linked to a general theory of cultural degradation. The application of each to France was sufficiently striking; but the application of both to England was terrifying. The radical Dissenters, as the vanguard of the philosophes in England, inevitably bore the brunt of the fear generated by these accounts of contemporary history.[53]

"National Love"

A good deal has been made of the importance of Burke's close connections with Ireland and with the peculiar stresses induced by his Irish Catholic background.[54] The psychological effects of his heritage are a matter of speculation, although they must have been as real then as they are now elusive. There is nonetheless tangible evidence of the influence of Ireland on his thought in his writings on Irish affairs, in the congruence between these and his commentary on the French Revolution.

In the first place there was, as an established part of the Anglo-Irish intellectual tradition, a long-standing debate about the dangers of freethinking and the corresponding virtue of supporting traditional normative values. Swift was of course the most brilliant exponent of the advantages of the "common forms"[55] over the crazed, if logically coherent, theories of projectors, experts, and speculators. In fact much of what he says in A Tale of a Tub about the extremism of Roman Catholic reasoning and the extravagance of Puritan emotionalism and enthusiasm was adopted by Burke in his contrast between the systematic reasoning of the Voltairean philosophes and the bogus sentimentality and benevolence of Rousseau and his disciples.[56] Burke's debt to Swift is great, but it is largely drawn from the most traditional materials in Swift's work, those homiletic and apologetic attitudes and techniques which can be found in the writings of the seventeenth-century divines.[57] Although each adapted these to the circumstances of his own time, the persistence of such features in their writings is, more than anything else, a mark of their innate conservatism and their alertness—unsurprising in their Ireland—to the implications for modern politics of the previous century's religious disputes. In other words, Burke's attack on the impractical theorizing of the philosophes was of a piece with the long series of attacks made on fanaticism—mostly of the Puritan kind—since the days of the Cambridge Platonists. He was very much an Anglican in this respect. Anglicanism had learned from Richard Hooker the polemical art of offering itself as the *via media* between two extremes. Burke saw the English character and Constitution in the same light, but his emphasis on local affections as the basis for the social and political system was derived from a different source.

In the Second Treatise of Francis Hutcheson's *Inquiry into the Original of Our Ideas of Beauty and Virtue* (1725), a work deeply indebted to Shaftesbury's *Characteristics of Men, Manners, Opinions, and Times* (1711), there is an attack on the effects of sectarianism on man's capacity for universal benevolence. Those who "cantonise men into several sects for the defence of very trifling causes," who "love the Zealots of their own sect" for the "Fury, Rage and Malice against opposite sects,"[58] impair moral feeling by providing an apparent justification for treating others as less than human and ratifying the most cruel and despotic behavior. The bearing of these remarks on the Irish situation is inescapable: the Penal Laws against Catholics and the coincidence of religious persuasion with political power or the lack of it made Ireland the most glaring example of that species of factionalism which perverts benevolence and damages those natural affections nourished in us by our earliest association with places and people. Faction breeds despotism; benevolence breeds freedom. This is an early version of the Burkean theory of local affections, "that narrow scheme of relations" which binds us to the "little platoon"[59] of society into which we are born:

> Here we may transiently remark the Foundation of what we call national love, or Love of one's native country. Whatever Place we have liv'd in for any considerable time, there we have most distinctly remark'd the various affections of human nature; we have known many lovely characters; we remember the associations, friendships, familys, natural affections, and other human sentiments: our moral sense determines us to approve these lovely dispositions, where we have most distinctly observ'd them; and our benevolence concerns us in the interests of those persons possess'd of them. When we come to observe the like as distinctly in another country we begin to acquire a national love towards it also; nor has our own country any other preference in our Idea, unless it be by an association of the pleasant ideas of our youth, with the Buildings, Fields and Woods where we receiv'd them. This may let us see how Tyranny, Faction, a neglect of Justice, a corruption of Manners, and anything which occasions the Misery of the subjects, destroys this national love and the dear idea of a country.[60]

It is, I suggest, from this Irish source that Burke received the basic elements of his political theory of the affections. It is also from his Irish experience that he learned to give that theory priority, because Ireland, ruled by a sectarian faction, deprived of the benefits of the British Constitution, was an exemplary instance of the instability bred by hatred. He knew of Catholics judicially murdered;[61] he knew bigotry and fanaticism in power; and he therefore saw a direct link between the Protestant Ascendancy in Ireland and Jacobinism in France. True benevolence of the Hutchesonian rather than the Rousseauistic type could not survive in a country so grievously maltreated. In his early *Tracts Relative to the Laws against Popery in Ireland* (written in 1765 but unpublished in his lifetime) Burke had objected to the stereotyped depiction of the Irish by English historians such as Temple and Clarendon as a rebellious people. Oppression had made them so, not nature. Ireland, made miserable by faction, could again be made rebellious by speculators whose theories would be more attractive to those who had nothing to gain from the preservation of the existing state of affairs.

Furthermore, in the spectacle of Irish Catholics fleeing persecution in Ireland and French Protestants fleeing persecution in France, Burke felt that he was witnessing a radical dislocation of natural feeling of the sort described by Francis Hutcheson.

> But to transfer humanity from its natural basis, our legitimate and home-bred connexions; to lose all feeling for those who have grown up by our sides, in our eyes, of the benefits of whose care and labours we have partaken from our birth, and meretriciously to hunt abroad after foreign affections, is such a disarrangement of the whole system of our duties, that I do not know whether benevolence so displaced is not almost the same thing as destroyed, or what effect bigotry could have produced that is more fatal to society.[62]

Bigotry at home stimulates benevolence toward "foreign affections." This is an early formulation of the attack on Rousseauistic benevolence. By 1782, the year of Irish legislative independence, Burke had decided that bigotry was merely an expression of a deeper form of injustice. "I have known men, to whom I am not uncharitable in saying, . . . that they would have become Papists in order to suppress Protestants; if, being Protestants, it was not in their power to oppress Papists. It is injustice, and not a mistaken conscience that has been the principle of persecution at least as far as it has fallen under my observation."[63]

This was in his *Letter to a Peer of Ireland on the Penal Laws against Irish Catholics.* Ten years later, in 1792, writing to Sir Hercules Langrishe on the question of admitting certain categories of Irish Catholics to the franchise, an increasingly urgent priority in the eyes of a British government now eager to appease them and win them over from revolutionary ideas, Burke gives further emphasis to the connection between the Protestant Ascendancy and the Jacobins. The Irish Protestants are not aristocratic; they are plebeian. And "a plebeian oligarchy is a monster: and no people, not absolutely domestic or predial slaves, will long endure it. The Protestants of Ireland are not *alone* sufficiently the people to form a democracy; and they are *too numerous* to answer the ends and purposes of an *aristocracy*."[64] By 1795, in his second letter to Langrishe, he launches his most direct attack on the Protestant Ascendancy, the Jacobins, and the Indian policy of Warren Hastings:

> I think I can hardly overrate the malignancy of the principles of Protestant ascendency, as they affect Ireland; or of Indianism as they affect these countries, and as they affect Asia; or of Jacobinism, as they affect all Europe and the state of human society itself. The last is the greatest evil. But it really combines with the others, and flows from them. Whatever breeds discontent at this time, will produce that great master-mischief most infallibly. Whatever tends to persuade the people, that the *few* called by whatever name you please, religious or political, are of opinion that their interest is not compatible with that of the *many,* is a great point gained to Jacobinism.[65]

Thus much of what had happened in Ireland was a standing rebuke to all that was being attempted in France. National love and political affections were being broken or vulgarized by a despotic, enterprising sect which had a persecuting edge to its deeply embedded fanaticism. The French were universalizing sectarianism into a theory of global benevolence and revolution. What the sect had been, the party would become. Neither the sect nor the party, the Ascendancy nor the Jacobins, was a true aristocracy. Each was "a plebeian monster." In the light of this analysis we can understand why Burke attacked the personnel of the French National Assembly. A country could not be ruled by lawyers, "friseurs" (hairdressers), and petty clergy. No traditional bond of affection or respect allied them with the people over whom they ruled. Where affection was lacking, power justified itself by terror.[66]

It has been pointed out that the Scottish philosopher James Beattie, in his *Essay on the Nature and Immutability of Truth* (1770), anticipated Burke's attack on the French Enlightenment. Beattie opposed abstract theorizing, the current debasement of taste, the cold-heartedness of the "metaphysician," abstruse research into the fundamentals of the human condition.[67] "The evidences of the philosophy of human nature are found in our own breasts; we need not roam abroad in quest of them; the unlearned are judges of them as well as the learned. Ambiguities have arisen when the feelings of the heart and understanding were expressed in words; but the feelings themselves were not ambiguous."[68] Beattie was a member of the Scottish Common Sense School of philosophy, of which Hutcheson was the founder, when he moved to Glasgow from Dublin in 1730, the year after Burke's birth. The use to which Burke put Hutcheson's ideas about "national love", tends to obscure the fact that Hutcheson's work was itself, politically speaking, one which united the more radical notions of Viscount Molesworth and Archbishop King, both of whom had defended the Glorious Revolution in Ireland and the right of the oppressed subject to rebel. Burke is uneasily caught between their views and those of Bishop Berkeley in *Passive Obedience* (1712), where the right of rebellion against constituted authority is firmly denied.[69] It is nevertheless clear that Burke's attitudes toward Ireland, and his knowledge of the central intellectual disputes of the day in Ireland, contributed a great deal to the formulation of his attitudes toward the French Enlightenment, the Revolution, and the English national character.

Natural Aristocracy, Moral Essence, and the European Order

In conclusion, it may be well to define a little more clearly what, in Burke's view, a true aristocracy was and how it related to the "national love" or idea of a nation which was clearly so important to his assertion of the English spirit in the Revolutionary period. An aristocracy embodied the "moral essence" of a nation. Since France had expelled its aristocracy, it had expelled its essence, and as a consequence Revolutionary France was not the true country at all: "Nation is a moral essence, not a geographical arrangement, or a denomination of the nomenclator. France, though out of her territorial possession, exists; because the sole possible claimant, I mean the proprietary, and the government to which the proprietary adheres, exists, and claims."[70] Such a proprietary interest was not elected by "literal representation." This could register the sum of individual wills without representing communal feeling and interest. Such feeling and interest would be registered instead by "virtual representation": "Virtual representation is that in which there is a communion of interest, and a sympathy in feeling and desires, between those who act in the name of any description of people, and the people in whose name they act, though the trustees are not actually chosen by them."[71]

This was a defense of the unreformed House of Commons as well as an attack on the Jacobins and the Protestant Ascendancy in Ireland. The French émigrés at Coblenz (or at Beaconsfield) were the true France in exile from its geographic actuality. It was such a system which gave Christian Europe the cohesion of a unified community. Although this had been modified by the Reformation, Burke, close to Montesquieu in this respect,[72] regarded the post-Reformation European system as a fundamentally united culture with different political variations corresponding to the different variations of a common faith. The collapse of Catholicism in France had, he believed, fearful implications for Protestantism in England.[73] His fury at the English Dissenters was provoked by what seemed to him their un-Christian exultation in disorder, their glee in the triumph of abstract right and actual ruin: "I am attached to Christianity at large; much from conviction; more from affection. I would risque a great deal to prevent its being extinguished any where or in any of its shapes."[74] In defending the old European comity of nations he was following in the footsteps of Montesquieu, who had argued in *Esprit des lois* for the reestablishment of the feudal privileges of the French nobility as a means of limiting the increasingly despotic power of the monarchy.[75] Montesquieu had also distinguished Europe from what he called Asiatic despotism by claiming that it had retained a diversity of laws, inherited by Christianity from Rome and humanized by the influence of Christian teaching. Although there are important differences between Montesquieu and Burke on the role of the family in the Christian political system, they are at one in their vision of a Europe of interdependent nations with France and England at its center.[76]

It was this system which Burke defended against the Revolution, and in the English national character he saw that system's values most effectively embodied. France was a threat, Ireland a dire warning, England the ideal middle term between the two. In a letter of 1791 he wrote:

> I have been baptised and educated in the Church of England; and have seen no cause to abandon that communion. When I do, I shall act upon my conviction or my mistake. I think that Church harmonises with our civil constitution, with the frame and fashion of our Society, and with the general temper of our people. I think it is better calculated, all circumstances considered, for keeping peace amongst the different sects, and affording to them a reasonable protection, than any other System. Being something in a middle, it is better disposed to moderate.[77]

Burke's renewed emphasis on the natural intimacy between the British Constitution, the national character, and the Anglican Church provided his own and the next generation with the composite elements of their attacks on the Revolution and their defense of the specifically British alternative to it. Coleridge, Wordsworth, and Southey were the most immediate inheritors of his analysis of the Revolution and his remedies against its fearsome influence.

2 National Character and the Conspiracy

As early as November 1789 Hannah More told Horace Walpole: "I am edified by your strictures on the French distractions. These people seem to be tending to the only two deeper evils than those they are involved in; for I can figure to myself no greater mischiefs than despotism and popery, except anarchy and atheism."[1] After a long vendetta against Burke, Walpole became so far reconciled to him after the publication of the *Reflections* that he declared himself a "Burkite."[2] By 1793 he had decided that the French "monsters" had passed so far beyond his own considerable powers of invective that he could do no more than restore to them their proper name: "But I have no words that can reach the criminality of such *inferno-human* beings— but must compose a term that aims at conveying my idea of them— for the future it will be sufficient to call them *the French.*"[3]

In the same year Fanny Burney published a pamphlet in support of the French émigré clergy. Surveying the events of the recent past, she found that contemporary history far exceeded the inventions of fiction:

> Already we look back on the past as on a dream, too wild in its horrors, too unnatural in its cruelties, too abrupt in its succession of terrors, even for the exaggerating pencil of the most eccentric and gloomy imagination; surpassing whatever has been heard, read, or thought; and admitting no similitude but to the feverish visions of delirium! so marvellous in fertility of incident, so improbable in excess of calamity, so monstrous in impunity of guilt! The witches of Shakespeare are less wanton in absurdity and the demons of Milton less horrible in denunciations.[4]

It must be assumed that the French priests on whose behalf Miss Burney made her plea were the same "coxcomb abbés" who, after the American Revolution, absorbed "something of the energy of the British character" and "were metamorphosed into reasonable beings."

Isaac d'Israeli, the witness to this transformation, which he had noticed "as far back as 1783," was ready to support them in 1793.[5] Even popery could be supported with propriety and profit at such a time. In D'Israeli's novel *Vaurien* a bookseller explains how it could be done: "And because I love free discussion, as every bookseller should, since the French emigrants arrived, to make trade a little brisker, I print their missals, masses, prayers etc. The established church can fear no great mischief from Catholicism in two-penny pamphlets."[6] *The Rights of Man* in sixpenny pamphlets would have been a different matter.

Burke, as a patron of the émigrés at Beaconsfield, set an example many were eager to follow. The fleeing French clergy were no longer papists; they were Christian fugitives from an atheistic and revolutionary France—old enemies become new friends. There was indeed nothing to fear from them except the thought of what they represented—Christianity on the run from Infidelity.[7] Their Catholicism was infinitely preferable to the new combination of "politics with metaphysics"[8] expounded by the French philosophes and their English disciples. The contrast between the émigrés and the revolutionaries became part of the contrast (already established by Burke) between the old and the new France.[9] Popery was no longer the enemy as such, but it was frequently cited as the influence that had created the despotic state of affairs from which the Revolution had emerged. Protestant England had made 1688 possible; Catholic France had made 1789 and 1792 inevitable.

The presence of the émigrés in England made the seriousness of the situation more immediately present to those who met them. They were living proof of the success of the anti-Christian conspiracy which their chief writer, the Abbé Barruel, had documented. They were also the counterparts in the propaganda war to the English Jacobins and philosophes, whom Burke believed to be numerous and all of the conspiracy theorists, such as John Robison, believed to be ubiquitous and ready to take advantage of "the present awful situation of Europe and the general fermentation of the public mind in all nations."[10] Although the panic fears of a conspiracy were real, they were also carefully nourished. To see that, one has only to note the prominence given to Barruel, Burke, and Robison in speeches, sermons, and magazines.[11] But the fear did not touch everyone. France had failed to emulate the events of 1688 in England; and the leveling tendencies of the Revolution would not, it was felt, gain much support in England. The English were too happy and sensible. Edward Gibbon expressed this view with great confidence in 1792, although it was held with less assurance by many of his compatriots in the bad years between 1793 and 1798.

Had the French improved their glorious opportunity to erect a free constitutional Monarchy on the ruins of arbitrary power and the Bastille, I should applaud their generous effort; but this total subversion of all rank, order and government could be productive only of a popular monster, which after devouring everything else, must finally devour itself. I was once apprehensive that this monster would propagate some imps in our happy island but they seem to have been crushed in the cradle, and I acknowledge with pleasure and pride the good sense of the English nation, who seem truly conscious of the blessings which they enjoy.[12]

Emigré Writings

English opposition to the French Revolution as it expressed itself in varying attitudes toward the French émigrés went through two distinct phases. The first was marked by the view that the Revolution was a crusade against Christianity itself and that the émigrés, especially the clergy, were the direct victims of it. The second, less melodramatic, began to replace the first after the Peace of Amiens (1802); it was governed by the sensible conviction that the new Napoleonic France threatened the existence of England. To support internal opposition to Napoleon was therefore a wise procedure. Hence it was the French *anglomanes* or constitutionalists who thereafter gained the bulk of English support rather than the proponents of royalism. As Barruel had been the dominant figure in the first phase, Mme. de Staël, who had been persecuted by Napoleon, was the dominant figure in the second. The two kinds of support are not as clearly separated as this description would indicate. Constitutionalists found support in England as early as 1790; conspiracy theorists remained popular into the 1820s and beyond. But in general the changing attitude toward France was reflected in the changing attitude toward the émigrés.

Support for the French liberal constitutionalists, such as J.-J. Mounier, Mallet du Pan, and Mme. de Staël, was firmly established by 1799. Du Pan's journal, *Mercure Britannique*, received support in public subscriptions from the Dukes of York, Kent, and Gloucester, among others. John Reeves and John Gifford, the two best government propagandists, provided technical advice and help; and it received encouragement, and possibly financial backing, from Lord Liverpool and William Windham.[13] It seems at first a little odd that a fortnightly paper with an eventual circulation of 750 should have received such careful attention. It was probably directed, though, at a specific audience—parliamentary and financial as well as the émigré audience itself—for the sake of weaning away support from the more fanatical royalists and conspiracy theorists and of guiding it toward a solution based on the notion of a restored constitutional monarchy in France. In brief, the journal implied that 1688 could be repeated after all— that or something close to it. By 1800, when the *Mercure* died, the conspiracy theory had effectively been discredited except in the minds of those who were beyond persuasion. By then too changes in the political and military situation had made British support for the émigrés, of whatever political conviction, less important than it had been.

Nevertheless, émigré literature did continue throughout this period to play an important part in the formulation of the notion of the contrasting French and English national characters. It was aided in this by the publication of a series of memoirs and collections of letters concerning the Enlightenment and the Revolution, frequently by people who had become disillusioned with both. Many of these were translated into English, and all were widely reviewed. The central historical question which they all, in their very different ways, posed was that of the relationship between the Enlightenment and the Revolution. The responsibility of the philosophes was of course widely canvassed; but even the constitutionalists, or intellectuals such as Mme. de Staël and historians such as Lacretelle the younger, paid close attention to this issue. In general they tended to see the revolutionaries as extremists who had abused and degraded the ideas of the philosophes, although it was inevitable, given their admiration for Montesquieu and their sometimes close ties with English Whigs such as Shelburne and Fox, that they should stress the liberal constitutional ideal as exemplified in France by Montesquieu himself and in England by Delolme and Blackstone.[14]

At first the weight of émigré writing favored the tactic of directly blaming the philosophes for the Revolution and claiming that the revolutionaries merely practiced what their forebears had preached. Stripped of all its Masonic and Rosicrucian elements (themselves a genuine part of the history of the Enlightenment), Barruel's *Memoirs* consist of the claim that the activities of Siéyes, Danton, Mirabeau, and Marat were applications of the writings of Voltaire, D'Alembert, Diderot, Helvétius, and others. The crepuscular world of Adam Weishaupt and his German Illuminati, of Mesmer, Cagliostro, and others merely threw the philosophes into high relief as the principal figures in the whole conspiracy. Most of the émigré writing thereafter simply abandoned the murky background Barruel had provided and concentrated instead on the specific activities of individual philosophes. Abbé Proyart, for instance, in a book on Marie Antoinette's mother, gives a dramatic account of how Helvétius, whose father had been surgeon to the Court, took advantage of his position there to spread corruption by disseminating the principles which he later incorporated into his book *De l'esprit*. We also hear that the queen was alert from an early stage to the dangers of the philosophes and their machinations and how she was the first to denounce the *Encyclopédie* for its attacks on religion.[15] J. B. Duvoisin, the former bishop of Nantes, attempts to demonstrate the deficiencies of Rousseau by comparing him unfavorably with Bossuet; he blames the whole "system of the Revolution" on Rousseau's "principle of the sovereignty of the people" and condemns him thereby in the eyes of history while excusing him as an individual who did not know what he did. He confirms the notion that the philosophes as a group conspired to bring about the Revolution and accuses Voltaire, Raynal, and Helvétius of having corrupted the youth of the country and of having demanded for themselves a toleration they would not grant to others, so fierce was their zeal to extinguish Christianity in France.[16] Even Sénac de Meilhan, a supporter of the philosophes and an advocate of Turgot in particular, admits a direct relationship between the writings of the philosophes and the excesses of the Revolution.[17] The well-known L.-S. Mercier, the *singe de Rousseau*, tells how he learned to look on the writings of Voltaire and Helvétius in a different light after he had seen what Baboeuf and his followers had made of them.[18] Louis Dutens supplies the conspiracy theory with graphic accounts of the atmosphere and conversation of the Parisian salons.[19] The more serious and complex work of Jean-Louis Soulavie the Elder is also governed by the central thesis that "the French Revolution is the principal product of the philosophical and metaphysical systems of the last years of the eighteenth century."[20]

Soulavie's more discriminating work, translated into English in 1802, is of a piece with the journalism of Mallet du Pan, Friedrich Gentz, and Jean-Joseph Mounier, all of whom about this time decried the notion of a conspiracy while affirming a causal relationship between the thought of the Enlightenment and the actions of the Revolution. In his *Mercure Britannique* Mallet divides the Enlightenment into two dominant groups. On the one hand is Voltaire and the Encyclopedists, who, in Mallet's view, would have regarded the Revolution as an absurd fantasy. On the other there is Rousseau and, more particularly, La Mettrie, Helvétius, and Holbach. Although his attribution of particular works to this latter group is inaccurate, his main point is sufficiently clear. The philosophes were composed of two groups; there was no overall conspiracy; one faction, led by Helvétius, bred all the disasters of the Revolution: "From this group of Hottentots came books like *Le Militaire Philosophe, Le Christianisme Dévoilé, Le Systéme de la Nature,* the complete revolutionary catechism, the clear anticipation of Jacobinism, the manual of all those lettered or unlettered gangsters who have subjugated France since 1789."[21]

Gentz, in an article translated from German and published in the *Mercure,* also in 1799, dismisses both the conspiracy theory and the direct account of the relationship between philosophic ideas and revolutionary actions. He argues for the need to set all that had happened against the background of the particular circumstances pertaining in France throughout the pre-Revolutionary period. It is in the interaction of these circumstances and the writings of the philosophes that the origins of 1789 are to be found.[22] This is the basis of the argument in Mounier's famous book *On the Influence Attributed to the Philosophers, Freemasons, and to the Illuminati on the Revolution in France* (1801; translated into English, 1801). He demolishes the conspiracy thesis with great efficiency; criticizes Voltaire and Rousseau but reminds his readers of the corrupt state of France when they were writing; allows them a certain, though not extravagant, greatness. Thereafter, like Sénac de Meilhan, he concentrates on the immediate causes of the Revolution: the weakness of the king, the dismissal of Turgot, the stifling of Necker's reforms.[23]

After Mounier the most important interpretations of the relationship between the Enlightenment and the Revolution no longer had to counter the outraged royalism of the first generation of émigrés or fears for the extinction of Christianity in France and throughout the rest of Europe. The Catholic reaction in France helped subdue this fear so effectively that Soulavie was able to boast that "Voltaire, and the philosophers, his disciples, have vainly contributed to overthrow, in the course of a few years, what our fathers held in veneration. That religion, and those gods, which you imagine ineffectual, abased, and annihilated, are again rising round us."[24]

In the new situation the apologists for French constitutionalism were able to give their attention to the defects of French political and ethical thought which had contributed to the predominance in recent French history of the influence of Rousseau over that of Montesquieu. Of the commentators so engaged the most influential was the historian J. D. C. Lacretelle, whose *Histoire de France* was widely reviewed as it appeared in eight successive volumes between 1808 and 1821.

To demonstrate his central thesis Lacretelle undertakes an examination of French prose style throughout the eighteenth century. Voltaire and Montesquieu occupy the phase of transition from former excellence to present decay, represented in its most extreme form by Holbach. In political terms the worst effect of the new and decadent situation in France was the ousting of Montesquieu by Rousseau as the most important political philosopher of the century.[25] Thus he reaffirms what Burke had lightly insinuated—that there was an old France which had slowly been undermined by the process of decay that culminated in the Revolution. Lacretelle's work was warmly welcomed in England.[26] The most interesting response came from those reviewers, most especially an anonymous writer for *The British Review*,[27] who saw in the contrast between the solidity of Montesquieu's scholarship and the dandified elegance of his style an instance of the transition from the old to the new France. His style, we are told, had been formed by the France of the Regency period. All its excessively ornate and discontinuous features, its "brilliance," were the characteristic product of the salons, while his serious weightiness was in conformity with what one would expect from a rustic squire of the old rural France. This is the most remarkable example of the manner in which a belief in the change in French national character—reinforced by the current belief in the difference between the English and French national characters—could inform the analysis of a writer's style. Some of the most famous of the reviewers for the *Edinburgh Review*—Jeffrey, Brougham, Mackintosh—commented on the difficulties which Montesquieu's "nervous and brilliant style" created while conceding the great achievement which his work represented.[28] In effect Montesquieu was recruited to the cause of the liberal constitutionalists with the help of Lacretelle and his reviewers, despite some objections from Scottish intellectuals of a more radical disposition such as Thomas Christie, editor of the *Analytical Review*.[29]

Mme. de Staël:
National Characteristics and Cosmopolitanism

Four countries constitute the coordinates of Mme. de Staël's thought. Two of them, England and Germany, are Protestant; two, France and Italy, are Catholic. Each of these pairings also exhibits a contrast between a single unified state and an amalgam of various kinds of political units. The northern Protestant states exemplify political liberty (England) and profound feeling (Germany). The Mediterranean Catholic states exemplify social sophistication (France) and communcal consciousness (Italy). She had been sufficiently influenced by Voltaire, Montesquieu, and Delolme to make the connection between Protestantism, liberty, and natural feeling, which was as important to the anti-Revolutionary propaganda outside France after 1793 as it had been to the pro-Revolutionary forces inside France before that date. Still she was not one of the anti-Revolutionary scribblers. She knew that a war of propaganda had broken out and was concerned to argue that the cultural changes taking place in Europe were signs of a new and promising unity rather than symptoms of a more complete separation between the nations. Since England was the country most vigorously devoted to the prosecution of this anti-French and sometimes anti-Continental campaign, her work had a particular application to it as well as to France. In his review of her *De l'Allemagne*, Sir James Mackintosh noticed how the war propaganda had reversed the old eighteenth-century Anglo-Continental attitudes. England had once been the revolutionary country; now it was France which starred in that role.[30] Anglophilia in France had been replaced by Francophobia, even xenophobia, in England. Mme. de Staël wanted to change this position by reconciling her admiration for the Protestant culture with her love for the Catholic. Politically this meant a repudiation of the Revolutionary constitutions which she, as her father, Necker, had done in his book *Du pouvoir exécutif* (1792), criticized for their failure to either concentrate or balance powers,[31] and an acceptance of the British constitutional system, which, she believed, did both admirably.[32]

It would have been difficult for a friend of Sismondi to ignore the virtues of the Mediterranean cultures, even though the drift of his great work is in favor of the "Romantic" and Protestant North.[33] If *De l'Allemagne* contains an implicit criticism of French provincialism, her novel *Corinne; ou, De l'Italie* is much more explicit about the disadvantages of English insularity, introverted family affections, and moralism. The heroine, Corinne, half-English by birth and Italian by choice and destiny, appears to her English suitor, Nelvil, to owe her incomparable charms "to the fusion of all the attractive characteristics of the different nations."[34] In effect De Staël claims that Protestant reserve, while it nourishes intensity of feeling, is dangerously introverted and egoistic. Yet Catholic display, while it fosters honor and public consciousness, lacks the strength of personal feeling which is a precondition of liberty. Here she is adapting to national terms the old eighteenth-century argument about the merits and demerits of selfish egoism and social altruism; she puts a moral dispute in the form of a contrast between national characteristics. Having done so, she needs to find a principle of reconciliation between them.

Her word for this principle is *enthousiasme*, the exemplary exponent of which, in her eyes, is Rousseau; its aim is the achievement of a cosmopolitan tolerance in place of particular national chauvinisms. Germany would renew France with a fresh impulse of that Romantic, intense feeling which the socially sophisticated French lacked; Italy would give to dull and reserved England some of the brio and energy it required. The two countries representing the broken republican traditions of old Europe would save the great nation-states, France and England, from calcifying, respectively, into dictatorship and fortressed isolation.[35] The principle of *enthousiasme* would be mobilized by literature. Rousseau's writings had shown the way from morbid egoism to cosmopolitan freedom, from self-love to benevolence.[36] Everything she finds attractive in Rousseau Burke had found repellent. Even so, there is a marked similarity in their analyses of the significance of Rousseau for the time.

A reading of Mme. de Staël's *Reflexions sur la paix* quickly shows how conscious she was of the frailty of her position, locked between the royalism of the reactionary émigrés (many of whom thought that Necker was responsible for much of their misfortune) and the demagogic Robespierrean democracy: "How can one make the balance of powers understood? How is one to write a chapter of Montesquieu under the standard of revolution?"[37]

In chaotic conditions such as those of the Revolution, she maintains, personal egoism flourishes to the detriment of public good.[38] Therefore what is needed is some force to raise mankind above the pettiness of such self-interest. Contemporary literature, especially the writings of Rousseau, provides that force because it is informed by the ideals of service to humanity at large, not to any particular individual, sect, or country. Egoism is the opponent of liberty; literature is its savior. France has lost its capacity for spontaneous feelings after half a century of mockery, satire, wit, and philosophies of selfishness. Now it is in a decadent state, similar to that of Rome before the barbarian nations came to invade and ultimately, through the influence of Christianity, to transform it.[39] Her comparison here is a double, not a single one. During the Revolution the Jacobins stood toward their opponents in France and the governments of Europe as the barbarian nations had stood toward Rome in its last days. The opponents of the Jacobins actually *needed* the martial and astringent energies of these redoubtable revolutionaries. (Burke had made the same point earlier.) Now the whole of French society needs a further transformation, which will come from the modern equivalents of the barbarian nations. The only difference is that Mme. de Staël imagines that their invasion will take a literary form only and is deeply distressed that it became an actual military invasion by barbarous Prussians.

Still, she remains faithful to the hope that French mockery and English austerity, both of which had undermined public sentiment in England and France, would be overcome by a revival of feeling which would form into a political system of justice. "Happy we would be if we were to find, as in the time of the barbarian invasions by the northern peoples, a philosophical system, a virtuous enthusiasm, a firm and just legal system, which would create, as Christianity did, a climate in which the victors and the vanquished could reunite with one another."[40] What Christianity had done then, cosmopolitanism would do now.

Literature can be the most effective means of bringing about this desirable situation, but only if it is imbued with the philosophical ideas which, in effect, will provide the basis for her new religion of mankind. Rousseau is the exemplary writer; but Germany is the exemplary country in which this fusion of ideas and literature has been achieved on a large scale. It is characteristic of the Germans, a meditative people, to be austere; austerity naturally allies itself with morality, a system of obligations and restraints. But when moral philosophy is fired by enthusiasm, the result is literature of the modern kind, of the new sensibility, "reveuse et profonde."[41] The melancholy of the new literature merely demonstrates the previously affirmed connection between intensity of feeling and liberty. England, Germany, and Geneva, all Protestant communities, had produced a Romantic literature which had beneficial social effects that were proportionate to its own innate sadness. "Happy is the country where the writers are sad."[42]

It is not altogether surprising that the English reviews of Mme. de Staël's *De l'Allemagne* (translated simply as *Germany*) concentrated more on her view of the French philosophes than on her accounts (garbled enough, to be sure) of Kant's philosophy; for in her writings, as in those of many other French émigrés, they found confirmation of the belief that the real degradation of philosophy in France and the truly dangerous political doctrines of the Revolution had come from the "materialist" thinkers, Helvétius, Holbach, Condillac, and Diderot.[43] By the close of the second decade of the century, the English unanimity about the appeal, charm, and general acceptability of Mme. de Staël was wonderful. The *Eclectic Review*, which had attacked her *De la littérature* quite savagely in 1812, could not find words enough to praise her in 1819.[44] It was not so much her discovery of Germany which won her such acclaim as it was her rediscovery of a France which Englishmen could again admire without feeling obliged to condone the Revolution, Napoleon, Infidelity, or Libertinism. The fact that she praised the British Constitution helped also. Indeed *Blackwood's Magazine* found it possible to hail her on the strength of this alone.[45] In her anglophilia, directly inherited from Voltaire and Montesquieu, lay another solution to the interpretation of the Revolution. It was an old one but no less valuable for its revival. It held that the French constitutional reformers had set out to make France a constitutional monarchy like England but had been defeated by sinister and radical figures much given to abstract theorizing of an extreme French kind which could not abide the sort of beautiful compromise achieved, in characteristic fashion, by the English. Mme. de Staël made the likes of Montesquieu, Turgot, and Necker (she included her father in all her benign citations) honorary Englishmen who had failed to make 1688 work in 1789. The persistence of this comparison between the two revolutions, inevitable at first, becomes monotonous at last.

In Mme. de Staël's writings émigré literature comes to terms with the fact that the Revolution has happened, that the ancien régime is gone, and that the conditions of existence in the new world have to be negotiated in the new language of the Romantic and "cosmopolitan" era.

The English Response:
Sermons, Pamphlets, Novels

As the opening quotations from Horace Walpole, Fanny Burney, and others suggest, the English response to the Revolution in the 1790s was an especially violent and frightened one. The French émigré clergy could not emulate their English counterparts in the force of their revulsion at the spectacle of the great conspiracy which Barruel had confirmed but which many English sermons had anticipated well before 1797. Beilby Porteus, bishop of London, claimed in 1794 that the Revolution was designed to supplant religion with philosophy.[46] A pamphlet by John Courtenay, a member of Parliament, provided the usual list of French philosophic criminals but then went on to claim that the English Dissenters had compressed French ideas into a "spiritual regenerating pill" which helped pregnant mothers to produce children capable of imbibing the "cursed doctrine" at the contaminated breast.[47] Two editions of this lunatic publication were absorbed by the public even before Barruel appeared on the scene. Other pamphleteers, including John Moore, had hinted at the European scale of Voltaire's operations; and the appearance in English of the works of Frederick II of Prussia put paid to the earlier claim that the philosophes had never intended to have their ideas translated into practice.[48]

After Barruel, the hysteria of anti-French feeling reached a comic pitch. John Bowles found Voltaire's slogan "Ecrasez l'infame" too shocking to repeat.[49] A writer for *The Gentleman's Magazine* in 1797 claimed that Voltaire looked "like an odious devil" in a portrait he had seen of him.[50] Bishop Samuel Horsley called the philosophes "those children of hell" in the course of a sermon in 1800; the language he used on other occasions was so much more violent that his sympathetic biographer did not reproduce it, saying that it had been "caught from the infection of the Time."[51] Henry Kett, another clergyman, saw Voltaire as the Antichrist.[52] Reviews such as *The British Critic*, *The Gentleman's Magazine*, and *The Anti-Jacobin Review* gave the works of Barruel, Robison, and Frederick II as much publicity as possible in order to alert the public to the dangers of this burgeoning conspiracy. Stories of Voltaire's cowardice, promiscuity, and irreligion began to appear, although they all gave pride of place to the various accounts of his excruciatingly painful and godless death, examples of which still appeared with regularity in the 1820s.[53] Pamphleteers issued into print with what was no more than a plagiarized summary of Barruel.[54] The Earl of Liverpool hoped that Richard Watson, the famous bishop of Llandaff, would publish another version of the Jesuit's *Memoirs*, suitably clothed "in a Protestant dress." Watson refused; he did not believe Barruel. But George Gleig, preaching at Stirling in 1803, when the vogue for Barruel had almost passed, suspected that those who doubted the existence of the conspiracy had been "duped by some of its emissaries" or were themselves eager to "promote the causes for which it was instituted." Even those who welcomed the achievement of the philosophes in exploding popish superstition could not go so far as to welcome the political doctrines with which they had done so.[55] Antipopery was not really a help in facing up to the implications of the Revolution, but it was often used as an explanation for the Revolution's having happened at all and for its being French.[56]

In Robert Bage's novel *Hermsprong; or, Man as He Is Not* (1796) Mr. Woodcock, the curate, declares: "Sermons, to succeed now, must either ascend to the heaven of heavens with Swedenborg or must pour out with pious effusion, and in the most vituperative terms the English tongue will afford, death and damnation to the French."[57] The hero of this novel, born in America among the Indians and then educated in France, was as unpopular as any French revolutionary. The political novel of the 1790s, dominated by Godwin, Bage, Holcroft, Mary Hays, and Mary Wollstonecraft, is fond of displaying the Man of Reason as hero, environed by a corrupt society which he proceeds to convert to his own views by a series of sermons and altruistic actions. The anti-Revolutionary novel manages to perform the almost unnecessary job of caricaturing the doctrinal heroes of Godwin and company. Often the authors themselves are caricatured. Richard Price turns up in D'Israeli's *Vaurien* as Dr. Bounce; Holcroft becomes Reverberator; Thelwall appears as Dragon. D'Israeli goes farther than almost any other novelist in emphasizing the relationship between the French and English philosophes. He quotes Holcroft and Helvétius with equal readiness and sneering accuracy; and he makes the basic comparison between his very English hero, Charles, and his very French villain, Vaurien, a real confrontation between national characters, out of which several memorable assertions of English superiority emerge. To Vaurien's support for divorce and general sexual freedom Charles replies: "Mr. Vaurien, this subject is always revolting to me; you treat it like a Frenchman, and never in your country was true connubial enjoyment found."[58]

This note is heard again and again in the popular novels of the day. The philosophe or intellectual, for all his sexual lasciviousness, is cut off from the natural affections which make marriage and the love of children possible. Charles Lloyd's *Edmund Oliver* (1798), dedicated to Charles Lamb, announces in the advertisement that its author is opposed to Godwin and modern philosophy, for he believes "that the domestic connections, which are only co-eval with the existence of marriage, are the necessary means of disciplining Beings, at first merely sentient, to a rational and enlarged benevolence."[59] Hannah More's *Coelebs in Search of a Wife* (1809) is an account of the hero's pursuit of an ideal perfection in womanhood. We learn that "the woman who derives her principles from the Bible" and her amusement from study and nature "will not pant for beholders." One of the reformed ladies surprises her husband by the cold reception she gives "to a large cargo of new French novels and German plays," which had been her staple diet in her former, decadent life.[60] Mrs. Elizabeth Hamilton's *Memoirs of Modern Philosophers* (1800) is even more laden with cautionary tales. Bridgetina Botherim finally emerges from "the gloomy masses of tenebrific shade" of modern philosophy to perceive the nature of true filial affection;[61] Julia Delmond gives a deathbed lecture on the false systems of Glib and Myope, the Holcroft and Godwin of the novel. Similarly, in her *Letters of a Hindooh Rajah* (1811), she attacks the new philosophy in the person of her heroine, Lady Grey, the epitome of English womanhood, who sees off the philosophical pundits with the remark that although "purity of heart, unfeigned humility, sanctity of morals and simplicity of manners" may be obnoxious to the modern philosopher, they nonetheless contribute to the cause of human happiness, something the philosopher will never know.[62] Fitzosborne, the philosophe-villain of Jane West's *Tale of the Times* (1799), is as cold-hearted and systematic in his designs on female virtue as one could hope. Sexual immorality and the attack on family life are, in the eyes of most of these novelists, the essential principles underlying the great conspiracy against throne and altar:

> Should it therefore be told to future ages, that the capricious dissolubility (if not the absolute nullity) of the nuptial tie and the annihilation of parental authority are among the blasphemies uttered by the *moral* instructors of these times: should they hear, that law was branded as a vain and even unjust attempt to bring individual actions under the restrictions of a general rule; that chastity was defined to mean only individuality of affection; that religion was degraded into a sentimental effusion; and that these doctrines do not proceed from the pen of *avowed* profligates, but from persons *apparently* actuated by the desire of improving the happiness of the world; should, I say, generations yet unborn hear this, they will not ascribe the annihilation of thrones and altars to the successful arms of France, but to those principles which, by dissolving domestic confidence and undermining private worth, paved the way for universal confusion.[63]

As sexual immorality became more closely identified with French philosophy and Revolutionary theory, so loyalty to hearth and home became more characteristic of England. The New Woman, a scandalous figure, was French, intellectual, and lascivious. One of the funniest parodies of Godwin has the hero say of his carefully named mistress, Pandora: "To her unrestrained prostitution, I ascribe all that ease of manner, flow of fancy, and graceful intrepidity of thinking which rendered her so amiable in my eyes."[64] Women of this kind were modeled on the hostesses of the great Parisian salons. The memoirs of Frenchwomen such as Mme. de Genlis and Mme. du Deffand and various gossipy reports about the *amours* of the philosophes were widely noted and eagerly reproduced as proof of the immorality of the French character.[65] What began in other areas as an investigation into the philosophic origins and bases of the Revolution became finally an explication of the differences between the French and English national character. The novels, although not alone in this, gave sexual behavior a prominent role in that differentiation. It is against this background that the views of writers such as Southey, John Wilson Croker, John Scott, and Wordsworth can be seen as entirely characteristic of the period.

From Southey to Carlyle

In Robert Southey's *Colloquies* of 1829 Montesinos, speaking of the alliance in Britain between the church and the Constitution, says, "If a breach be made in our sanctuary, it will be by the combined forces of Popery, Dissent, and Unbelief, fighting under a political flag."[66] Infidelity was not, as in the 1790s, plotting the downfall of Christianity. Instead, in the year of Catholic Emancipation and one year before the revolution of July 1830 in Paris, it had joined with Catholicism and Dissent to destroy Anglicanism. Nothing associates Southey more closely with Wordsworth and Coleridge than his sense that the unique character of English national feeling depended on the preservation of the church-state relationship. His feudalism, like Wordsworth's, was in part a reaction against the new industrial and economic conditions which had changed England so profoundly in their lifetime.[67] All through his work he makes it clear that he believed that he had lived through a cataclysm which originated in France and was producing endless repercussions in England. It was his lot, as More says to Montesinos in the *Colloquies*, "to live during one of the grand climacterics of the world."[68] Although the crisis expressed itself socially in the poverty and brutality of the new poor in the industrial towns, Southey consistently thought of it as political rather than social in nature and French rather than English in origin. The pattern of events in France was being reproduced in England. Men of talent there, such as Voltaire and Rousseau, had been replaced by men without it, such as Marat and Hébert. So in England "Mr. Examiner Hunt" ushers in "Mr. Orator Hunt."[69] In England as in France chief among the "engines of mischief" was the press.[70] Southey, therefore, could justify his support for reviving the bill against seditious assemblies and steepening the penalty for seditious libel to exile. Although he was able to provide himself with an excuse for his earlier republican opinions, this is in itself of less consequence than his success in providing an interpretation of the Revolution and of contemporary English history which demonstrates that the first was a cautionary tale and a horrific premonition of the other. The interpretation is not without contradictions; but its combination of fierce moral passion and weak analysis is exactly typical of the period. If one wishes to find a position which includes characteristic English reactions to Barruel, the French émigrés, and the English Jacobins and equally typical definitions and descriptions of the war between Infidelity and Christianity, English domestic virtues and French sexual license, local patriotism and the "wild cosmopolite character"[71] of French democracy, the French national character, the French Enlightenment, French Catholicism, the significance of Napoleon, and the ultimate relevance of all these to the issue of English nationality, then Southey's works will provide it.

This becomes clearer if we compare Southey's achievement in this relation with that of John Wilson Croker and John Scott. Along with

Southey, Croker gave to the *Quarterly Review* through his writings and to a whole range of government-inspired papers and magazines through his views the typical tone of the English rejection of France.[72] Yet, although Croker was a much greater authority on the Revolution than Southey (or indeed than anyone else in England), the range of his attack is much narrower. He did not, like Southey, seek parallels between French and English experience. He was probably too good a historian to do so with Southey's facility. But without these or compensatory interpretive efforts Croker has nothing to offer on the significance of the Revolution other than what a rank, vindictive anti-French feeling would lead one to expect. Even that feeling has its limitations, for he confines its expression almost entirely to the contrast between the sexual immorality of the French and the domestic bliss and chastity of the English. It is as astonishing as it is instructive to find such extensive information as Croker had at his command in the grip of such restricting prejudice.[73]

In his reviews of French novels in the *Quarterly* he dismisses the whole tradition of French fiction—Crébillon, Laclos, Louvet, Voltaire, Rousseau—as licentious at best, and worse when the licentiousness becomes political. No "baser, meaner, filthier scoundrel" ever "polluted society" than Rousseau, whose novel *La nouvelle Héloise* he characterizes as "an apology for incontinence and adultery." The later generation of Balzac, Paul de Kock, Hugo, and George Sand "pervert not only private but public morals" and "are alternately the cause and consequence of a spirit which threatens the whole fabric of European society."[74] Lady Morgan, an old enemy of Croker's, receives predictable maltreatment at his hands, but his review of her *France* is also a sketch of the chaste British female, which, in its censorious and censoring spirit, is wholly of the age of Bowdler: "Some of our readers may have heard the title of a most profligate French novel called *Les Liaisons Dangereuses.* We had hoped no British female had ever seen this detestable book; it seems we were mistaken."[75] Lady Morgan had. This is good enough reason for Croker to rebuke her for her Bonapartist sympathies—though Napoleon I could have loved Laclos's novel no better than Croker himself. For Croker, however, political conviction was inescapably allied to sexual purity. Before George III died anti-French reaction had created Victorianism.

Croker had no republican past to live down, as Southey had; but he would have supported Southey's contention that he had at least escaped "the atheism and leprous immorality" which generally accompanied such opinions. Although both men were very much in discipleship to Burke on this point, they labor it with such persistence that it begins to appear obsessional. Croker was conscious of his debt to Burke and felt himself to be part of a tradition, which included Mackintosh, of continuing the historical interpretation of 1688 as a contrast to 1789—one soon to be brought to a culmination by Macaulay.[76] Croker makes the intimacy between the interests of the professional historian and the requirements of political propaganda startlingly clear. The two interests or vocations converged in this period, not merely because of the enlarged audience which read the new reviews such as the *Edinburgh* and the *Quarterly* but also because historical writing and reviewing were the most sensitive of all discourses to the current crisis. The uniqueness of the English tradition was being defined there against the threat of Revolutionary and Napoleonic France. Croker's odd contribution to that definition was to make prudery a function of true English national feeling. It is a strange, cantankerous, yet important achievement, although one he has to share with some of his brilliant contemporaries.

John Scott, best known as editor of the outstanding *London Magazine*, also deserves to be remembered for *A Visit to Paris in 1814* (1815), *Paris Revisited* (1816), and *Sketches of Manners* (1821). His books and reviews perfectly complement those of Croker on the issue of the French and the Revolution. As early as 1811 he announced his preference for Englishwomen such as Hannah More and Sarah Trimmer over Mlle. de l'Espinasse or Mme. de Genlis.[77] He admired Mme. de Staël for her genius but believed that her immoral and indelicate writings would "create a class of women of a different order from those who have long cheered the fireside, doubled the joys and divided the sorrows of Englishmen."[78] Paris was the glittering capital with that "mart of sin and seduction," that "point of union for every thing that is evil"— the Palais Royal—at its heart.[79] In the years after Waterloo, when the English returned to gaze upon the country whose influence had "been unbounded on the continent for the last twenty years,"[80] the French seemed to be remarkably unrepentant about the recent past and still incorrigibly themselves. Scott was taken aback to find that a nation degraded first by the pernicious philosophy of the Enlightenment and then, further, by the Napoleonic dictatorship could be so unchastened. The old French sense of honor and chivalry had finally been removed by Napoleon: his "stripping off of the soldier's moral lace and feather,"[81] as he called it in 1816, had affected the whole populace by 1821. Yet even with that and the "vast blot" and "hurtful influence" of the Revolution, the French people at large "have caught neither modesty nor caution from their disgraces: they are still as light, as confident, as insolent, and as rash as ever. To reduce them to their proper low level, is really a moral duty: for this alone can reduce the hurtfulness of their example, and, in some measure, obliterate the stain they have affixed on the character of mankind."[82]

The Hundred Days did not improve Scott's (or England's) opinion of the French, and their apparently ready acceptance of Napoleon's defeat and the return of the Bourbons puzzled him as much as it disgusted Hazlitt. He returns again and again to the theme of France's guilt for the wars of the preceding twenty years and more and of the national failure to accept this guilt because of a radical lack of moral sensibility. Irresponsible and licentious, corrupted by the philosophes and by Napoleon, the French remained a painful enigma to Scott. No wonder, claimed the *Quarterly Review* in 1813, that people had believed something as absurd as Barruel's theories a generation before.[83] Some explanation was needed for what had happened, some account of the "unexampled rottenness in the Church and State" which had preceded the collapse of the ancien régime. The conspiracy theory was thus shelved and replaced by the theory of the French national character, an entity which had been either always suspect or recently degraded. Men otherwise as different in their political views as Scott, Hazlitt, and Francis Jeffrey were at one on the French national character. The French were too light, volatile, profligate, and corrupt to achieve liberty, and their vaunted sophistication was never free of what Jeffrey calls "voluptuousness and sensuality." That "species of indelicacy which is peculiar, we think, to their nation"[84] was most pronounced in its writers. The philosophes were thus guilty either of having corrupted the national character of their countrymen or of having expressed it in a typical manner. There was no escape from such circular accusations.

"Disaster opens the eyes of conscience,"[85] wrote Wordsworth; the 1790s had driven this lesson home to him and Southey time and again. The story of their recantation of earlier political beliefs is well known and needs no further rehearsal.[86] It is easier to understand the form their recantation took, however, if the anti-French spirit of the time is realized in all its intensity. Southey, for instance, claimed that the violence of French republicanism had forced him back to the seventeenth-century English republican tradition and that it was to it that he had remained faithful while earning the reputation of having been faithless to the French cause. Writing to Coleridge in 1800 he declared that "Sièyes and the Corsican have trod upon my Jacobine corns—and I am a thorough English republican."[87]

Both Southey and Wordsworth appear more treacherous toward their early opinions because neither made the grounds of his convictions clear until after he had lost faith in the Revolution. One of their premises, shared by many of quite different political opinions—for example Hazlitt—was that the French were not truly fit for liberty, even though, for a glorious moment, it had seemed that they were. This is a prejudice neither ever recanted. It emerged more prominently as the initial hopes disappeared with the September massacres, the Terror, the invasion of Switzerland, and the emergence of Napoleon. The true face of France had reappeared out of the Revolutionary glow. In 1821 Southey could speak of the difficulty of establishing a free government "among a people altogether unused to freedom" and how much more difficult it is if they are "as in France and Italy, a corrupt people."[88] France was as much a victim of its history of authoritarian and Roman Catholic rule as was England the beneficiary of its history of Protestantism and freedom. Given such a governing prejudice about France and England, disillusion with the Revolution was bound to lead to an even stronger pride in and loyalty to England and its uniquely fortunate traditions. Southey and Wordsworth believed themselves, then, to be English republicans and therefore hostile to the French and English Jacobins. A republican was what the Jacobin should have been. But what more could one expect? "No man who was acquainted with the history of the *Fronde* could have expected any happy result from a revolution in France, the French being what they were."[89] The Jacobinism of "that stirring season" of the nineties, when young and old had been led to hope for "indefinite pro-gression"[90] for the human race, had been more effectively destroyed by French excesses than by repressive legislation in England. For Southey the inheritance of that tragedy was the failure of the dis-illusioned to support the true popular revolution of the time, the revolt of the Spanish against Napoleon.[91] In the meantime, at home, in the new industrial condition, the Church and King mobs of 1791 were fast becoming the Luddite mobs of 1812.[92]

Wordsworth's case is not radically different. He had always opposed the first war against the Revolutionary French and supported the sec-ond against Napoleon. He never forgave Pitt, nor could he ever abide "the Corsican." In his poetry many of the clichés of anti-French feeling are found in almost the same form as in Southey or even Croker and Scott. Local patriotism, the emphasis on domesticity, chastity, the so-lidity and endurance of the reserved and austere character of the Eng-lish are all there in conjunction with the portrayal of the French scoffer and mocker, the cold-hearted sensualist, and the ruminations on the spirit of irreligion or Infidelity and the dangers of abstract theorizing. The flight to the seclusion of the natural world from the turmoil and uproar of the turbulent life of the city and of the Revolution is a central theme not only in Wordsworth's poetry but in the counter-Revolutionary literature of the whole period. The seeking-out of Nature is ultimately a seeking for a deeper formulation of the essential English spirit and tradition unpolluted by the influences of modern industrial expansion and political doctrine. Books II and IV of *The Excursion* put the experience of disillusion within the French frame; the feting of Voltaire by the Parisians on his famous last visit is ironically commented on by the Wanderer:

> Yet so it pleased a fond, a vain, old Man
> And a most frivolous people.[93]

The Spanish uprising was crucial for Wordsworth, as it was for Southey. Even if the Spanish were Catholic and overly submissive to their king, "in all these things we judged them gently: and taught by the reverses of the French Revolution we looked upon these dispositions as more human—more social—and therefore as wiser, and of better omen, than if they had stood forth the zealots of abstract principles, drawn out of the laboratory of unfeeling philosophists."[94] *The Convention of Cintra* makes it clear that after 1802 the Spanish rebels had taken on the role of the French émigrés in the English counter-Revolutionary polity. They too were Catholics, people of a traditional and conservative cast of mind, who, despite the ill-effects of their religion, were preferable to, and fairly immune to, the appeal of Jacobinism and the "pestilential philosophism of France": "No flight of infidel harpies has alighted upon their ground. A Spanish understanding is a hold too strong to give way to the meagre tactics of the 'Systeme de la Nature'; or to the pellets of logic which Condillac has cast in the foundry of national vanity . . . the paradoxical reveries of Rousseau and the flippancies of Voltaire are plants which will not naturalise in the country of Calderon and Cervantes."[95] This passage could have been taken from any of the standard reviews of the period; it does not, of course, wholly typify Wordsworth's conception of nationality, but it shows its conventional basis. In the process of rejecting France, Southey absorbed almost everything that was negative, while Wordsworth transformed these elements into a vision which has the moral range of Burke, though a gentler, more "Anglican" tone. What Burke began, Wordsworth and Coleridge brought to completion. Southey, Croker, and Scott and reviews such as the *Quarterly* and *The British Critic* never really discovered how to articulate English national self-assertion in a wholly positive way. For them the distinction of being English was almost coincident with being anti-French.

Part of the anxiety of Southey and others lay in the recognition that the political effects of the French Revolution were resonating in an England undergoing transformation by the Industrial Revolution. It seemed possible that the new urban populations in England could in the new climate become as fickle and ferocious as the so-called Parisian mob. In 1837 Carlyle gave the specter of that mob its most memorable description in his account of October 6, 1789, and in his prefatory account of the September Massacres.[96] His theatricalized version of the Revolution is matched by an equally histrionic account of the forces which produced the philosophes and transformed the French character. His essay of 1833 on Diderot is a striking instance of his method and of his adherence to the old view that something mysterious had to be the cause of the French cataclysm. He dismisses Barruel (at some length) but then merely substitutes for the anti-Christian conspiracy a very typical amalgamation of subterranean forces, all the more potent for being inchoate:

> Meanwhile, whether in constituted association or not, French Philosophy resided in the persons of the French Philosophes; and, as a mighty deep-struggling Force, was at work there. Deep-struggling, irrepressible; the subterranean fire, which long heaved unquietly, and shook all things with an ominous motion, was here, we can say, forming itself a decided spiracle;—which, by and by as French Revolution, became that volcano-crater, world-famous, world-appalling, world-maddening, as yet very far from closed! . . .
>
> Why France became such a volcano-crater, what specialities there were in the French national character, and political, moral, intellectual condition, by virtue whereof French Philosophy there and not elsewhere, then and not sooner or later, evolved itself,—is an inquiry that has often been put, and cheerfully answered; the true answer of which might lead us far. Still deeper than this *Whence* were the question of *Whither;*—with which, also, we intermeddle not here.[97]

These were indeed the questions. In trying to answer the question of *Whither* the Revolution would go, Carlyle, of course, had rather apocalyptic answers. Perhaps these struck a chord in Southey, for he too was inclined to despair that the state of the world and the state of England had been irredeemably damaged by 1789. In his *Reminiscences* Carlyle tells how sympathetic he found Southey toward the views he had expressed in his great book. The last time the two met, they sat on a sofa together and had a long talk:

> Topic ultimately the usual one, steady approach of democracy, with revolution (probably explosive) and a finis incomputable to man; steady decay of all morality, political, social, individual; this once noble England

getting more and more ignoble and untrue in every fibre of it, till the gold . . . would all be eaten out, and noble England would have to collapse in shapeless ruin, whether for ever or not none of us could know. Our perfect consent on these matters gave animation to the dialogue.[98]

In the end the whole discussion of France is a tribute to the inaugurating power of Burke's analysis. All the elements which constitute the later commentaries and critiques are to be found in his writings of 1790–1797. His objections to the philosophes and to Rousseau, his attacks on the coarsening of the sexual relationship, the threat to the family and marriage, the existence of a conspiracy against throne and altar, the seductions of abstract theory, the attractions of the English character and its close bond with church and Constitution, the contrast between 1688 and 1789, the plight and the importance of the émigrés, the ruthlessness of the new philosophy and the prominence of the men of letters, the new urban intelligentsia in the new world which had come to replace the old—all of these survive intact into the age of Carlyle and beyond. In molding an attitude toward France, Burke molded an attitude toward the Revolution and gave to the anti-Revolutionary forces the potent weapon of conservative nationalism. He taught his generation and the next the importance of being English. It was a lesson they deeply absorbed. "What," asked John Scott in 1814, "is the character of a philosophy"—meaning the French nation's philosophy—"that hesitates to acknowledge a national superiority so constituted?"—meaning the superiority of the British.[99]

3 Mackintosh and France: The Age of Anxiety

James Mackintosh was a young man of promise in 1790, but his great potential remained a matter of speculation, a good deal of it his own, during his lifetime. He was unfortunate in many respects. His enemies were much more distinguished as a group than his far fewer friends. He received a bad press from the likes of Coleridge, Hazlitt, and James Mill,[1] while the great admiration in which he was held by the Scottish Whigs, particularly Francis Jeffrey,[2] by the French liberals, especially Benjamin Constant and Mme. de Staël, and in the Holland House circle[3] was always modified by the recognition of his incapacity to do justice in writing to those talents that shone so brilliantly in conversation. Fundamentally, though, Mackintosh's reputation and career were blighted by his apparent volte-face on the French Revolution. Even after his death in 1832 we find Macaulay, Plumer Ward, and the anonymous author of *Notice to the Life of Sir James Mackintosh* (which introduced his unfinished work on the 1688 revolution) referring to the important and famous change in Mackintosh's opinions between 1791 and 1798—that is, between the publication of his best-known work, *Vindiciae Gallicae*, and the publication of his *Introductory Discourse to the Law of Nature and Nations*, a prospectus for a series of lectures delivered at Lincoln's Inn.[4] This was the crisis of his career. No recantation in this period elicited greater shock or bitterness. Only Southey compares with him in this respect, but Southey was less exposed because he was a man of letters only. Mackintosh wanted to be that, and a philosopher and politician too.[5]

A disciple by education and inclination of the French and Scottish Enlightenment, he exemplified in his career the difficulty of retaining belief in the basic tenets of Enlightenment thought during the hectic years between 1789 and 1832. He was in some measure a victim of the increasingly ideological quarrels which split the Whigs internally, at times bringing them close to and at times separating them from the Tories, Radical Dissenters, Westminster Reformers, and Philosophical Radicals. His own intellectual allegiances were fissiparous too. They included Burke and Montesquieu, the tradition of international lawyers—Grotius, Pufendorf—Hartley, Locke, and the Scottish Common Sense School. His liberalism was closer to the Continental kind, represented among his friends and correspondents by Degérando, Royer-Collard, Benjamin Constant, and Mme. de Staël. But in England the future belonged to Benthamite utilitarianism, not Continental liberalism, which was nonetheless to have a brief success in 1830. Mackintosh, a Scottish liberal émigré of the eighteenth century, found in the *Edinburgh Review* no more than a partial focus for his views; ultimately, like most émigrés, he confided himself more fully to his diary and journal—and, he may have hoped, to a more sympathetic posterity.

His published work lives in the shadow of more famous names. His unfinished book on the 1688 revolution, for which he had gathered immense quantities of material, much of it original, was kindly reviewed and then entirely outdone in popular esteem by Macaulay. So too his curious brand of modified utilitarianism, which, when published by Macvey Napier in the *Encyclopaedia Britannica*, was so fiercely attacked by James Mill in his *Fragment on Mackintosh* that his work on ethics, like that on history, is chiefly remembered for what it provoked others to say rather than for what it said itself. His *Vindiciae* lives parasitically off the great name of Burke, and his thirty-nine lectures on the law of nature and nations (to which only the general prospectus was published) are known now primarily for what Hazlitt said of them in *The Spirit of the Age* a quarter-century later.

The eclectic fury which Mackintosh displays in his reading is governed by an overwhelming anxiety over finding some system of belief which would effectively replace the collapse of his early convictions. He tried to pursue Coleridge through the labyrinths of German philosophy but was soon quite hopelessly lost; he tried to follow Burke's reading of 1789 in the light of 1688 but could not find in the analogy the grounds for condemnation of 1789 which Burke discovered; Continental liberalism, particularly Mme. de Staël, was intellectually attractive to him, but it seemed to include an attitude toward sexual matters which profoundly shocked and alienated him; utilitarianism seemed morally insufficient and in need of some supplement from the moral sense theories of Shaftesbury, Hutcheson, and others. Yet he could not provide this himself, and he could not belong to any of the groups with which he dallied. He was the last figure in the great line of Scottish academic philosophers; its decline is well represented by Mackintosh's politically dictated refusal of the chair of moral philosophy at Edinburgh in 1818 as successor to Thomas Brown.[6] He wanted a career in public life, for which he was singularly ill-equipped.

The fame he won with the publication of *Vindiciae Gallicae* in 1791 widened Mackintosh's circle of acquaintance immeasurably. Dr. Samuel Parr brought him to Birmingham in that year to show him the smoldering ruins of the houses burned in the political riots. As a further political lesson he accompanied Godwin and Parr on a visit to Joseph Gerrald in prison in 1793, before Gerrald was transported for sedition. Yet despite his Whig and radical friends, Mackintosh was already beginning to undergo a change of heart. The turn of events in France, especially the September Massacres of 1792, had begun to change his view of the Revolution so that by 1795, when he was called to the bar, his attitude was perceptibly closer to Burke's than it had been earlier. This was publicly revealed in 1796 in his *Monthly Review* notice of Burke's *Thoughts on a Regicide Peace;* in December of that year he wrote privately to Burke pleading for an interview and announcing, "I can with truth affirm that I subscribe to your general Principles & am prepared to shed my blood in defence of the Laws and Constitution of my Country."[7] Burke invited Mackintosh to Beaconsfield that Christmas; an account of the interview between them survives, later confirmed as accurate by Mackintosh himself.[8]

In 1799 Mackintosh began his series of lectures at Lincoln's Inn,[9] in which he made his rejection of the Revolution and of all radical notions painfully clear. He was particularly unfair to Godwin, who was in the audience. This provoked a memorable reply from the enraged Godwin.[10] Thereafter Mackintosh was regarded as the archapostate by Charles James Fox, Coleridge, Parr, Godwin, and others. The government greeted him as a recruit, and after Mackintosh had published a series of articles in the *Morning Post* in support of the war against France, Prime Minister Henry Addington offered him a knighthood and the recordership of Bombay. Foolishly Mackintosh accepted both. He left for Bombay in 1803, having given a last display of his power in his *Defence of Jean Peltier,* a case remembered for the final speech, in which Mackintosh attacked Napoleon, the Revolution, and despotism in general. The speech was translated by Mme. de Staël, and the two were close friends thereafter.

In the nine years he spent abroad Mackintosh lamented his choice in terms only slightly less bitter than his erstwhile friends at home used in denouncing it. Estranged from Parr, Coleridge, Godwin, and Fox, he was consistently portrayed as a man who had denied the

Revolution for the sake of government patronage. He was persecuted for this change of attitude by men who had changed with him.[11] In a sense Mackintosh became the whipping boy for his generation's remorse and disillusion, in part because he had so effectively articulated its early hopes. For a man who published only three pamphlets and a couple of dozen anonymous articles between 1791 and 1830, he drew an abnormal amount of attention. This was not on account of any extraordinarily repellent characteristics on his part, although in reading the evidence one might be tempted to believe so. It happened because Mackintosh, like Southey but more fully, embodied the new phenomenon of betrayal in an ideological war.

His diaries bear witness to his efforts to overcome his sense of betrayal, to understand all over again what the French Revolution meant, to regain the fame he had won for so brief a space and write a distinguished work in which he would explain the age to itself. But these efforts were to no avail; although he frequently laments that his temper was not suited to the tempestuous times, he was in fact a typical product of the age's turmoil. The sense of political betrayal is greater than that associated with a party or group. It is a sense of having helped rob the world of a once youthful feeling of hope and universal brotherhood. Mackintosh is the purest example of the effects of such political remorse in an age when that phenomenon had gained a new prominence. Despite his great abilities, he was so overcome by Burke's reading of the Revolution and by the Revolution's own developments that he spent much of his life trying to regain a position from which he could comprehend the transformation which Burke's opposition to France had produced in his own and in the English consciousness. This he never achieved.

The Romantic outcast plagued by a profound remorse is often a figure who has renounced human sympathy for the gloomy pleasures of a diabolical misanthropy or selfishness. He is first cousin to the political recanter, the man who has betrayed the Revolutionary doctrine of universal sympathy for a meaner and more selfish alternative. The so-called "cimmerian intelligences"[12] of the contemporary literature move through a political gloom which has become as all-encompassing as was the hope of political renovation which had briefly preceded it.[13] The various and vicious pen portraits of Mackintosh manifest this association quite clearly. In them he is exposed as a hard-hearted metaphysician, a man without normal feelings, a venal cynic.[14] He became, by freakish and unfortunate circumstance, an exemplary image of the age's guilt in the eyes of many. Although by no means alone in this respect, he was central to the immense mass of hostile commentary which surrounded most of the important writers of the time. Burke, Paine, Godwin, Southey, Byron, and Shelley were all at different stages cast by their opponents in the demonic role of creatures ultimately deficient in the basic human feelings and thus imprisoned in the fastness of their selfishness. Part of the difficulty in reading this commentary arises from the fact that the same image can represent quite different political views, for the recanter, like the revolutionary himself, was thought to be immune to human sympathy. This rapidly transposed image indicates the bearing of the whole post-Revolutionary dispute about the relationship between reason and feeling and, by extension, between patriotism and cosmopolitanism, natural loyalty and philosophical theory, wisdom and sophistication.

Mackintosh's position was not, of course, that of the glamorous or demonic Romantic misanthrope; but he was bedeviled by an issue which this age was fond of debating to the point of exhaustion. That was the reformulation of the roles to be assigned in political as well as in moral philosophy to feeling and reason. Initially Mackintosh believed that the hostile reception accorded the Revolution was the result of a damagingly heightened emotionalism. Later he came to believe that too great a reliance on rational and abstract theorizing had much to do with the violence which the Revolution had generated. These were the standard positions of commentators on both sides of the fence, but Mackintosh wanted to find a reconciliation between what he thought were extreme positions. Only by doing so could the cause of moderate Whig liberalism be saved. Yet the torrid climate in which he exercised his "coquetry between an active and a meditative life"[15] did not allow for a resolution of the issue. As a conversationalist he belonged to the salon, to the Holland House circle, where he was at his ease with men such as Samuel Rogers, Richard Sharp, "Bobus" Smith, and John Allen.[16] As an academic scholar he would have been in his element in the chair at Edinburgh. Instead he chose the world of politics and the great reviews, where the stereotyped attitudes toward the question of feeling and reason had hardened into the versions of French and English national character which had become central to the propaganda war. Moreover, on his return from Bombay in 1812—in broken health—he was himself subject to the caricaturing which had become an inevitable result of the fixed positions in the national dispute. He was a radical who had been bought by the government, a man who had betrayed generosity of feeling for selfish ends. He could not reestablish either his own reputation or his thought. In *Vindiciae Gallicae* he had defended good sense against excessive Burkean emotionalism; in his late writings he found himself compelled to give feeling a more prominent role without at the same time going over into irrationalism. Yet the irrational fears and furies of the time made it impossible for him to achieve the balance he sought. Much of his time in India was spent in agonizing over the loss of his reputation and the means whereby he might recover it.[17] At home he found that the life of a reviewer and minor politician allowed for no opportunity to establish a moderate position between the extremes of sentimental English conservatism and doctrinal, radical rationality.

From Vindiciae Gallicae *to the Lincoln's Inn Lectures*

The evolution of Mackintosh's attitude toward Burke is the key to his early development. *Vindiciae Gallicae* was a rebuke to Burke's emotionalism, but this was not its central concern. One of the reviews described it as having two main political objects: "first to defend the French Revolution, next to vindicate its English admirers. The great schism among the Whigs may be reduced to the question, which of the two parties,—the opponents or the admirers of the French Revolution of 1789—were the true Whigs of the English Revolution of 1688?"[18] This was well enough to the point. Burke had helped to force the issue in this direction, although the parallel between the two revolutions was an inevitable one, especially after the centenary celebrations of 1788. In a later review of Burke's *Letter to a Noble Lord* Mackintosh extends the parallel to embrace Burke's earlier career, particularly his defense of the American colonies against Britain and his part in obtaining the reforms of 1782.[19] But there is another strain in this pamphlet which opens wider issues than these points of British domestic controversy. The French Revolution demonstrated, says Mackintosh, that "it was time . . . that Legislators, instead of that narrow and dastardly coasting which never ventures to lose sight of usage and precedent, should, guided by the *polarity* of reason, hazard a bolder navigation, and discover in unexplored regions, the treasure of public felicity."[20] There is nothing here, or anywhere else in *Vindiciae*, which would have been strange to the ears of an eighteenth-century Whig, although he might not have agreed with it. It is the date which gives the passage its impact; or, more accurately, it is the retrospect provided by 1792 which makes this rather harmless advocacy for reason over custom appear more revolutionary than it is. The Foxite Whigs may have liked *Vindiciae* and preferred it to *The Rights of Man* because it seemed to hit the moderate center between

Burke and Paine. But the situation was moving so rapidly that within four years Mackintosh himself would believe that his pamphlet had been revolutionary. It did not change; but the feelings of its author and its audience did.

On another issue—the causes of the Revolution—Mackintosh also opposed Burke and took a cooler view of the matter: "In the French Revolution, all is to be attributed to general causes influencing the whole body of the people, and almost nothing to the schemes and the ascendant of individuals."[21] Burke won this argument too, at least in the short term. The whole conspiracy thesis helped mobilize the belief that the Revolution was a ruthless triumph of cunning intellect over unsuspecting and innocent feeling. Mackintosh consistently argues that the personal beliefs of the philosophes had nothing to do with the soundness or otherwise of their political analysis of the pre-Revolutionary situation.[22] This point, however, strong in itself, was weakened as the Revolution progressed and as the evidence did seem to point to some ulterior, if not frankly explicit, connection between the alleged atheism and licentiousness of the philosophes and the violence and shock of the Revolution. By 1796 Mackintosh was defending the philosophes on the grounds that their ideas had been abandoned, not put into effect, by the revolutionaries and that they had tried to avert the Revolution by converting the French king "from his scandalous indolence" and by trying "to sow in his frozen heart some seeds of virtue."[23] Thus he was already yielding ground before Burke, conceding that individuals could and did have as much influence on history as impersonal forces. In addition, Mackintosh's attempt to portray Burke as overemotional in his interpretation foundered when Burke claimed that it was precisely this failure to be galvanized by the threat of France which was a characteristic of the too tepid English reaction. England *needed* to be emotional to combat the hot conviction of the revolutionaries. So, although Mackintosh never believed the conspiracy theory as such,[24] he found no satisfactory alternative explanation for the Revolution. The sarcasm with which he had addressed Burke's exaggerated feelings in 1791[25] was sadly inept from the perspective of 1800. In that year he avowed to George Moore, on hearing of the formation of consular government in France:

> I have too long submitted to mean and evasive compromise. It is my intention, in this winter's lectures, to profess publicly and unequivocally that I abhor, abjure, and for ever renounce the French revolution, with all its sanguinary history, its abominable principles, and for ever execrable leaders. I hope I shall be able to wipe off the disgrace of having been

once betrayed into an approbation of that conspiracy against God and man, the greatest scourge of the world, and the chief stain upon human annals. But I feel that I am transported by my subject to the borders of rant.[26]

This tone is recurrent in Mackintosh's writings up to 1804, when Bombay had finally helped lend perspective if not enchantment to his view. His eagerness to get back to England and a parliamentary career was provoked by the memory of passages such as this, produced publicly, as he had promised, in his Lincoln's Inn lectures. He wanted to show that there was a consistency in his attitudes between 1791 and 1800—but this was not possible. He could not prove consistency where there was none to prove. Yet he wished to recover his reputation from the charge of betrayal. In a letter to Richard Sharp he writes: "But I own to you that my strongest motive was of a different kind . . . I wished for an opportunity of acting a strongly popular part in a conspicuous theatre, that I might be known in the latter part of life to be actuated by the same Principles which animated my youth. I was desirous of removing all ambiguities & fixing a consistent and decisive character."[27]

Out of the excitements of the years 1791–1798 Mackintosh emerged, before an audience of about 150 in Lincoln's Inn, as the lecturer on "The Law of Nature and Nations."[28] The audience was full of peers and Tory M.P.s; none of Mackintosh's Whig friends appeared.[29] Coleridge turned up for the repetition of five of the lectures in this highly successful course in the first three months of 1800, and he heard the strong anti-Revolutionary remarks which had apparently been omitted on the first occasion, in 1799. The introductory *Discourse* had led Godwin to break off his close friendship with Mackintosh because of its attacks on visionary philosophers and systems of universal benevolence. Hazlitt accused him of plagiarism;[30] Mackintosh's son, naturally, saw the matter differently. Whereas in *Vindiciae Gallicae* "he rose up to defend freedom against the attacks of high aristocratic and despotic principles; he now came forward to defend the very foundations of society against the fury of a wild enthusiasm, which usurped the name of reason."[31] Coleridge, writing in 1801, put the change in Mackintosh's principles down to rank ambition rather than intellectual conversion. To him Mackintosh was a rogue who wanted money, fame, and the smiles of the great.[32] His penetrating rancor ignores the nature of the intellectual change Mackintosh had undergone, one no less complete than his own.

The most important feature of the lectures is not their overt political content but their total rejection of the system of universal benevolence, which Mackintosh identified with some of the French philosophes and their English disciples, particularly Godwin. In its place he gives a highly Burkean account of the sources and preservers of authentic feeling. He has surrendered his earlier attraction to simple political forms for a belief in the slowly evolving complexity of human institutions and their intimate bond with ancestral and basic human feelings.[33] Man is now viewed in history, not in abstraction. Feeling is the ground of morality.

> No system of moral philosophy can, surely, disregard the general feelings of human nature and the according judgment of all ages and nations . . . The usages and laws of nations, the events of history, the opinions of philosophers, the sentiments of orators and poets, as well as the observations of common life, are, in truth, the materials out of which the science of morality is formed; and those who neglect them are justly chargeable with a vain attempt to philosophise without regard to fact and experience,—the sole foundation of all true philosophy.[34]

This is Burke, without much modification and with no apology. The only difference is that Mackintosh's claim that the French Revolution was brought about by the prevailing influence of false systems of ethical belief condemns him to reinterpret eighteenth-century ethical philosophy in order to show what had gone wrong. In effect his aim was to demonstrate how French thought had turned the English tradition from its true course.

Thus Mackintosh's account of ethical thought can be seen to have a political bias, just as his political thought can be described as having an ethical bias. He was persuaded by Burke that 1789 could be understood as a violation of the spirit of 1688; but he was hard put to find a satisfactory explanation for this belief. He recognized that a history of thought would be more difficult to write than a political history because "the circumstances which determine the Revolutions of Speculation are of so Subtile and evanescent a kind that the most refined politics of the most ingenious Statesmen are comparatively gross and palpable."[35] Yet there is nothing especially subtle in Mackintosh's treatment of the issue. In effect he claims that Condillac and Helvétius vulgarized the philosophy of Locke in both its moral and political aspects, and that these French developments were in no way implicit in the English tradition from which they derived, a tradition which also includes Bacon and Hobbes. The Continental contributions to the theory of liberty which England had helped to formulate include those of Grotius, Pufendorf, and Montesquieu, the great intelligences of international law, and in modern times Mme. de Staël. France posed a threat to liberty because from there came false reason (Helvétius) and inauthentic feeling (Rousseau). Their political descendants were Robespierre and Napoleon. Opposing them in the recent crisis were the forces of custom, precedent, accumulated wisdom, and natural feeling, preserved in the British Constitution, the most effective and monumental of all European institutions.

All this is a rather weak attempt to give intellectual respectability to the Anglo-French war of national types. The details of the argument are even less persuasive than its general outlines (one wonders if he had read Hobbes), but the simplifications to which Mackintosh subjected the issue are not ridiculous. They are important and telling features of the general relationship between French and English culture at that time. Elements of his arguments are to be found widely distributed throughout the writings of the period. He registered in compact form much of what was generally believed in intellectual circles. Coleridge, for instance, although he was a far more brilliant intellectual historian than Mackintosh, could not have disagreed with his conclusions. Precisely because he lacks Coleridge's penetration but agrees with his general description of the eighteenth-century philosophical tradition Mackintosh reveals more clearly the political bias which informed it.

By 1805 Mackintosh had decided to write three books: the history of the 1688 revolution; an important "system of ethics"; and the life of Burke. He did not start the last nor did he finish the first two, even though he admitted in 1810 that he was better equipped to write the life of Burke than the other projects.[36] In fact Mackintosh spent a good deal of time lamenting his inability to realize his own promise and his avowed aims.[37] His extensive knowledge was never shaped by clear convictions. Whatever his personal problems may have been, it is evident from his notes and scattered writings that the French Revolution created an impasse to his thought. He admired the American and English Revolutions; how could he explain his hatred for the French Revolution? Like everyone else he could ascribe the Revolution to the ill-effects of Enlightenment thought; or he could blame it on the Jacobins. He wrote to Lord Holland in 1805 about his famous Peltier speech, to which Lord Holland had obviously demurred:

> You complain a little of my saying too much against the Jacobins . . . because you fear that the world may confound them with the Revolution & the Revolution with the Principles of Liberty . . . Certainly the world is too apt to make this confusion . . . It has made it & it is one of the active enemies of whatever is liberal or generous among men . . . But what are we to endeavour? It seems to me that instead of making a vain attempt to preserve the Revolution and the Jacobins by endangering lib-

erty we must labour to preserve Liberty by sacrificing the Revolution and the Jacobins . . . This at least has appeared to me for several years to be the true policy of the Friends of Liberty in England. I acted on that notion in my little way & for so doing some of them more attached to sounds and names than to Principles were almost ready to cast me out of their number.[38]

This is a clear statement. Mackintosh had to sacrifice the Revolution for the sake of his principles rather than his principles to the cause of the counter-Revolution. This was the key to his consistency; but with it he had to unlock the still unanswered question, why had the French produced the Jacobins—or the philosophes? Whatever the "beginnings of such an unhappy state" may have been in France, the convulsions of the Revolution are more usefully seen as the result of "general causes, than as vices peculiar to that great nation."[39]

Sexual Morality and Ethical Philosophy

As late as 1805, then, Mackintosh was still prepared to argue that in following Burke he was a true Whig. His opposition to France was only partly articulated in his hostile account of the French philosophical tradition, and he remained uncomfortable with the popular notion that the whole issue could be explained in terms of national character. What he sought was a series of "general causes" which would explain why the French had behaved in so terrifying a manner. In his pursuit of these he took up the reading of the abundant memoirs of eighteenth-century France. He regarded the memoir as a literary genre in which the French excelled particularly. In these works he hoped to find the solution to his question. In 1807 he wrote to Richard Sharp:

> You must have read the Mémoires of Bezenval. I hailed in them the resurrection of French Mémoires which had I thought been buried under the vast piles of our declamation & metaphysics. They are it is true smutty & slovenly, very often trifling and intolerably tedious. But the frivolity characterises an old courtier—even the grossness represents the manner of Paris from the time of the Regent till the full ripeness and rottenness of Mme. Dubarry's reign. After having read myself blind about the Revolution I had no pictures of poor Louis & his Court in my fancy till I read this old intrigue.[40]

Six months later, having read the Vie privée du Vicomte de Mirabeau, he speaks of it and the memoirs of Bezenval as "the most valuable documents relating to that moral condition of France out of which the Revolution arose."[41]

Mackintosh also reacted strongly to the memoirs of Mme. Roland

and the letters of Mlle. de Lespinasse in 1811. He transcribed parts of the memoirs of Mme. de Montespan, which he read in 1820, taking immense care in recording them. After the death of Mme. de Staël, her son Auguste wrote to ask Mackintosh for help in publishing her book on the Revolution (the *Considérations*), commenting on the debased eagerness with which the English public swallowed biographies, anecdotes, and other material on the private lives of public figures.[42] Mackintosh is by implication innocent of this charge. He read this material for its historical interest, for an account of what he called the "moral condition" of France before the Revolution, and came to the conclusion that it was the very sexual license, begun under the Regency, which so sapped the French character that it became vulnerable to the infection of dangerous ideas. Others such as Southey and Croker were willing to treat this licentiousness as a national characteristic of the French; but Mackintosh saw it as a historical fact of the French eighteenth century. He was nonetheless horrified by it.

The letters of Julie de Lespinasse, one of the great hostesses of the Enlightenment salons of Paris, impressed him with their eloquence on the subject of love. But since the love described was adulterous, Mackintosh wished that they had been written by a man, since for a woman to write so "is such an outrage upon our Sentiments that it is difficult for us to consider it dispassionately." He goes on:

> If I were to value myself upon any thing it would be upon having better showed than other moralists the immense importance of female purity & its tendency to produce every other virtue . . .
> However justly we may reprobate the Parisian morals every individual at Paris must be tried by a reference to that standard. It is almost as unreasonable . . . to blame a Parisian Lady in the eighteenth century for offending against the rules of purity as it would be to think ill of a Mahometan for Polygamy.[43]

The next day he recorded in his journal the opinion that "the Palace of Louis XV was for forty years a brothel. Licentiousness in this triumphant State easily found immoral theory."[44]

So there it is in a nutshell. Like the other "high Protestant alarmists for social order in England,"[45] Mackintosh was convinced that sexual purity was a necessary condition for the attainment of liberty. This was the reason for the French failure after 1789. Lasciviousness denied liberty; French society had become decadent, and the Revolution was the culmination of that decay, not a recuperation from it. In believing this he failed completely to see the differences between the French aristocracy and the middle classes, although the sexual immorality of the one might have been a sufficient explanation of the increasing religious disbelief of the other.[46] It is little wonder that for all his admiration of Mme. de Staël he could never quite warm to her failure to submit to the "rules of morality."[47] Having shown that English hearts were truer than French, he was obliged to demonstrate why this was so. It was a moral as well as a historical question. Historically, he seemed to feel, the question had been answered. Morally it was still to be explained. This was the task of his proposed work on ethics.

Sexual immorality in France was, in Mackintosh's view, a product of selfishness or of the philosophies of egoism, which he believed to be both cause and consequence of the long trail of ruin. This was why he welcomed the revival of sentiment in counter-Revolutionary Europe. As early as 1807 he greeted the renewal of what he thought was the old association between religion, sentiment, and liberty.[48] Mme. de Staël, with her crusade for a new *enthousiasme*, represented the most influential elements in French liberalism, so conceived; despite his reservations about her private life and her fiction, Mackintosh regarded her as the prophet of a new and healthier dispensation in France. So in his ethical thought he had to argue that sentiment, different from selfish egoism and false benevolence, was the ground of liberty and that their natural alliance was cemented by religion. In his *Dissertation on Ethical Philosophy* he makes his disapproval of the "selfish system" quite clear, claiming that its results in France were sexual license, revolution, and despotism, while in England it had produced closet theories and cold-hearted radicalism. By these references he meant utilitarianism. In more positive terms he tried to demonstrate that there was a connection between true feeling and liberal government. Morality, sexual and otherwise, created the conditions for liberty. His attempt to demonstrate this, however, was a failure. He could provide no proof whatsoever of the necessary connection.

James Mill went straight to the heart of the matter in his rather brutal *Fragment on Mackintosh:* "There is no peculiar fitness, in what is called the selfish system of morals, to form the ground work of the despotic system of government. The sentimental system, which Sir James professes, is far better adapted to that end, and far more frequently worked with a view to its accomplishment."[49] The *Dissertation* was given short shrift by Mill because it was an attack on utilitarianism. Mackintosh had argued that utility was not a novel idea but a traditional and "generally an essential part of moral systems."[50] Bentham was more insistent than usual in his application of the principle, but he had made the error of confusing ethics with jurisprudence and, worse, of excluding feeling from any vital role in his calculation of the consequences as a criterion of the moral worth of an action. "The cultivation of all the habitual sentiments" is absolutely necessary;[51] these are so complex in their operation that a system such as Benthamite utilitarianism is, like the extreme political theories of the French, better at laying down rules abstractly conceived than at taking account of circumstances and difficulties. Moreover, feeling has its source in the family; the family is the basic unit of society; the security of the family is based on marital fidelity and chaste habits. Suddenly the attack on utilitarianism comes full circle to the earlier attacks on the French. They meet on the same issue: "Purity is the sole school of domestic fidelity and domestic fidelity is the only nursery of the affections between parents and children, from children towards each other, and, through these affections, of all the kindness which renders the world habitable."[52] Mackintosh goes on to demonstrate that conscience "must be a universal principle" to which the will is subsidiary.[53] This too aroused Mill's savage anger. Mackintosh always had the gift of making enemies. Once he had been accused of lacking feeling. Mill, knowing this, rejoins: "We know, however, by experience, that when Sir James talks of a want of feeling, he talks of it as a great blemish. He cannot bear that intellectual things should be spoken of in the language of intellect."[54]

Mill seemed partly to apprehend the problem with Mackintosh's moral philosophy. His distrust of abstract ideas, his defense of the family, chastity, circumstance, religion, cultural variety—these were Burke's historical arguments seeking to redefine themselves in the language of philosophy. Mackintosh could never free himself from Burke's thrall, even though he knew that his reputation for consistency depended on distinguishing between Burke's liberal position and his own. But he had absorbed Burke more deeply and was closer to him than he seemed to realize. To admit as much was to accept that he had in fact repudiated the ideas of *Vindiciae Gallicae*. He had recanted, but he could not wholly admit this to himself, partly because it had become such a public issue and the subject of so much hostile comment.

Mackintosh's parliamentary career, dominated by his zeal to introduce a reform of the penal system, was not sufficient compensation for his broken promise as a writer.[55] Coleridge called him "king of the men of talent,"[56] but it was a cruel phrase for someone who had once believed himself to have genius. Still it was accurate, and it helps to establish Mackintosh's significance. Caught, in his own phrase, "between the sage and the multitude,"[57] he was able to combine elements of the response of each to France and to illuminate the coherence between them. His native moderation had lost its historical setting once Burke engaged with the French Revolution in the new ideological dispute which so dominated Mackintosh's life. In 1823, in his inaugural address as Lord Rector of Glasgow University, he praised Burke (one of his predecessors as rector in 1784) and went on to mention his own much smaller achievement. His words are a sufficient conclusion to his blighted career and the stressful times in which he lived: "My life has been variegated and has left little time for the prosecution of projects that were formed in my early life; and the age of repose has been converted into an age of anxiety."[58]

4   Coleridge and Rousseau: A Philosophy for the Nation

Writing to his brother George in 1798 Samuel Taylor Coleridge announced that he had discarded his former enthusiasm for the French Revolution: "I have snapped my squeaking baby trumpet of Sedition & the fragments lie scattered in the lumber-room of Penitence."[1] At this point he was sure that his opinions "are utterly untainted with French Metaphysics, French Politics, French Ethics, and French Theology."[2] In fact Coleridge had never blown the trumpet very loudly, although he had gained sufficient prominence as a man of Jacobin sympathies among the supporters of government to be described in *The Beauties of the Anti-Jacobin* (1799) as one who had "left his native country, commenced citizen of the world, left his poor children fatherless and his wife destitute."[3] There are echoes here of Burke's attack on Rousseau for abandoning his children and making a mockery of the ideals of family life. This must have been especially bitter to Coleridge, who the year before had begun to turn against the "modern patriotism" represented in England by Godwin's opinion that "filial affection" was "folly, gratitude a crime, marriage injustice, and the promiscuous intercourse of the sexes right and wise."[4] Coleridge wanted to make "truth spread from the understanding to the affections;"[5] benevolence arises from the domestic feelings and informs the quest for truth. "The searcher after Truth must love and be beloved; for general Benevolence is a necessary motive to constancy of pursuit; and this general Benevolence is begotten and rendered permanent by social and domestic affections."[6] It is characteristic of Coleridge in the period 1796 to 1800, when he was moving from his early Unitarian faith and sympathy for France to his later anti-French and ultimately Anglican position, that he should dwell on the issue of the domestic affections, sexual promiscuity, and benevolence, which were integral to the dispute between Burke and Rousseau.

In March 1796 Coleridge protested the manner in which the "aristocratic faction" sneered at the "French writers" and at Burke.[7] By May his onslaught on Godwin had begun, even though he still felt able to recommend Benjamin Flower's *Cambridge Intelligencer* and the *New Monthly Magazine*, both of which were favorable to the Revolution, to readers who gained comfort from even if they did not give practical support to his own paper, *The Watchman*.[8] At this stage he was still vacillating between his former dissenting loyalties and his increasingly anti-Revolutionary conviction, no doubt influenced by the increasingly ominous climate of repression in England.[9] His intellectual allegiances were becoming more emphatically English. His comment on Southey's sonnet for Rousseau's cenotaph is one indication: "I do not particularly admire Rosseau [sic]—Bishop Taylor, Old Baxter, David Hartley & the Bishop of Cloyne are *my men*."[10]

The invasion of Switzerland, the somewhat exaggerated pose of disillusion in *France: An Ode*, and his discovery of German thought quickly followed. Coleridge, more concerned than ever "to evince the necessity of bottoming on fixed Principles,"[11] in the midst of this change placed feeling at the center of his moral and political universe: "My philosophical opinions are blended with, or deduced from, my feelings: & this, I think, peculiarizes my style of writing."[12] In the subsequent formulation of his political philosophy, Coleridge aimed to retain this priority of feeling while defining its historical role more fully than Burke and its philosophical role less abstractly than Rousseau. He wanted to make Burke's thought complete by making it more philosophical; the deficiencies of Rousseau were to be illuminated by a critique rooted in the actualities of historical circumstance. No doubt the Revolution affected Coleridge's view of Rousseau. It was a common belief that the ideas of the French intellectuals had been realized in Paris. The cult of Rousseau was especially associated with Robespierrean democracy and terror, and Burke had singled him out for attack as the most dangerous French thinker of all, largely because he corrupted feeling and morals. He was, therefore, an unavoidable challenge. Recognizing the power of his thought and his increasing influence in England,[13] Coleridge determined to refute him. The argument was fully under way by 1809 in *The Friend*.[14]

The Rejection of Rousseau

Coleridge objected to Rousseau's political philosophy on two counts: its reliance on abstract reason alone and the claim implicit in such reliance, that one system applicable to all possible combinations of

circumstances can be devised.[15] Against that he puts forward a Burkean notion of prudence: God can foresee all consequences, and
therefore his "infinite Wisdom" is "one with that Almighty Will on
which all consequences depend."[16] Man cannot; and so to achieve
harmony between his reason and his will, he needs prudence in order
to adapt to changing historical circumstances. A theory such as Rousseau's is inhumanly rigid and strict. That which is politically right "is
capable of being demonstrated out of the original laws of pure reason";
nothing else will do.[17] Yet the extreme rigor and purity of Rousseau's
thought is not countered by a corresponding concession of all things
to expedience. This is the defect in Burke.[18] Rousseau's thought has
great merit, especially on the question of "a *rightful* constitution of
government."[19] It is not enough to regard his doctrines as the characteristic products of an unbalanced personality, as Burke did.[20] Coleridge therefore had to negotiate a position between the peremptory
claims of abstract theory and the ad hoc responses of expedience. He
saw the first phase of the dispute between England and France in
philosophical terms. Although his aim, like that of so many of his
contemporaries, was to resolve the dispute by defining a specifically
English vision of the alternative to French radicalism, he was the only
one among them to devise a political philosophy which was not damagingly provincial in its range and application.

The most vulnerable of all Rousseau's distinctions, in Coleridge's
view, is that between the General Will *(volonté générale)* and the Will
of All *(volonté de tous)*:

> He admits the possibility, he is compelled by History to allow even the
> *probability*, that the most numerous popular assemblies, nay even whole
> nations, may at times be hurried away by the same passions, and under
> the dominance of a common error. This will of all is *then* of no more
> value than the humours of any one individual: and must therefore be
> sacredly distinguished from the pure will which flows from universal
> Reason. To this point then I entreat the Reader's particular attention:
> for in this distinction, established by Rousseau himself, between the *Vo-
> lonté de tous* and the *Volonté générale*, (i.e. between the collective will,
> and a casual over-balance of wills) the falsehood or nothingness of the
> whole system becomes manifest.[21]

The failed distinction here is itself the consequence of a failure to distinguish between Reason and Understanding.[22] Coleridge is not, of
course, denying Reason itself, simply because Rousseau assigns such
sovereignty to it. Reason, while keeping its own identity, must learn
to "clothe itself in the substance of the individual Understanding and
specific Inclination, in order to become a reality and an object of con-

sciousness and experience."[23] By descending to particulars, Universal Reason manifests itself as the Understanding while not being identical with it. By virtue of this distinction, Coleridge admits the necessity of reconciling what he called Theory and Expedience within a political system. Theory provides principles, understanding provides the means of acting upon them. Rousseau had offered the principles only; the means of acting upon them were nonexistent. The General Will in effect is a fiction. It is merely a way of claiming that the actual has no meaningful existence until it is coincident with the idea or theory that Reason has created. To Coleridge this is both totalitarian and impractical.

While the effect of this argument is damaging to Rousseau, it has another aim. Coleridge may have turned his back on his dissenting and radical past, but he did not thereby condone the excesses of the English Tory reaction to the Revolution and to the English Jacobins. He knew the evils of expedience without Reason as much as he feared those of Reason without expedience. He wanted

> an enforcement of the absolute necessity of principles grounded in reason as the basis or rather as the living root of all genuine expedience. Where these are despised or at best regarded as aliens from the actual business of life, and consigned to the ideal world of speculative philosophy and utopian politics, instead of state-wisdom we shall have statecraft, and for the talent of the governor the cleverness of an embarrassed spend-thrift.[24]

The embodiment of this kind of statecraft was William Pitt the Younger. Pitt had opposed the Revolution on grounds of contingency and for selfish motives rather than on the grounds of fundamental principle. Coleridge then makes an important distinction. Motives, which Pitt had followed, are so complex and mutable that they can never be safely identified and known; but motives are the occasions of action, not its ground. The ground of action is Reason, which forms the basic personality of an individual; character, one's social and variable guise, is molded by motive. Personality wills action, motive justifies it. When a man such as Pitt is entirely given to motive, he shows his lack of principle: "It is not the motives govern the man but it is the man that makes the motives."[25] Pitt lives entirely in the world of circumstance; Rousseau thinks entirely in the world of universal Reason. One has produced repression, the other terror. The distinctions Coleridge makes between these worlds are not academic; they are part of his attempt to find a political world in which neither prevails—French Revolution nor English Reaction.

Yet Coleridge's critique of Rousseau, although powerful, is also polemical. It is no final dismissal of Rousseau's political philosophy to point up the confusion between the General Will and the Will of All, or to say that it is a verbal distinction only, without substance. Coleridge's distinction between Reason and Understanding, his division of the world into its noumenal and phenomenal aspects, was borrowed from Immanuel Kant, whom he read while in Germany in 1798–99.[26] But he did not know—indeed he could not have known—that Kant had found this very distinction in Rousseau.[27] He was therefore unwittingly using Rousseau's own distinction to reduce him. This does not mean that Coleridge's commentary on Rousseau is any less valid; but it does expose its polemical intent, for Coleridge had cast Rousseau in a role which did not do justice to Rousseau's thought. For Burke he had been the great sentimentalist, the hypocritical preacher of cosmopolitan benevolence. For Coleridge he was the apostle of pure Reason, the forerunner of Robespierre. Each view was determined by considerations that had more to do with the defensive requirements of English culture than with the range of Rousseau's writings.

Rousseau did in fact make precisely the distinction Coleridge found lacking. In *Emile* he gives an account of the ideal development of the understanding and of feeling while admitting that the universal idea of Man must always be encountered in its diverse forms in different cultures.[28] The aim of education is to develop what he calls *amour de soi*, a recognition that the good of all coincides with one's own good—as opposed to *amour-propre*, a selfish form of interest exercised at the expense of the community. The development of *amour de soi* leads to the formation of Conscience. Conscience can then cooperate with Reason, which knows the good. Conscience makes that knowledge effective. The *sentiment intérieur*, the native human feeling for the good, precedes Reason.[29] When Reason is perfected by feeling, virtue is achieved. It is a cultural triumph, distinct but also ultimately deriving from the natural goodness *(la bonté)* which belongs to the state of nature, not the state of civil society.[30] Man is educated to a state of grace after the loss of his original happiness in the fall from nature to society. Rousseau's philosophy has within it the distinction between Reason and Understanding (or, in his terms, Intelligent and Sensitive Reason)[31] which Coleridge thought of as his own or as having originated in Kant. In Kant it has much greater rigor. It is true, however, that initially the distinction was strongest in Rousseau's ethical philosophy, but it was so much weakened by the time of *Du contrat social* (1762) that Coleridge, whose main interest was the political aspect of Rousseau, could be excused for having failed to see its ghostlier presence there or in *Economie politique* (1755).

Yet in *Contrat social* Rousseau suggests that a community has a corporate self which would be as damaged by the predominance within it of selfish impulses as would the individual who had developed *amour-propre* rather than *amour de soi*. Therefore a community which follows its better nature is a community determined by the General Will; the Will of All would predominate only where the community was in danger of disintegrating as a political or social idea.[32] He is here formulating a version and a vision of the ideal community which is not far removed from Coleridge's final version in *Church and State*. Common to both is the moral notion that Reason and public feeling share an accord which it is the purpose of education to confirm. Furthermore, the expression of a community's best self in the concept of the General Will is neither necessarily totalitarian nor remote from the notion of an educated elite which would in a sense be its expression.

This does not entirely dispose of Coleridge's objection. He may be right in saying that the General Will is in practice indistinguishable from the Will of All and that it is on that account a political nullity; but he is wrong in his reasons for saying so. The General Will is not a notion which belongs solely in the domain of abstraction. It is a form of Public Conscience. The cooperation of conscience and reason produces morality, and in the civil sphere, which is the only sphere in which the General Will can exist, morality takes the form of *la vertu*— that is, *political* virtue, the intentions and conduct proper to a good citizen. Moreover, the individual stands in a reciprocal relation to the General Will; he surrenders to it the whole of his natural freedom and receives in return his civic freedom. This relationship is translated into action by the Law, the creation of the Legislator. It is here that the weakness for which Coleridge had been probing lies. The Legislator is a Solon or a Moses or a Messiah. He redeems the civic state from sin and rewards it with grace or virtue, the civic correlative of the lost state of innocence. Such a Legislator could also be Robespierre—or Napoleon. Coleridge seems to have sensed the danger in Rousseau's thought without being altogether sure where it lay. That is one of the traditional problems of reading Coleridge. His texts are commentaries on other texts rather than formal expositions themselves. There is consequently a degree of overlap and confusion between his own ideas and those of the writers he discusses.[33]

Rousseau insisted that the individual will is both sovereign and subject when it functions as part of the General Will. The ideal integration of the individual within the social grouping, prepared for in *Emile*, is realized in his novel *La nouvelle Heloise*, in which the idealized Julie is both a rebuke to and a reconciler of the extremes of sentiment and reason represented by Saint-Preux and Wolmar.[34] The paradoxical element in Rousseau, the derivation of his political and ethical thought from fundamental positions which are clear and yet elusive at the same time,[35] was not looked upon kindly by Coleridge. In this he followed tradition. Diderot, D'Alembert, Voltaire had all preceded Burke in regarding Rousseau as a sophist, a cynic, a moralist who dazzled with paradoxes but left nothing of value.[36] In Coleridge's writings Rousseau the moralist is secondary to Rousseau the political theorist; so intent is he on stressing the despotic tendency of the *Contrat social* that he sees little or nothing of the idea of a community which is offered in that and in many other works of the period.

This blindness to important aspects of Rousseau's thought is surprising, given the attention Coleridge paid, especially after 1817 to the issues involved in the description and revival of a national community. Part of the reason, as I have indicated, is that Coleridge came to know Kant's political philosophy without being aware of Kant's debt to Rousseau. Going by what Kant had written in *Zum ewigen Frieden* and in *Metaphysische Anfangsgrunde der Rechtslehre*, Coleridge must have found a much more formal and complete separation of the unconditioned and intelligible from the contingent and sensible world than Rousseau would have recommended. Although he frequently mentioned with a mixture of delight and awe the system of "trichotomy," which he had discovered in Kant and through that rediscovered in his favorite seventeenth-century Anglican divines,[37] Coleridge was pleased with a technique characteristic of Kant's approach rather than with the substance of his thought. For he has substantially the same objection to Kant as to Rousseau, even though Kant wholeheartedly defends the radical autonomy of the individual will. In *Rechtslehre (The Science of Right)* Kant demonstrates that autonomy and the realization of it in society by the free acceptance of social responsibilities. He rewrites Rousseau:

> And thus it is not to be said that the individual in the State has sacrificed a *part* of his inborn external freedom for a particular purpose; but he has abandoned his wild lawless Freedom wholly, in order to find all his proper Freedom again entire and undiminished, but in the form of a regulated order of dependence, that is, in a Civil State regulated by laws of Right. This relation of Dependence thus arises out of his own regulative lawgiving Will.[38]

This too would deserve Coleridge's criticism of the General Will in Rousseau, although Kant changed the emphasis from the problem of will in relation to universal reason to the problem of freedom in relation to the state. If the individual surrendered his whole freedom to the state in exchange for civic freedom, in what sense (other than the merely verbal) could freedom be said any longer to exist? And by whom could it be said to exist at any given moment? The paradox at the heart of Rousseau's General Will and of Kant's regulated and "proper Freedom" is that they imply that one *must* choose to be free. The very radical nature of their idea of freedom is tainted by the necessity for coercion in realizing it. Receiving these problems, one from Rousseau, the other from Kant, Coleridge sought a way of resolving them which would be applicable to England and would not have the terrible effects they had had in France, whose citizens had forgotten that "reason . . . in perfect purity is found in no man and in no body of men."

> This distinction the latter disciples of Rousseau chose completely to forget, and,—far more melancholy case—the constituent legislators of France forgot it likewise. With a wretched *parrotry* they wrote and harangued without ceasing of the *Volonté générale*—the *inalienable sovereignty* of the people: and by these high-sounding phrases led on the vain, ignorant, and intoxicated populace to wild excesses and wilder expectations, which entailing on them the bitterness of disappointment cleared the way for military despotism, for the satanic Government of Horror under the Jacobins, and of Terror under the Corsican.[39]

The purity of Rousseau's doctrine made it dangerous. Yet Kant's capacity for abstracting from circumstances for the purpose of formulating a general Law, while powerfully attractive to Coleridge in his search for "fixed principles," was also antipathetic to his search for a way of combining principle with circumstance. Kant's separation of the world of actual circumstance from the world of Law was much sharper than Rousseau's.[40] The Law of Right, for instance, stated: "Act externally in such a manner that the free exercise of thy Will may be able to co-exist with the Freedom of all others, according to a Universal Law."[41] This Law of Right can also ratify the justice of making offenders submit to its precepts.[42] This is close to Rousseau's idea of the General Will forcing man to be free by educing his best self.[43] In fact Kant was not in the least unwilling to concede that a political community has force as its governing principle. The individual will "must become collective" if a civic community is to be formed.

> As therefore a uniting cause is necessary over and above the individual wills of all in order to blend them into a general will, which no one of them can do alone—the fulfillment of this idea in practice can be based on no other factor in a polity than on force, on the compulsion of which public law is afterwards founded. This, indeed, leads one to expect great divergences in practice from the theoretical conception, since one can

little trust the moral disposition of the legislator to leave the formation of a just constitution to the general will of the people, after he has united the uncivilised mob to form a nation.[44]

From this point it is not far to Kant's final denial of resistance.[45] The radical autonomy of the individual will is philosophically secure; on the political level it is transformed into a collective will, in which form it is denied the right to resist established power, for in doing so it would become merely capricious and make force supreme over Law (even though Law may initially owe its existence to force). This is a political philosophy developed in the light of the French Revolution. The element of compulsion is inseparable from the idea of freedom. It is this element in each instance, Rousseau and Kant, which made Coleridge uncomfortable. He did not recognize the close kinship between the two, but he did recognize that they were in their different ways formulating a political ideal which owed as much to Geneva and Prussia as his own owed to England. He looked for a way of asserting the political system appropriate to a state which had evolved historically as a community rather than to the more abstractly conceived collective notion of the State expounded by Rousseau and Kant. He emerged from the debate with Rousseau and from the engagement with the issues of Reason and Burkean Expedience convinced that a political philosophy specifically English in its origins and application but more universal in its significance urgently needed to be developed.

Anglican Nationalism

Coleridge's theology bears the impress of both Kant and the Anglican divines of the seventeenth century. He accepts the division of the noumenal and the phenomenal worlds, one governed by Reason and the other by the Understanding; but he also wants some principle which connects them. Christianity provides, in the mystery of the Incarnation, the paradigm of such a connection. The *Treatise on Method*, with its famous "reconciliation of opposites," offers the classic exposition of the system of "trichotomy," the method whereby two worlds schismatically divided are reunited by a principle which partakes of each of them.[46] Coleridge is in effect converting a dualistic into a monistic vision of the world. There remains, however, an insoluble problem. In *The Statesman's Manual* the phenomenal world is denied any autonomous existence; only the noumenal world has real existence, given it by God. This was the guarantee of its freedom. Here the distinction between Rousseau and Coleridge is glaringly obvious. For Rousseau the idea of society represented in the *Contrat social* is a world of freedom because it has been chosen by man as in accord with his own best nature. But in Coleridge the ideal world is free only to the extent that we participate in God's nature, that our will is in accord with the will of God. This accord is the basis of personality. But man, considered in his phenomenal aspect, as a character in society, is completely determined, an object in a world of objects. The two worlds remain separate. Freedom belongs to one as surely as the lack of freedom characterizes the other. It is clear that in Christian terms the only means by which this unhappy division can be overcome is by faith. Coleridge attempts to describe this:

> Faith seems to me the coadunation of the individual will with the Reason, enforcing adherence of Thought, Act, and Affection to the Universal Will, whether revealed in the Conscience, or by the Light of Reason, however the same may contravene or apparently contradict, the will and mind of the flesh, the presumed experience of the senses & the understanding, as the faculty, or intelligential yet animal instinct, by which we generalize the notices of the senses, and sub*stantiate* their *spectra* or *phaenomena*.[47]

Thomas Carlyle was among the first to claim that Coleridge lacked the intellectual courage to live through to a solution of the fundamental problem his earlier career had left to him. Having "skirted the howling deserts of Infidelity," he failed to press on to the "new firm lands of faith beyond"; instead he preferred to "create logical fatamorganas for himself on the hither side."[48] This is to the point. All of his wrestlings with the doctrines of the Incarnation and the Trinity, all of his assertions of congruence between reason and religion, and even his definition of faith in the *Essay on Faith* do not help Coleridge escape from the Kantian prison to which he had too readily surrendered. There was no means by which, given the distinction between noumenal and phenomenal, the idea of freedom which supervened in the first could modify the fact of determinism which prevailed in the second. Coleridge, rather than Kant, had become subject to the obsession which stimulated his reading of Rousseau's political thought— the obsession which conceived of the world in terms of a contrast between theoretical perfection and chaotic meaninglessness. Burke had taught him something of the idea of prudence as a means of diminishing, even abolishing, this contrast; and Coleridge knew that it could not be sustained in any system of political philosophy which he could expound, since it was on precisely this point that he had rejected Rousseau and French theory in general. It was also on this point that he had been so fatally attracted to Kant, who, having shown him how to repudiate Rousseau, had entrapped him in the very same dilemma Coleridge had found so damaging in the *Contrat social*. He was at an intellectual impasse in 1819, a decade after he had determined to combat Rousseau. It was at this point that he turned, in his *Philosophical Lectures*, from theology to history. In evolving a philosophy of history he managed to find an exit and thereby a means of formulating his political philosophy.

The basis of Coleridge's philosophy of history is the conviction that the social and political characteristics of an era are dependent on the prevalent philosophical climate. Systems of philosophy are

> highly influencive and connected with the manners, nay with the great political events, of mankind, in a degree and in a manner which ought to impress on the minds of all statesmen that without a congenial philosophy there can be no general religion, that a philosophy among the higher classes is an essential condition to the true state of religion among all classes, and that religion is the great centre of gravity in all countries and in all ages, and accordingly as it is good or bad, whether religion or irreligion, so all the powers of the state necessarily accommodate themselves to it.[49]

Two conclusions follow. History has a discernible pattern which is traceable through an examination of the predominant philosophical systems of the past. A philosophy of history can be educed from a history of philosophy. Coleridge likens the process of interaction and reiteration in these great systems to a symphony by Cimarosa, with stated themes being repeated and reinterpreted until they form one harmonious and satisfying unity.[50] Furthermore, the intervention of Christianity in this historical process was decisive. Philosophy as such had completed itself before Christ; his coming gave it another dimension in which to develop. Here Coleridge allows his theological convictions an opportunity to reexpress themselves. If the Greeks had Reason, the Christians surpassed them by having Religion as well.[51] History is, then, a perpetual ebb and flow between polarities, never achieving rest in any one but being periodically characterized by the chief features of the predominating polarity. Thus the pattern of Greek thought is reproduced in Christian Europe, with the essential difference that it has now a recognizable end. It is purposive. Within that framework all history, ancient as well as modern, has passed from dark eras of materialism into sunlit periods of Platonism. Thus the age of materialism, which according to Coleridge reached its climax in the French Revolution, has begun to pass over into a new Platonism, heralded by the rise of the philosophy of idealism in Germany. From the English Restoration to the French Revolution the "mechanico-corpuscular" theories of philosophy had predominated, with all the attendant and unfortunate consequences in the social and political life of Europe. Now the new age was beginning.[52]

One may suspect the dichotomies which are the organizing principles of the *Philosophical Lectures*. They may be regarded as a reversion to a historical defense of Anglicanism, a return more sophisticated but no less passionate to the example set by Burke.[53] Having failed to make theology philosophical or philosophy theological through his attempted fusion of English neo-Platonism and Kant,[54] he provides instead an account of the development of philosophy which has as its polemical interest the exposure of modern French philosophy as a fading example of a degrading and gross materialism. This is all the more pronounced in Coleridge's assigning to the golden age of Anglican civilization in the seventeenth century an exemplary role in his subsidiary argument in favor of local patriotism and against cosmopolitanism.[55] In this light Coleridge is reduced in these lectures to falling back on a highly tendentious analysis of past history for the defense of Christianity and idealism against the secular materialism of the Enlightenment.

This account of the *Philosophical Lectures* fails in only one respect, although that is central. It does not take as a serious consideration the need, recognized by Coleridge, for a truly philosophical interpretation of the French Revolution in England by those who were opposed to it. In making Rousseau's political philosophy central to the whole issue, he had identified what seemed to him the feature which made that revolution different from any other—a challenge ill met by most of his contemporaries. The doctrine of the General Will, a form of coercion in the disguise of unanimity, cleared the way, in his opinion, for the titanism of the individual will as the will of the State. This new religion of the State seemed to him the typical product of a revolution which had been prepared for by intellectuals. He was not at all concerned with the conspiracy theory about the philosophes. His concern was for the larger view which would demonstrate a connection between the theories of such a group and the politics in which they would eventuate. Since he found Burke's analysis persuasive, he wanted to build on it while compensating for what seemed to him its overemphasis on the circumstances of a specific historical situation. He did not want to ignore these; he wanted to find a way of incorporating that kind of political empiricism into a philosophy which would meet the Enlightenment vision of man on the high ground of principle as well as on the lower ground of experience. Christianity, with its inherent dualism, reconciled by the Incarnation, was a religion which showed how the unification of the two worlds of what he sometimes called Idea and Image could be achieved. Kant's method had shown how general law could be derived from circumstance. Anglican theology had insisted on the supremacy of the "supersensuous" to the "sensuous" world. In attempting to combine all these features within one system of thought Coleridge had run into difficulties to which the *Philosophical Lectures* provided a solution. The statism of the modern intellectuals had to be countered by another version of the ideal political polity. Otherwise there was no rational argument against the implicit authoritarianism of theories which had already had highly explicit and frightening authoritarian consequences in France with the Jacobins, Robespierre, and Napoleon.

Thus *On the Constitution of the Church and State* (1830) has as its central and most enduring suggestion the need for a *clerisy*, a body of learned men in charge of cultivating the nation. Supported by what he calls the *Nationalty*, this body constitutes the National Church, distinct from but inevitably involved with the existing Anglican Church. This elite group is a counter to the philosophes. Its function is not to subvert and corrode existing institutions but to educate the people to become loyal citizens, to reconcile the idea of the State with that of the Nation. This "virtual aristocracy," as Burke would have called it, is the connecting principle between Permanence and Progression, Civilization and Cultivation. Through it modern industrial England would be able to resist the doctrines of the French Revolution and reassume the Anglican heritage of the seventeenth-century divines—Baxter, Hooker, Jeremy Taylor—who seemed to Coleridge to prefigure his concept of the clerisy. In its defense of the alliance between Property and Power, in its regard for the historical evolution of the culture and the Constitution, the whole work is heavily indebted to Burke. Along with Burke, however, there are other possible influences and models— Schiller among them.[56] The differentiating element, though, is evident in the title. Coleridge is insistent on the governing power of an Idea to bring into existence something—a state—which always stands to the original Idea as an approximation but is never fully its embodiment. In this account the bifurcated world which had been so unbridgeable for him before is finally rejoined. History is a demonstration of the "continued influence" of the idea of a Constitution. It exists as a principle in the minds of its subjects and therefore has a reality which is as great as that of the Constitution which existed at any given time in English history. There is therefore no longer any separation between a noumenal and a phenomenal world. Both exist; both are real; they are interdependent, although they are also distinct. Their various embodiments throughout history, together with the principle or Idea itself, constitute the specific English tradition. Coleridge goes to quite unnecessary trouble in the opening chapter to attack Rousseau for having believed the original social contract to have been a historical fact. For Rousseau, as for Coleridge, it is a juridical fiction. But this glancing attack (and its accompanying footnote on German Illuminati and the framers of the 1791 French Constitution) indicate the central point I have been addressing—Coleridge's eagerness to distinguish between the English and the French traditions in political thought, to affirm the heritage of liberty which distinguishes the former as against the new-minted theories of abstract tyranny that characterize the latter.[57]

Church and State is the most sustained exposition of Coleridge's political philosophy. It lacks some of the richness of the *Philosophical Lectures*; it is disappointingly fragmentary at times; but it is a solution to a crucial series of questions posed by the Revolution and the Enlightenment. Coleridge *did* complete or at least extend Burke's thought. He *did* see something of the dangers of Rousseau's political theory. Most of all, to the general clamor for a definition of the English national spirit he gave the only notable response. In doing so he defined the limits of conservative thought in that period.

5   Godwin, Helvétius, and Holbach: Crime and Punishment

In 1798 Robert Fellowes, an Anglican curate, protested, as Burke had done before him, that a new spirit of universal philanthropy had been lately recommended by certain philosophers to replace traditional local patriotisms. He singled out William Godwin for special comment: "Among the most singular of these is Mr. Godwin, author of an elaborate work called "Political Justice." His system is totally impracticable; and even if it were practicable it would be pernicious:—it would abolish all the endearments of love and charity, and steel the human heart against its best sympathies, with a more than stoical insensibility."[1]

Godwin won notoriety as the exponent of a rigorously inhuman utilitarianism in the years immediately following publication of his *Enquiry Concerning Political Justice and Its Influence on Morals and Happiness*. This contemporary caricature of his thought has endured ever since.[2] The fact is that Godwin was not at all a utilitarian in any strict sense of the word, although he was obviously indebted to certain features of the utilitarian theory of moral obligation. Among his contemporaries he is closer to Thomas Holcroft than to anyone else, and even the most cursory reading of Holcroft's writings would reveal how far he is from recommending any system of moral obligation which does not give primacy to the force of human feeling. It is, however, still customary to describe *Political Justice* as a treatise in which the author expounds an unrelenting intellectualism and to read the novels which came later as exercises in a compensatory sentimentalism, stimulated by Godwin's marriage to Mary Wollstonecraft.[3] This constitutes a complete misreading of Godwin and a failure to recognize the nature of the problems which he and Thomas Holcroft attempted, in their different ways, to solve.

Their work is characterized by three main convictions: first, that Necessity rules the world, or in other terms, that we inhabit a world governed by immutable physical laws; second, that man is naturally altruistic or benevolent; and third, a corollary to the preceding, that it is to man's benefit to exercise this benevolence because in doing so he increases the sum of human happiness and recognizes the reality of the physical laws which govern our being. One could make this sound more utilitarian than it is by saying that Godwin and Holcroft, recognizing that we are physical beings and that we therefore seek pleasure and shun pain, claim that we have a natural tendency, which is in accord with the physical laws of the universe, to do that which will increase pleasure and diminish pain. It is perfectly possible also to see in this a justification of the utilitarian calculus of pleasure and pain, which is more closely associated with Bentham. The major difference between Benthamite utilitarianism and the Godwinian system is that Bentham believes man to be naturally selfish; Godwin does not. Bentham's system demands that society be so organized that love of self, in seeking satisfaction, will have no harmful effect on others. Godwin and Holcroft by contrast believe that love of others, when expressed in action, is in fact the most sublime form of self-love. Society in their view need not be reorganized to make this belief effective; the moral education of the individual in this belief would in itself lead to a reorganization of society. They are not reformers like Bentham; they are moral revolutionaries whose most passionate plea is that we should be sincere both with ourselves and with respect to others. The effect of this would be to dissolve the amalgam of class distinctions and regulations which we call society, replacing it with a universe in which human relationships would spontaneously develop without the intervention of laws, regulations, or customs arising from distinctions of wealth. They are moral anarchists for whom society as such is little more than the expression of an irrationality in man arising from his failure to be sincere and to realize the fundamental and rational benevolence of his nature in a world where the only binding laws are those of physical nature.

Given these premises, Godwin could not view the French Revolution with approbation. His diary reveals his dislike for the violence and mob rule in Paris: where such disorder exists rational behavior is next to impossible. Yet he was deeply involved in the events in England which arose from the Revolution. He was an approving member of the audience which heard Dr. Richard Price welcome the Revolution in that high biblical strain which so angered Burke. He was also a member of the committee which accepted Paine's *Rights of Man* for publication; he played an important part in the discussions provoked by the famous treason trials of 1795, and he managed to be as friendly for a time with Coleridge and Mackintosh as he was with Holcroft.[4] Besides, few Englishmen were as well versed in the writings of the French Enlightenment. He had read Rousseau and Montesquieu with care and was, by his own admission, so deeply affected by Holbach's *Système de la nature* and Helvétius's *De l'esprit* that the reading of them led eventually to his outright rejection of Christianity in 1787.[5] It is clear that Godwin came to regard the Revolution as a force opposed to much that was best in the thought of the Enlightenment. While he rejected the course of one, he retained his belief in the principles of free inquiry and discussion underlying the other. His notion of an elite composed of "literati," a rational group of publicists with the good of mankind as their goal and the lucidly persuasive pen as their means, found its ideal in the philosophes.

This is by no means to say that Godwin was so influenced by the thought of the French Enlightenment that he can be understood only as one of its offshoots. He is very clearly part of that utilitarian tradition of English thought which includes Hobbes, Mandeville, Hartley, and Bentham; equally, he has affinities with the tradition of moral thought which gives preeminence to an intuitive moral sense and which includes Bishop Butler and Samuel Clarke.[6] Godwin attempted to blend these traditions into one system of thought and in doing so sought the aid of Helvétius and Holbach. By looking at the work of these writers, we can judge what Godwin learned from them and allow their influence on his work the prominence it deserves. First, though, a brief account of the moral theory which Godwin develops in *Political Justice* may help to distinguish it from the kind of utilitarian morality with which it has so often been confused.

Godwin's Moral Theory

It is certainly possible to select passages from *Political Justice* which would seem to prove that Godwin's morality is, *au fond*, Benthamite. For example: "Morality, as has already been frequently observed, consists in an estimate of consequences; he is the truly virtuous man, who produces the greatest portion of benefit his situation will admit."[7] Godwin goes on to prove that the impartial estimate of the consequences which flow from any proposed action is a display of benevolent altruism, not of selfishness. The detachment which appears to be so impersonal is in fact the prerequisite of true benevolence, since benevolence directs itself primarily toward the welfare of others, not of oneself: "The soundest criterion of virtue is, to put ourselves in place of an impartial spectator, of an angelic nature, suppose, and uninfluenced by our prejudices, conceiving what would be his estimate of the intrinsic circumstances of our neighbour, and acting accordingly."[8] In other words, a complete knowledge of the circumstances is necessary for the practice of benevolence in any single case. Godwin claims that to see the truth is to love it and therefore to act in accord with it. To be totally rational is to be totally benevolent. Such a claim demonstrates the obtuseness of the point of view which regards him as a writer who extols reason at the expense of feeling. Right reason spontaneously produces right feeling; the wish to behave well is gratified by the capacity of reason in showing us how to behave best: "Virtue, sincerity, justice, and all those principles which, begotten and cherished in us by a due exercise of reason, will never be strenuously espoused, till they are ardently understood. In this sense nothing is necessary, but to show that a thing is truly good and worthy to be desired, in order to excite in us a passion for its attainment."[9]

Godwin, far from being a man fanatically devoted to some machinelike model of reason, reserves his most eloquent pleas for the disciplining of feeling in order to attain the happiness of both the individual and mankind. Feeling so disciplined constitutes his idea of virtue:

> Virtue is nothing else but kind and sympathetic feeling reduced into principle. Undisciplined feeling would induce me, now to interest myself exclusively for one man, and now for another, to be eagerly solicitous for those who are present to me, and to forget the absent. Feeling ripened into virtue, embraces the interests of the whole human race, and constantly proposes to itself the production of the greatest quantity of happiness. But, while it anxiously adjusts the balance of interests, and yields in no case, however urgent, to the prejudice of the whole, it keeps aloof from the unmeaning rant of romance, and uniformly recollects that happiness, in order to be real, must necessarily be individual.[10]

The innate generosity of man must be disciplined into a rational program of behavior. *Political Justice* is exactly that. It is a blueprint for the ideal state; but equally it is clear that such a state can never become an actuality unless the difficulties of actual circumstances are taken into account. In other words *Political Justice* is a prolegomenon to the novels and, in a lesser degree, to *The Enquirer*, as well as to some of the other multifarious works which Godwin was later to produce. Godwin believed passionately in the possibility of perfection, but only if perfection is taken to mean all that can be achieved within the limits of the necessary laws of the physical universe. He was also aware, as who could not be, of imperfection, an awareness heightened no doubt by the collapse of so many utopian hopes during the Revolu-

tionary period. To travel from one state to the other, man needs Will—
or, as Godwin and Holcroft would have called it, the exercise of Mind.
This is not to be confused with either caprice or the Kantian notion
of the autonomous free will; neither is it to be rejected in favor of that
"scheme of material automatism" with which, in Godwin's opinion,
the system of Hartley (and of Helvétius and Holbach) was "unne-
cessarily clogged."[11] Man is neither free nor determined, but he can
determine to make himself as free as necessity allows.[12]

Therefore, in leaving the theoretical purity of *Political Justice* behind,
Godwin was not in any sense commencing a long recantation of principles the extravagance of which had become apparent even to him.
In his own words: "It is true that no theory, accurately speaking, can
possibly be practical. It is the business of theory, to collect the circumstances of a certain set of cases, and arrange them. It would cease
to be theory, if it did not leave out many circumstances; it collects
such as are general and leaves out such as are particular."[13]

Godwin turned to literature in order to examine in specific form
representative circumstances by which his theory would be tested.
Those circumstances all relate to one issue—the issue of power and
its abuse in the name of self-love. Allied to these are ancillary questions
such as those of public reputation, delusions of freedom of the will,
the causes of evil in an imperfect society, and the complexity of motive.
After 1798 Godwin moved closer to these questions, although the
general drift of his interest in that direction was already visible in the
changes made between the three editions of *Political Justice*. In *The
Enquirer* we read:

> But though reputation will never constitute, with a man of wisdom and
> virtue, the first and leading motive of his actions, it will certainly enter
> into his considerations. Virtue is a calculation of the consequences, is a
> means to an end, is a balance carefully adjusted between opposite evils
> and benefits. Perhaps there is no action, in a state of civilisation and
> refinement, that is not influenced by innumerable motives; and there is
> no reason to believe that virtue will tend to diminish the subtlety and
> delicacy of intellectual sensation. Reputation is valuable; and whatever
> is of value enters into our estimates. A just and reasonable man will be
> anxious so to conduct himself as that he may not be misunderstood . . .
> it is a spirit of false bravado that will not descend to vindicate itself from
> misrepresentation.[14]

The world of Godwin's novels is adjacent to this. It is also, however,
in this area, where Godwin attempts to show how his theories apply
in actual circumstances, that the influence of Helvétius and Holbach
is most apparent. There are important differences between them, to

be sure. But Godwin is indebted to both of them because he, like them, attempted to develop a secular morality based on the conviction that in a world of otherwise unchangeable physical laws there is also an unchangeable moral law which determines that there will always be a reciprocal relationship between the gratifications of self-love and the general good of mankind. Helvétius and Holbach approached this problem from different angles; Godwin was influenced by both, and it shows in his novels more than anywhere else.

Helvétius: Self-Love and Power

It might be well to begin a consideration of Claude-Adrien Helvétius with a quotation from *Political Justice* which should remind us of the differences between him and Godwin. Godwin's consistent interest in the motives for action—an important consideration in his novels— gives his writing an emphasis which Helvétius, in his constant preoc- cupation with the consequences of action, avoids:

> If self-love be the only principle of action, there can be no such thing as virtue. Benevolent intention is essential to virtue. Virtue, where it exists in any eminence, is a species of conduct, modelled upon a true estimate of the different reasons inviting us to preference. He that makes a false estimate, and prefers a trivial and a partial good to an impartial and comprehensive one, is vicious. Virtue requires a certain disposition and view of the mind, and does not belong to the good which may accidentally and unintentionally result from our proceeding.[15]

Against that, on the subject of virtue, Helvétius declares: "The virtuous man is by no means he who sacrifices his pleasures, habits, and strongest feelings in the public interest, for such a man is impossible. Rather it is he whose strongest desire is so much in conformity with the general interest tha⁺ he is almost always obliged to be virtuous."[16]

The utilitarianism of Helvétius, with its emphasis on the conse- quences of action and on self-love as its only source, leads inevitably to the notion that man in order to be happy must live in a rationally controlled environment. After all, the environment determines the degree of coincidence possible between self-love and public interest. To Helvétius it seemed obvious that the influence of the Catholic Church in France severely reduced the possibility of such coincidence, not only by its system of laws and punishments but also by its various attacks on the (to him) legitimate selfishness of the individual. Edu- cation was all-powerful, and therefore control over it had to be ab- solute. The totalitarian implications of this are clear now, but Helvétius would have defended his system on the grounds that the philosopher-king, or Legislator, who would lead the people from ignorance to enlightenment would do so in their own best interest, since he would be acting rationally in accord with the nature of things.[17] Nevertheless, his whole emphasis is on the formulation of a legislative system based entirely on his redaction of the epistemology of Locke and Condillac. The essence of his whole system is that every area of human life is controlled by necessary forces, that knowledge reveals their workings to man, who then adapts himself to these known surroundings in a manner calculated to give him the greatest possible pleasure and the least possible pain. This type of thinking produced many books which were in fact blueprints for a new society, such as *De l'esprit* and *Political Justice*, in which the prejudices of the past and the accumulations of history were regarded with a uniform hostility. It is typical of Helvétius that he should use the simile of a religious order to illustrate his conception of what the new legislator would need initially to do: "Therefore, the first step in the formulation of an excellent legal system, is to pay no attention to the hostility of prejudiced views, nor to the friction of competing personal interests, nor to already established customs, laws, or usages. One must look upon oneself as the founder of a religious order who, in dictating his monastic rule, has no regard whatsoever for the conventions and prejudices of his future subjects."[18]

Although the Godwinian concepts of virtue with its altruistic bias and of Mind with its spontaneous and, from a political point of view, anarchic capacity to create relationships free from the interference of laws or systems are both far removed from this philosophy, there are on other levels many points of contact. They share a belief in the unimportance of heredity, in the identification of vice with error, and in the pernicious effect of vested interests in the state. More important, though, Helvétius sketched out a genealogy of the passions which led him directly to confront the problem of self-love in its severest form; that is, when self-love takes the shape of the desire to dominate others. If self-love is conceived of as nothing more than a rather petty selfishness, it is a politically manageable problem, given the possibility of creating a controlled environment which would actually help to promote that selfishness toward consequences which were never part of its intentions. But Helvétius, looking for a Newtonian coherence in the moral as in the physical world, announces that "the passions are in the moral world what movement is in the physical universe. It creates, destroys, conserves, and animates all; without movement, all is dead. So too, the passions inform the moral universe."[19]

It follows that the intensity of moral compulsion is in proportion to the extent to which the self-love of the agent is involved. Legislation could indeed stimulate human progress by recognizing this fact.[20] All this holds, though, only as long as Helvétius can keep his epistemology and his political philosophy anchored in the conviction that happiness is identical with pleasure.[21] He does, however, describe other and more complex passions, and these are not so readily referred to a physical basis. There is for Helvétius a natural and automatic desire for physical pleasure; but passion in becoming more complicated becomes less natural and, one would think, less dependent for its satisfaction on anything which could be called physical. He sketches the stages of a psychological development which, deriving from our physical nature, passes from love of pleasure and fear of pain to a condition of self-love in which the wish for happiness is born. This in turn leads to a longing for power so that happiness may be achieved. This wish for power is the agent of all the dangerous and artificial passions which derive from "natural" self-love.[22] Power has close connections with reputation, and reputation is itself closely related to self-esteem, since the public and the private image of a man often supplement each other. Helvétius at this point completely evades the serious questions which his description of the power drive involves by asserting that true greatness consists in its pursuit, since to attain power is to forsake the esteem of tiny cliques in society for the sake of gaining the esteem of the whole social world.[23] To seek fame is to seek self-respect, and to despise fame is a sign of failure.[24] Still a problem remains. If power can be so justified as a legitimate human impulse, then how can its abuse be punished? It is possible that a man in power could commit a crime against society which would remain secret.[25] His reputation would be untarnished, yet it would not correspond to his worth. Helvétius can give no answer to this problem, since he makes worth and reputation *necessarily* coincident. It is no complete answer to say that wickedness is caused by the laws and mores of a society.

Godwin realized this in part. He inherited from Helvétius the problem of power and its relation to secret crime. For Helvétius there was no real answer; for Godwin, with his belief in the natural altruism of man, there was. To act selfishly or cruelly involves a self-contradiction for a man who is constituted to act benevolently. A criminal therefore in hurting others, even secretly, also hurts himself. At this point Godwin enters the territory of crime, remorse, and punishment, which would later be mapped out by the various Romantic movements. First, though, he found that it had already been to some extent explored by Holbach. It is clear that a good deal of the scrutiny to which ques-

tions of power, reputation, self-esteem, secrecy, and remorse are subjected in Godwin's novels is owing to what he read in Holbach's *Système social* and *Morale universelle*. I would also suggest that Godwin's
political philosophy is only fully developed in his novels and his ov-
ertly political and theoretical writings taken together; and that a certain
hesitancy in his thought is exposed by the way in which he vacillates
between a kind of environmental determinism, which is borrowed
straight from Helvétius and does not at all consort with other elements
in his own thought, and an intense preoccupation with the complex-
ities of human motive, which arises fundamentally from his interest
in the perversions of a conscience afflicted by false notions of its own
welfare. Yet the subject of the novels is an uncomfortable one for
Godwin; although he did not evade the issue of crime and concealment
as Helvétius had done, he did evade the possibility that evil is radical
and innate, not simply artificial and the result of error. Besides, the
circumstances of his life also account for a certain final deterioration
in the quality of his work, and this must be taken into account in any
criticism of his failure to go far beyond the problems and solutions
he inherited from Holbach and Helvétius.

   In any event, the problem which Godwin faced in his novels was
that of evolving a morality which could exert pressure on a man's
private conscience as effectively as on his public actions. It was a crucial
question for those who wished, like Helvétius and Holbach, to found
a secular ethic which could rival the Christian system of sin and grace,
reward and punishment. Although the similarity between the thought
of Helvétius and Holbach is remarkably striking in almost all other
respects, on this issue the two differ.[26] Holbach and Godwin both
seek a safeguard against hypocrisy, especially when it is practiced by
men in socially or politically powerful positions. It is a moral problem
with profound political implications which Helvétius had ignored or
failed to see.[27] Its inherent difficulties make the possibility of formulating a law or set of laws which would control the sphere of morals,
public and private, extremely remote.

Crime and Punishment in Holbach's Philosophy

The Abbé Bergier, Holbach's most formidable contemporary critic,
accused him of destroying morality by reducing all things to the level
of the physical and the useful: "It is evident that the confounding of
the moral with the useful, virtue with physical well-being, duty with
desire, moral obligation with the forever renewed wishes of our hearts,
leads to the destruction, not the establishment of a moral system; to

do this is to form a code for brute-animals, not for men."[28] In one sense this is true; but then Holbach's terminology and that of the Abbé were based on entirely different assumptions about the nature of man and the world. No one was more ardent or hectoring in his desire to create a new ethical system based on exclusively materialist premises than was Holbach.[29]

The remorseless aggression of his writing gives his work the appearance of consistency; yet despite the uniformity of its expression, his thought is a tissue of contradictions. Nevertheless, his works had a profound influence in nineteenth-century England,[30] and Godwin was attracted to one of their most striking anomalies—Holbach's concept of conscience.[31] This embraced precisely those relationships between honor, reputation, self-respect, and the guilt of secret crime which Helvétius had failed to develop.

According to Holbach, disorder results when some person or thing acts in contradiction to its nature. Chance or accident is only apparent; knowledge would reveal the interaction of cause and effect.[32] All is linked in the great chain of necessity: "There is nothing accidental or fortuitous in nature."[33] In this tightly constructed world, man seems to have little possible margin of error. He is nothing more than a transient combination of particles of matter who must adapt to his environment or perish.[34] His intellectual and moral life is rooted in the physical and, like it, is part of the inescapably determined and determining system of the universe. Freedom is out of the question: "Man is no more free to think than to act."[35]

The Helvétian reciprocity between private and public good takes its place quite naturally in this system: the good is what is socially useful, evil what is socially harmful.[36] But Holbach, unlike Helvétius, also paid attention to the internal harmony of the personality. His *Système de la nature* acknowledges the Helvétian system of external harmony and determinism; but *Système social* and *La Morale universelle* both concentrate on the psychology of the individual who acts in a moral manner and, more interestingly in the present case, on the individual who acts immorally toward his environment and his fellows. Good and evil are not measured in this internal world by beneficial and harmful effects. Order in the internal world, like order in the adjacent world outside, is dependent on each person's abiding by the principles of his nature; good and evil are then defined in those terms: "The Good is that which is in conformity with our nature; Evil is anything contrary to it."[37]

Just as enlightened reason reveals the source of disorder in the external world, conscience examines the shortcomings of the internal universe. The perceptions of conscience seem, according to Holbach, to be limited to a privileged elite:

> The voice of conscience is heard only by those who are introspective, who reason about their actions and in whom a sound education has nurtured the wish to please and the habitual fear of being despised or hated. A person formed in this manner becomes capable of judging himself; he reproaches himself when he commits an action which he knows might alter the feelings which he wants constantly to arouse in those whose esteem and affection are necessary to his happiness. Every time he behaves badly, he feels shame, remorse, repentance; he examines his behaviour, he corrects himself, out of fear of undergoing again the painful recognitions which often force him to hate himself, because at such times he sees himself as he is seen by others.[38]

The conscience-striken man is acutely conscious of the loss of his reputation in the eyes of those whom he has injured; and this loss disturbs his own well-being. Holbach was obviously trying to build up an internal world of reciprocal relationships to balance the deterministic external system which he had adopted from Helvétius and others.[39]

Conscience, then, is the internal faculty by which man becomes aware of any contravention of his own nature. Similarly, it alone can impart that feeling of satisfaction which a good reputation, an unblemished honor, deserves. Holbach was careful to distinguish this from the traditional aristocratic honor, with all its military and religious connotations. True honor consists in a balance between self-respect and the respect of others: "No force on earth can deprive the good man of that true honour which belongs to him alone."[40] The possession or loss of reputation becomes a barometer of the moral climate in which man lives.[41] As long as a man follows his nature and acts morally, he will feel at peace with himself and is at home everywhere. He is integrated into his milieu and is part of the great natural process of life.[42] If society at large has become vicious, the virtuous man, like Godwin's St. Leon, retreats to the bosom of his family. In this as in many other details of Holbach's philosophy a religious shadow is visible; Holbach tends to think of his virtuous men of conscience as a persecuted elite or sect.[43] This contrasts sharply with Helvétius's idea of the great man rising above the praise of particular societies to bask in the esteem of the general public.[44] Both writers have in common a preoccupation with the issues of self-esteem and public reputation and the need to make these congruent with each other. The emphasis is different in each case, largely because Holbach confronts the problem of secret crime which Helvétius ignores. As a consequence he is much more involved with the dilemma of the private conscience and its system of internal censorship and punishment.[45]

To put it bluntly—as Holbach does—the issue of the undetected crime is resolved by the claim that the criminal punishes himself with a severity which society could not equal. "Laws can only punish visible crimes and public misdemeanours; they cannot deal with hidden faults and unknown crimes. Nevertheless, these do not remain unpunished on that account. Man's very nature punishes him for them. The wrongdoer is always in a state of fear, while the good man, even in the midst of misfortune and despite human injustice, enjoys the respect of men of good will, and savours the sweetness of a clear conscience."[46] The good man enjoys the respect of his comrades in belief and the pleasure of his own clear conscience in the midst of a hostile and corrupt world.

Just as the good man enjoys reputation and status wherever he goes, the criminal, conversely, becomes an outcast throughout the civilized world. Having lost the esteem of others, he loses self-esteem; these are interdependent. The predictable result is that he learns to despise himself.[47] Trapped in this unequal struggle against society and against his own nature, the criminal becomes a social outcast: "Only the good man is a truly social being. The criminal is always anti-social . . . Wickedness is a constant struggle of one man against all and against his own happiness."[48] The criminal is guilty not of sin but of social immorality. Yet this itself is nothing more than a new version of what had been called sinfulness, with reputation, public opinion, and the fear of dislike acting as the deterrents instead of wild superstitions; and as deterrents they are, in Holbach's view, much more effective than the vague terrors of religion.[49] Yet the tortures of the criminal are as vividly portrayed and as excruciating as those provided by conventional religion:

> Nature's law decrees that the criminal can never know a pure happiness in this world. His wealth, his power do not save him from his own nature. In the lucid moments spared him by his passions, if he dwells on his interior state, he suffers the reproach of a conscience troubled by the dreadful spectacles which his imagination presents to him. Thus it is that the murderer, during the night, even when awake, believes he sees the mourning ghosts of those whose throats he has cruelly cut; he sees the horrified stare of the enraged crowd which cries aloud for vengeance.[50]

Not surprisingly, such wretches give themselves up or commit suicide. Holbach here delivers a cautionary tale with some notably Gothic touches. The conclusion is that criminals succumb to despair because they cannot be reconciled to themselves. They have broken nature's law, and nature's law in turn breaks them.[51]

Godwin adapted most of Holbach's theory on this matter to the plots and purposes of his novels. Yet he frequently finds himself tempted to blame all forms of criminal action and alienation on the defects of his hero's society, rather than to investigate the nature of alienation and remorse in a society which by its very nature breeds such diseases. Holbach, for instance, also accepts the common notion that the criminal is very rarely a completely evil person—strictly speaking he should say never completely evil—since, according to the utilitarian or any other morality, he must benefit someone at some stage of his life.[52] In one sense we can understand Godwin's heroes as exemplars of the lesson that evil cannot avoid producing good. At the same time, it is hard to be entirely convinced that the Godwinian belief in benevolence is a more powerful antidote to the illness of his heroes than the environmental determinism of Helvétius (to which Godwin sometimes retreats). His heroes are emotionally disturbed criminals because their society has rendered them morally incompetent to see either their own or the society's good. They are in flight from their recognition of a criminality of which they themselves are victims. Godwin seeks the motive for evil in his criminals while at the same time wishing to say that criminality is socially determined. He cannot have it both ways at once, so he has it both ways alternately throughout his novelistic career. In Holbach he discovered the image of the criminal, the man whose isolation and torture represent the antithesis of that Godwinian and Holcroftian calm and peace of mind which we find in the implacably confident heroes of their novels and plays. In passages like the following we find concentrated the entire system of emotional conflict in Godwin's novels, one in which the guilty man feels "fear, shame, remorse; painful feelings which make us hate ourselves and which are perpetually revived in us by a troubled imagination and a disturbed mind. We harbour within ourselves our own enemy from whom we cannot escape. 'Where can we escape to,' said Anthony, "when we are unhappy with ourselves?"[53]

We must also remember, however, the presence of Holcroft and his almost fanatical hatred of secrecy, itself deeply connected to his interest in the relationship between crime, with all its subtle prevarications, and virtue, with its straightforward simplicity. In the advertisement to his play *Knave or Not?* he speaks of the nature of his villain Monrose:

> Persons, who have made the human mind their study, have discovered that guilty men exert the whole force of their faculties to justify their own course of action to themselves. To this principle the writer was strictly attentive, in pourtraying the character of Monrose. His design

was to draw a man of genius, misled by his passions, reasoning on his actions, systematising them, condemning them in principle, but justifying them in practice, and heating his imagination by contemplating the crimes of others; that he might still maintain that respect for himself of which the strongest minds, even in the last stages of vice, are so tenacious.[54]

So on the one hand we have the just man in a corrupt society, filled with Senecan confidence in his own righteousness; on the other we have the tortured, powerful, diseased criminal clinging desperately to the phantom of public reputation. We are already in the middle of *Caleb Williams*.

Godwin's Philosophic Parables

Godwin's first novel, *Things as They Are; or, The Adventures of Caleb Williams*, generally known by its subtitle, was published in 1794; it became one of the most popular books of the age.[55] Even Godwin's opponents were agreeably surprised by the imaginative power he displayed, although the hostility to *Political Justice* still lingered and made itself manifest in almost every notice or review. One anonymous commentator admirably summarized the general response: "We found romance in his philosophy; and it is but candid to own that we find philosophy in his romance. Fancy is a faculty which we should not have expected to find in the brain of a philosopher who had struck his hand upon his heart and felt it stone; yet fancy Mr. Godwin possesses in no common degree."[56]

The gloomy power of all of Godwin's novels disturbed many; his skill was admired, but his subject matter seemed odd: "He delights to explore the dark recesses of the heart. Still it is by this strange predilection that Godwin in prose, and Byron in poetry, are distinguished from all other writers of the present age, not less than by the eminent talent; which both of them devote to this uninviting branch of the anatomy of mind."[57] Even though in his preface to the novel Godwin emphasizes the work's political bearing, "the anatomy of mind" remains its most memorable achievement. In pursuing this Godwin registers the influence of Holbach, which reveals itself in two forms. The first is an extension of Holbach's attack on the aristocratic and feudal interpretation of honor and its replacement by the code of true honor, which is rooted in a clear conscience. A social fiction is replaced by a moral conviction. The second is an adaptation of Holbach's portrait of the man who, guilty of a secret crime against both his own nature and society, is punished by the terrors and remorse of his afflicted conscience. Both these ideas are welded together in

Caleb Williams to compose a work which is at once a recast of *Political Justice* in the form of a parable, an exploration of extreme psychological states, and a development from the Gothic romance toward the beginnings of the modern detective novel.[58]

The political background of *Caleb Williams* has some bearing on the novel's purpose. Godwin did not dare include his preface in the first edition of 1794, when the witch hunt against liberals and radicals reached its peak with the arrest of Thomas Hardy, Horne Tooke, and Thomas Holcroft on charges of treason. Their acquittal eased the situation, and the preface appeared in the editions of 1795 and 1797. In it Godwin explains his attempt to combine the didactic and the narrative elements:

> It was proposed, in the invention of the following work, to comprehend, as far as the progressive nature of a single story would allow, a general review of the modes of domestic and unrecorded despotism, by which man becomes the destroyer of man. If the author shall have taught a valuable lesson, without subtracting from the interest and passion, by which a performance of this sort ought to be characterised, he will have reason to congratulate himself upon the vehicle he has chosen.[59]

Caleb Williams was a story particularly appropriate to the England of the 1790s; its connections with the contemporary political scene emphasize its social preoccupations.[60]

The urgently confessional tone of the book is established in the opening lines; its onward movement scarcely falters after that.[61] The complex figure of Ferdinando Falkland dominates the eponymous hero; psychologically Falkland is a morbid psychotic upon whom intolerable pressures are brought to bear. In fact these pressures are related to the reader at secondhand through Williams, whose own sufferings are the physical counterpart to Falkland's mental agonies. Falkland murders the brutal Tyrrel; others are executed for the crime. Williams is persecuted because he knows of Falkland's guilt. Godwin elicits sympathy for Williams as the victim of social injustice while at the same time portraying the sufferings of the criminal. At a deeper level Williams and Falkland merge; they are both victims. Falkland is the victim of his prejudices, which are the basis of society; Williams is the victim of society, which supports Falkland's prejudices. It is a vicious circle, and the grief of both victim and persecutor at the denouement of the novel testifies to Godwin's bleak sense of the waste and destruction engendered by the system. In an unenlightened age victory belongs to no one.

Falkland's aristocratic leanings are quickly revealed.[62] Godwin is careful to portray him as a man who is attractive and sympathetic in many ways but corrupted by the prejudices of his social class. The threatened duel between him and Count Malvesi over a ridiculous point of honor betrays the absurdity of the aristocratic code; it also anticipates Williams's fate. Falkland warns Malvesi that their dispute has almost had a tragic outcome, because

the laws of honour are in the utmost degree rigid, and there was reason to fear that, however anxious I were to be your friend, I might be obliged to be your murderer. Fortunately the reputation of my courage is sufficiently established, not to expose it to any impeachment by declining your present defiance. It was lucky, however, that in our interview of yesterday you found me alone, and that accident by that means threw the management of the affair into my disposal . . . But, if the challenge had been public, the proofs I had formerly given of courage would not have excused my present moderation; and, though desirous to have avoided the combat, it would not have been in my power.[63]

All of the concepts with which Holbach struggled in his attempt to construct a secular ethic are explicit here. Self-love, the interaction between it and public opinion, reputation, aristocratic honor, the destruction of human happiness by the regulations of an inhuman code—all of these are so faithfully reproduced by Godwin that *Caleb Williams* reads at times like a novelistic version of the *Système social*.

The Malvesi incident foreshadows the arrogant Tyrrel's public humiliation of Falkland. Struck down by the brutal squire, Falkland feels that his reputation is violated. At once he enters the long night of horror and crime. Although this horror is genuine, its most damning aspect in Godwin's eyes is that it derives from an overweening respect for an artificial code and is so powerful that it overcomes the horror Falkland should properly feel for his unjust persecution of Williams.[64] But outraged virtue is compensated by two considerations. The first is that Falkland's conscience will torture him more implacably than he and society can torture Williams: "The vigilance even of a public and systematical despotism is poor, compared with a vigilance which is thus goaded by the most anxious passions of the soul."[65] The moral, found also in Holbach, is that we cannot escape ourselves; Williams's picaresque flights from the pursuing Falkland are also symbolic of Falkland's flights from the Furies of his own conscience.[66]

The second consideration which helps the virtuous Williams overcome the tyranny that besets him is the internal conviction of his own rectitude, his faith that he is one of the few elect to whom is granted the paradise of Truth. Armored in this belief he feels impregnable, and Falkland's apparently omnipotent influence is reduced to nothing: "I exult, said I, and reasonably, over the impotence of my persecutor.

Is not that impotence greater than I have yet imagined? I say, he may cut off my existence, but cannot disturb my serenity. It is true: my mind, the clearness of my spirit, the firmness of my temper, are beyond his reach.''[67]

The contrasts in *Caleb Williams* are stark, as rigid in some respects as those in *Political Justice*. We have Truth pitched against Error, Candor against Secrecy, uncalculating benevolence against calculating policy. The bliss of candor, that very Holcroftian notion, is the reward granted to a man who allows the spirit of universal benevolence to animate his conduct. It is not a very sophisticated philosophy, but it is an interesting attempt at one, especially in the light of what Shelley later did with this nucleus of convictions. It is easy to exaggerate the psychological abnormalities of Godwin's characters and ignore or underrate the fact that they represent, in a rather diagrammatic fashion, the answer to a problem in moral philosophy. Godwin was, like Holcroft and Holbach, worried about crime because its secrecy could have very disturbing effects on an ethical theory which presumes that self-esteem is as much dependent on the esteem of others as is self-love on the happiness of others. He would have agreed with Joseph Priestley that ''no person, who is not entirely divested of the common feeling of mankind, will bear to live abhorred by his fellow citizens, and to die with infamy entailed upon his name and posterity.''[68] But if, as in *Caleb Williams*, an innocent man must be persecuted for the preservation of another's public reputation, then surely the assumed ratio between self-love and the happiness of others is called into question. Perhaps it may be said that Godwin treated the problem rather melodramatically under the combined influences of Holcroft and his belief in the capacity of truth to prevail over all complications; of Mary Wollstonecraft and the image of the harmonious family unit which his brief marriage with her seems to have left permanently with him (as a memory only); and of the Sandemanian sect, of which he had been a member before 1787, with its primitivism, an element more pronounced in *St. Leon* and *Fleetwood* than in *Caleb Williams*.[69] The moral problem still remains unsettled, however, and it is further emphasized by the irresolution of *Caleb Williams*. Neither simple sincerity nor illicit power wins in the struggle; the ambiguity of the novel reveals a hesitation on Godwin's part which may do him credit as a novelist but is not to his advantage as a philosopher.

In fact, after *Caleb Williams* Godwin's powers visibly declined. *St. Leon* repeats the pattern of a vain physical pursuit which mirrors a spiritual odyssey. Once again the hero is beguiled by the false charms of wealth and rank from the cultivation of his moral nature and is cut off from intercourse with society. The painfulness of this exclusion is all the greater here because of Godwin's new-found desire to promote the family as a basic image for humankind. Candor is seen as the most necessary of all virtues in the preservation of the domestic affections; St. Leon destroys the intimate relationship between his family and himself by his secrecy. This secrecy to Godwin and Holcroft amounts to untruth.[70] There is a moral here which tends to alter the bias of Godwin's thought: "Philanthropy is a godlike virtue, and can never be too loudly recommended, or too ardently enjoined: but natural affection winds itself in so many folds about the heart, and is the parent of so complicated, so various and so exquisite emotions, that he who should attempt to divest himself of it, will find that he is divesting himself of all that is most to be coveted in existence."[71] This outburst occurs when St. Leon decides to forsake his role of the impartial philanthropist to mankind for a life of service to his son Charles as recompense for having destroyed domestic harmony and ruined the boy's family life. This could be regarded as a symbolic decision by Godwin himself. Released from the prison of his own theories by the affection of Mary Wollstonecraft, he decided to make amends to an area of human experience which he had unjustly ignored. This is the main emphasis of the novel; the theme of secret guilt is subsidiary to it and does not develop the Holbachian ideas of secret guilt with the fullness or with the vehemence of *Caleb Williams*.

In the preface to *St. Leon* Godwin declares his intentions of giving personal affections a more prominent place in his philosophy than they had achieved in *Political Justice*. He does so in the conviction that they would not distort the sense of justice in the mind.[72] His rather Sandemanian admission that feeling and justice are "jarring principles" which have to be reconciled is ominous, however, for in the next novel, *Fleetwood; or, The New Man of Feeling*, the division which Godwin had made earlier in *Political Justice* between theory and practice becomes more apparent than ever. The difference now is that theory, as epitomized in the mountain-dwelling sage, Ruffigny, is clearly identified with the cerebral, detached, and unemotionally philosophic attitude toward life, while practice, exemplified by the MacNeil family, old friends of Rousseau, is identified with feeling. A rigid dichotomy is set up. Fleetwood himself wavers between these two ideals until, after Ruffigny's death, he marries Mary MacNeil. The choice for domestic bliss has been made; but as in *St. Leon* the relationship is poisoned. Estrangement and flight, guilt, anger, remorse, and desire for revenge succeed in the now-established Godwinian pattern before Enlightenment belatedly dawns to resolve all the terrors that inhabit the darkness of Error. Once again the tortures of secret guilt plague the hero; once again he is punished by his own suffering for his failure to grasp the truth. Just as Falkland was the victim of aristocratic prejudice and St. Leon the victim of a social system that threatened to starve his children, Fleetwood is the victim of a harmful education which allowed full rein to his willfulness and deprived him of the checks and restraints which the presence of others imposed. The moral of *Fleetwood*, for all its touches of Rousseauistic pastoral, is that society is natural and necessary to man and that misanthropy is, as Holbach declared, hurtful to the misanthrope and to the society he spurns. Ambrose Fleetwood, the hero's father, explains the position to Ruffigny; here Godwin fuses his utilitarian idea of the interaction of individuals in society with his comparatively new theory of domestic and private affections: "This is the great distribution of human society; every one who stands in need of assistance appertains to some one individual, upon whom he has a stronger claim than upon any other of his fellow-creatures. My son belongs to me, because I was the occasion of his coming into existence; you belong to me, because you were hungry and I fed you, because you wanted an education and a protector, and found them in me."[73] This was as near as Godwin ever got to reconciling general benevolence and private affection. The vague figure of Ambrose Fleetwood unites theory and practice briefly; but his son divides them again in his warped and misanthropic career.

Mandeville, published twelve years after *Fleetwood*, marked Godwin's return to the social determinism of Helvétius. The internal torment of the criminal, as described by Holbach, is now borne by Mandeville, not because of any secret crime but because of the pernicious influence of a rigidly Calvinistic education. The novel is a study of the deforming effects of a bad education. The religion of Hilkiah Bradford, Mandeville's tutor, is described as a religion of hate, concerned only with the "chosen few which were elected and separated from the world,"[74] whereas the religion of Henrietta, his spiritual guide in the aptly named environment of Beaulieu, is one of love. But Henrietta's idea of man's nature is nothing more than a summary of Helvétius. In an attack on misanthropy she declares:

> Consider, that man is but a machine! He is just what his nature and his circumstances have made him: he obeys the necessities which he cannot resist. If he is corrupt, it is because he has been corrupted . . . Give him a different education, place him under other circumstances . . . and he would be altogether a different creature. He is to be pitied therefore, not regarded with hatred; to be considered with indulgence, not made an object of revenge; to be reclaimed with mildness.[75]

The careful enumeration of the most trivial incidents in Mandeville's early life is also defended on Helvétian grounds.[76] The hero is to be understood in relation to his determining environment. Supreme among these influences is education; Mandeville, therefore, is a victim of prejudice like all of Godwin's protagonists. His hatred for the Shelleyan figure Clifford is seen as a result of his early upbringing; the whole apparatus of the Holbachian ethic of reputation, guilt, and conscience is brought into play to demonstrate the tragic but vain struggles of the hero to evade the laws of social determinism. Mandeville's consciousness of his reputation recalls Falkland's attachment to a false code of honor; like Falkland, Mandeville is a noble spirit blinded by his prejudice, which cuts him off from the society of others: "I felt that inborn pride of soul, which, like an insurmountable barrier, seemed to cut me off forever from every thing mean, despicable, and little. With all this pride, I could not endure the thought of a slur or an inglorious reputation, and, . . . I could die for very spite and shame at the bare idea, that any thing sordid and vile should pollute the whiteness of my name."[77] This contrasts with the society of benevolent altruism at Beaulieu: "It was like the society of 'just men made perfect' where all sought the good of all, and no one lived for himself, or studied for himself."[78]

Here the tradition of the philosophes, especially of Holbach, and that of the Rational Dissenters, especially Holcroft, are juxtaposed. Godwin's idea of hell is Holbach's idea of the torments of the guilty conscience; his idea of heaven is the Dissenting Platonism of Price and Holcroft with its emphasis on an absolute Truth;[79] and his idea of society on this earth is the Helvétian application of associationist psychology and social determinism, blended with the Dissenting faith in universal altruism and benevolence. As his novels decline in quality, the proportion of abstract theorizing increases at the expense of the concrete expression of particular situations. Theory and generalization dominate practice and particularity; but the theory no longer possesses the monolithic unity and logic of the three editions of *Political Justice*. Godwin is visibly straining to reconcile the different traditions and elements of his thought in *Mandeville*. The result is an increase in the utilitarian emphasis he took from Helvétius.

Mandeville was no final solution. Godwin's last two novels, *Cloudesley* and *Deloraine*, bear witness to the disintegration of a philosophy which had once seemed impregnable in its unity and consistency. *Cloudesley* is distinguished by presenting three solitaries: Lord Danvers, an echo of Ruffigny in *Fleetwood*, and Cloudesley and Borromeo, two misanthropes. The intricacies of the plot are bewildering; and when some clear philosophic statement does emerge, it appears incidental to a series of events which have no visible connection with it. The preface does declare a belief in the complexity of the motives for action[80]— acknowledged and exemplified in the best of Godwin's earlier work— but there is little psychological exploration to follow in the novel itself. Three standard themes in his thought do receive some form of development. The theory of education as the universal molder of character is discussed in relation to Julian, the adopted son of Arthur Danvers, who had been sent by Lord Danvers, his uncle, to be educated in the 'natural' surroundings of rural Italy rather than the 'artificial' institutions of the British Isles.[81] Cloudesley himself is an example of the formative influences of education; but he is also an example of the theme of the impulsive, warm-hearted man whose feelings have never been disciplined by any guiding principles. In this instance Godwin reverts to the opinions he expressed in *Political Justice* while showing further symptoms of the renewed influence of Helvétius on his thought: "The history of this man affords a striking example of the disadvantages arising from a defective and neglected education." A good education would have given Cloudesley principles; but, "accurately speaking, he had never had principles; his good impulses were merely the creatures of feeling, and arose from his ascribing to others the uncorrupt sentiments he found in his own breast; and when experience . . . had shown him his mistake, he no longer found anything within him to control his misanthropy."[82] Feeling is once more subjugated to Reason.

The third assertion of philosophical belief is the most forthright of all; it declares the reconciliation of self-love and universal benevolence: "The one thing that most exalts and illustrates man is disinterested affection. We are never so truly what we are capable of being, as when we are ready to sacrifice ourselves for others, and immolate our self-love on the altar of beneficence. There is no joy like the joy of a glorious sentiment, to go about doing good, to make it our meat and drink to promote the happiness of others."[83] But the novel as a whole affords no reconciliation or combination of any of these elements of Godwin's philosophy. His thought has consistency in that the elements remain the same; yet their relation to each other is incoherent.

In *Deloraine*, his last novel, Godwin returns to the black, misanthropic pessimism of *Caleb Williams* and *Mandeville*. As a result the influence of Helvétius recedes, and the nexus of Holbach's ethical concepts reappears. The mass of mankind, we are told,

> are held in awe by the opinions and censure of each other. Reputation is the breath of their nostrils, the element by which they respire. The construction that shall be made of their proceedings is the thought that

awes them; and even the judgement they shall make of themselves is regulated by the judgement of their neighbours. We are members of a community, and can be scarcely said, any one of us, to have a rational existence independent of our Fellows.[84]

Thus the struggle between Helvétius and Holbach ebbs and flows in Godwin's novels. In fact their influence is complementary, since Holbach gives the utilitarian theory of Helvétius a moral and psychological insight which compensates for its automatism. Godwin, however, although intellectually aware of this connection between the two, never managed to fuse them into one credible and memorable character or novel. His most striking portraits are, like Falkland and Williams of *Caleb Williams*, extreme examples of either the Helvétian automaton or Holbach's conscience-stricken criminal. Catherine, the heroine of *Deloraine*, exemplifies the puzzlement of Rational Dissent in the face of the perversions of human evil when she asks, "Oh, why have not human creatures a confidence in the force of truth and justice? Why do they not believe that there is a power in these, which, addressed to an ingenuous spirit, cannot fail to overcome every obstacle?"[85]

In conclusion one may say that Godwin reached an impasse. He believed that human action is determined by the conditions and laws of the physical world, but he could not explain the complicated means by which this determination is achieved. He tended more and more to see the gap between his conviction and his experience as the traditional one between reason and feeling. This was not very persuasive or even flattering to himself. The intricacy of human motive which he had examined in his novels was in fact altogether too great to coexist with the rudimentary psychology and epistemology upon which he, like Helvétius and Holbach before him, had based his moral theories. In his last theoretical work, *Thoughts on Man*, he continued his attack on the Helvétian notion of self-love and the whole "chilling and wretched philosophy of the reign of Louis the Fourteenth."[86] The major contrast in all his work had been that between universal altruism and the monstrous selfishness of the Holbachian criminal—a figure who reappears in passages such as the following, both of which could have come either from Holbach or from the novels:

> The principal circumstance that divides our feelings for others from our feelings for ourselves, and that gives, to satirical observers, and superficial thinkers, an air of exclusive selfishness to the human mind, lies in this, that we can fly from others, but cannot fly from ourselves.[87]

and,

> What the desperate man hates is his own identity. But he knows that, if for a few moments he loses himself in forgetfulness, he will presently

awake to all that distracted him. He knows that he must act his part to the end, and drink the bitter cup to the dregs. He can do none of these things by proxy. It is the consciousness of the indubitable future, from which we can never be divorced, that gives to our present calamity its most fearful empire.[88]

To insist on this contrast is consistent, but to admit its depth is worrying. Experience, as Godwin demonstrated in his novels, and primarily the experience of evil, has so many ramifications that it is difficult to absorb it fully and, at the same time, to retain one's theoretical convictions about it in all their purity. In attempting to do both these things he leaned, sometimes heavily, on Holbach, sometimes on Helvétius. Finally, while admitting the difficulty of his position, he recognized that whatever tenability it had could be assured only by his alliance with the view of morality which "has been supported by Shaftesbury, Butler, Hutcheson and Hume."[89] The doctrines of the French, absorbed by Godwin, led him into contradictions which he could not solve. They also opened up to him problems which his future son-in-law would take farther than Godwin or his French mentors ever dreamed of going. In the meantime Godwin was left with the spectacle of a world the nature of which could be understood but the experience of which made understanding seem almost irrelevant. There was no way to correlate the complexity of motives with the complexity of consequences, especially when he attempted to do so in the exemplary case histories of his criminal protagonists. Neither Godwin, Holcroft, Helvétius, nor Holbach learned to deal with the political or psychological problem of the power complex, although they did at times have insights into its obscure depths. Perhaps they were too devoted to the principle of the triumph of goodness in the world, ensured either by careful social engineering or by man's own naturally benevolent nature.

6 Shelley, La Mettrie, and Cabanis: Remorse and Sympathy

No English writer of the period 1789–1832 absorbed the thought of the French Enlightenment more deeply than Percy Bysshe Shelley. Unlike the earlier generation, which had committed itself initially to the Revolution and finally, in shock, to hostility toward it and almost all things French, the generation to which Shelley belonged did not wholly regard the betrayal of Revolutionary ideals as a necessary consequence of the dangerous and naive quality of the ideas themselves. In Shelley's view, violence and revenge had perverted the Revolutionary spirit so thoroughly that a new despotism had emerged to replace the old. But he did not condemn revolution on this basis; he condemned instead violent and vengeful revolution and repression.[1] He sought a means by which the potency of the governing ideas of the French Enlightenment might be restored to a Europe and an England that had come to regard the Holy Alliance and Tory administrations as necessary guardians against not only Napoleon, the Luddites, and the Radicals but also against those Revolutionary principles of which these factions seemed, or were said to be, the inevitable consequence.[2] Shelley regarded such a view of recent history as nothing more than an excuse for repression seized upon by those who wished to discredit the very idea of revolution itself. To him the spirit of the Enlightenment had almost been quenched in England by the opportunistic revenge of those who could point to that spirit's bloody (though not in his view inevitable) consequences in France.[3]

But revenge was the mark of despotism in France and England. The revolution Shelley envisioned sought to extirpate revenge from the human spirit. If those who had suffered from injustice took revenge on their victimizers, they themselves became victims again of the vicious cycle of repression, hatred, and bloody revolution. The revolutionary had to set the despot a moral example; his civilization

had to be more advanced and noble than the regime he was pledged
to overthrow. Even in his Gothic fiction Shelley makes this plain. For
instance, the unwitting victim Verezzi shakes the vengeful Zastrozzi
when he declares:

> "I fear nothing . . . from your vain threats and empty denunciations of
> vengeance: justice, Heaven! is on my side and I must eventually
> triumph."
>   What can be a greater proof of the superiority of virtue, than that the
> terrible, the dauntless Zastrozzi trembled: for he did tremble: and, con-
> quered by the emotions of the moment, paced the circumscribed apart-
> ment with unequal steps. For an instant he shrank within himself: he
> thought of his past life, and his awakened conscience reflected images
> of horror. But again revenge drowned the voice of virtue—again passion
> obscured the light of reason, and his steeled soul persisted in its scheme.[4]

Despite the Gothic environment, this is really more reminiscent of
the novels of Holcroft and Godwin and of the atmosphere of discussion
among the Radical Dissenters of the 1790s than of Monk Lewis or
Ann Radcliffe. It is in fact so unremarkable a sentiment that easy parallels can be found in contexts ideologically foreign to its own. Southey's Thalaba, for instance, has the same puritannical conviction in his
own and in God's goodness that we find in Verezzi; and he learns
too, when he refuses to kill Laila and later her father, Okba (who had
murdered Thalaba's father), how barren revenge is.[5]
    What differentiates Shelley so clearly from others on this issue is
the primacy which he gave to revolution, or rather to a series of revolutions which would, in moving against the entrenched positions of
obscurantism, dissolve them. Revolution, as he envisaged it as early
as 1814 or 1815, had to be philosophically grounded in order to become
politically effective.[6] What the foundations for such a grounding are
has always been a matter of some dispute among his commentators,
although the disagreements have largely been centered on the proportions of French materialism and Greek idealism in his thought.[7]
Without going into the details of such disputes, it seems possible to
refocus them to some degree by investigating an issue rather than a
combination of influences. The issue (which of course has its ramifications) can be conceived of in this way: given Shelley's belief in
revolution and his abhorrence of revenge, is there any means by which
we can describe the evolution in his work of an ethical system in
which these are reconcilable and governing ideas?
    This question can perhaps be answered by reconsidering Shelley's
adaptation of the amalgam of ideas which he inherited from the French
Enlightenment, keeping in mind that such an adaptation was affected

by his view of the French Revolution and by the previous adaptations of those ideas in the work of other writers who had lived through the Revolution and the reaction to it, especially Godwin and, to a lesser extent, Cabanis and Volney.[8] His debts to various Enlightenment thinkers have been assessed before now. Holbach, Helvétius, Condorcet, and Rousseau are the most widely acknowledged;[9] their influence is further magnified and complicated by their evident presence in Godwin's thought as well.[10] The importance of others, such as Cabanis, has been underrated.[11] Furthermore the nature of the link between Shelley's ethical preoccupations and his materialism is surprisingly anticipated in La Mettrie. Although there is no clear and unambiguous evidence that Shelley read La Mettrie,[12] the affinity between them demonstrates a crisis in the thought of the French Enlightenment which was prolonged into and provides a context for the thought of both Godwin and Shelley in England.

As in Godwin, the crisis concerns crime and punishment, although Shelley alters the geography of the issue by surveying it from a higher vantage point than any to be found in Holbach, Helvétius, Cabanis, La Mettrie, or Godwin. He accepts much that was, even in his youth, traditional in the dispute. The terminology of self-love, self-esteem, reputation, benevolence, and altruism is recurrent throughout his work; so too are the standard tenets of materialist thought, closely linked as they had been in the Enlightenment with anticlericalism, atheism, doctrinaire notions of necessity, and educational theory.[13] These last are more prevalent in his earlier works—*Queen Mab* and *Laon and Cythna*—than are the former, but neither entirely disappears at any point. Yet Shelley's innovation was to take these notions and their associated idioms out of the realm of political philosophy and into the realm of metaphysics without at all subduing their revolutionary appeal. This is one of the major achievements of his poetry. The revolutionary element in Shelley's thought is at once its most obvious and its most typical element—his theory of the imagination. The inclusion of the imagination and his definition of its role subject the crime-and-punishment issue to a sea change, relieving it of an inertness which had become almost total in Godwin and lending it a power which fostered contact with a form of Platonism or neo-Platonism that could vivify but never overwhelm that central concern. The works in which this achievement is most fully demonstrated are *The Cenci* and *Prometheus Unbound*. But before they can be viewed in this light, it is necessary to trace the evolution of Shelley's thought and, particularly, to show how the imprint of French materialism gradually faded into but always remained part of the mature poetry of his last four years.

The Question of Evil

Shelley's work reveals a deep involvement with the problem of evil. The acceptance of evil as an element of human existence differentiates him from most radicals of the time, since to them evil was not intrinsic to the human condition but merely the expression of its unnecessary imperfections, most of which were political or social in their origins and structure. The utilitarian strain in contemporary radicalism ensured the absence of a metaphysical dimension; and it also ensured the presence of a very rudimentary model of human psychology. One of Shelley's early influences, Constantin Volney, represents this strain very clearly: "Self-love, the desire of happiness, and an aversion to pain, are the essential and primary laws that nature herself imposed in man, that the ruling power, whatever it be, has established to govern him: and these laws, like those of motion in the physical world, are the simple and prolific principle of every thing that takes place in the moral world."[14] Volney has greater importance for Shelley than this merely representative quality, for he also broaches the question of evil and its operations in the kind of panoramic context of vanishing civilizations which we meet in *Queen Mab* and in *Laon and Cythna*. The protagonist in *The Ruins* is chided by the Apparition for blaming the miseries of man on Fate: "Falsely do you accuse Fate and Divinity: injuriously do you refer to God the cause of your evils."[15] His reply, in the next chapter, is interesting because in it he invokes the language of torment and crime even while acknowledging the supremacy of reason: "Pardon my ignorance. Alas! if man is blind, can that which constitutes his torment be also his crime? I was unable to distinguish the voice of reason; but the moment it was known to me, I gave it welcome."[16] Here is a miniature and rather tepid version of the issue which was to become central in Shelley's thought. It is worth noting at this stage in order to recognize how much a part of the common currency of contemporary thought it had become. Volney's book was original in none of its ideas; it gained much of its influence from the spectacular view of the downfall of despotism and the utopian possibilities of the new age which it based on the well-favored European contrast between ancient Oriental autocracies and modern European republics.[17] It had also a certain poignancy for those who were initially struck by its novel combination of the traditional cyclical view of history, pervasive throughout the eighteenth century, and the revolutionary, utopian view.

Volney combined the sentiments of regret evoked by the spectacle of the transience of (despotic) grandeur with the sentiments of joy awakened by the declaration of the more enduring prospects of democratic government. But the elements in Volney's work—the idiom of crime and torment, the panoramic survey of human history, the cyclical view of despotism, the linear view of revolution—are found easily in Shelley, not simply because Shelley read Volney but because these were widely available and widely dispersed materials. It was their combination, its force, and its sequence which mattered.

Sir William Drummond's *Academical Questions* also supplied the problems which for Shelley came to possess such coercive power. In the chapter on Leibniz he produces this well-worn query: "The necessarian has been often asked, how he can pretend to applaud virtue, and to censure vice, while he acknowledges both to be inevitable. That which necessity ordains, necessity justifies." Then, more pertinently: "In contemplating the existence of evil, I feel that I am unable to account for it. But let me ask, why philosophers have rashly imputed the being of all things to God?"[18] Drummond goes on to admit that the "ideal system," his alternative to "materialism," leads to perplexing conclusions, among which he mentions the question of evil, the belief in a benevolent Creator, and the relationship between liberty and necessity.[19] No penetrating discussion illuminates any of these subjects; but once more we see raised in a book known to be a favorite with the young Shelley the kinds of question which would engage him for the remainder of his life. As an atheistic materialist Shelley had to find an explanation for evil which would allow him to retain his faith in man's ultimately perfectible nature; and as a revolutionary he had to demonstrate how that perfectibility could become actual in a new program of human behavior. In England only he and Godwin faced this question squarely; but Godwin's attempt to resolve it had achieved temporary success only because it depended on a severe demarcation between the reflective and the affective faculties, one which he had been unable to sustain for long. Shelley was alone in his willingness to found his ethical system on materialism; just as he was equally alone in attempting to repudiate the dreariness of conventional materialistic thought by granting it a paradisal vision of the coming utopia, which he placed not at the horizon where time meets infinity but within man himself. It was attainable by the exercise of the faculty which, so to speak, gave reason its raison d'être—the imagination, the power in man which overcame his major limitation, his egoism.

Since 1770 various thinkers of the French Enlightenment had made a systematic attempt to offer as a credible alternative to the regimes and attitudes they attacked the idea of a wholly secular human society. The radicalism of Paine, Godwin, and Shelley, and to some extent Bentham, has its roots in Boulanger, Holbach, Helvétius, Mably, Morellet, Dom Deschamps, and before that La Mettrie. The young Shelley's position is unequivocally one of discipleship, especially to Holbach. He also, however, absorbed a good deal from Cabanis and in one particular respect went beyond both these authors (and beyond Godwin too) in formulating an ethical theory based, on the one hand, on the common assumption that goodness was a matter of social utility and, on the other, on the idea that the conventional notions of guilt and remorse were nothing more than a neurotic inheritance from the old penal systems which the Enlightenment had wished to humanize. If physical punishment was no more than a system of legalized revenge, the punitive effects of guilt and remorse were no less brutal and no less unnecessary.

Shelley's perception that feelings of remorse could be located in a culturally determined attitude toward crime had far-reaching implications: he always associated remorse with egoism or with the malevolent effects of institutional belief. For him remorse is a form of self-hatred, the emotion by which we undertake revenge on ourselves. It is a deep neurotic tendency in individuals who have not been given fulfillment through the doctrine of benevolence, the love of mankind that gives reason its definitive impulse toward developing both the techniques by which society may be improved and the concept of the perfect society toward which these improvements might be directed. When reason devotes itself to this latter aim, it is raised to a higher power; it becomes the visionary imagination.

In striking out from Godwin's and Holbach's entirely different conceptions of the role of remorse in the new ethical system, Shelley was not, after all, being entirely original. Eighteenth-century France had, in a curious way, anticipated him. In the work of La Mettrie we find the first attempt to describe traditional ethical behavior as a form of nervous disorder created by deliberate and despotic (mostly clerical) propaganda; and with that a serious effort to replace this with a form of rational behavior which, rather than meriting the usual attacks on its unemotional, automatic character, is sustained by its joyful commitment to the demands of our animal nature. Sexual liberty is for La Mettrie as much as for Shelley an avenue of escape from repression, a source of legitimate joy and pleasure, and a natural consequence of a reason that looks benevolently to the general and "natural" needs of man for its guidelines and not selfishly or stupidly to the power lusts of a few disguised as the proper rules for all.

The problem of evil is solved if evil can be legitimately regarded as the accumulated deposit in the human nervous system of centuries of exploitation. It is appropriate that two of Shelley's French mentors were physicians, for as a vegetarian and an atheist, Shelley was bound to look for a physiological basis for human behavior. Yet this was not in itself entirely satisfactory, because it led directly to the Holbachian and Godwinian doctrine of necessity. It was possible to assert human freedom by positing a human nature distinguished by its capacity to desire and to call the satisfaction of that capacity freedom. Equally, it was possible to assert determinism on those grounds. Shelley saw this impasse and attempted to find a way out.

He conceives of freedom in a number of interconnected ways. There is freedom from irrational tyranny, which he often imagines in terms of a brother and sister or a pair of epicene twins orphaned or confronted by monstrous parents. There is its interior equivalent—freedom from the guilts and anxieties bred in an individual by the values and mores of an unjust society. Then, in an ascending scale, there is the freedom from egoism and all the variations of self-love and self-hate which egoism produces in the individual and all the injustices which it produces in society once it is allowed to become a governing principle. Through this last freedom the individual aspires to benevolence, that summit of the utopian thought of Holcroft and Godwin and the goal of the moral theories of Richard Price. Shelley, however, goes further with his insistence on the presence in the world of a universal spirit of love, into harmony with which the benevolent man enters. Benevolence thereby becomes transformed from a feeling with a merely social utility (and therefore a moral force) to a metaphysical experience of union with the guiding principle of the world. On this level all the other freedoms are subsumed. Yet if benevolence can be metaphysically sanctioned by the existence of a universal spirit of love in the world, of which man is the expression, so too can egoism claim for itself a metaphysical sanction in the existence of a contrary spirit of evil. Shelley moves rapidly from a passionate and simple defense of atheistic secularism to an elaborate form of neo-Platonism, without at any point yielding his faith in the certainty of a revolutionary renovation of mankind. His dualism is a battle between good and evil in which the fortunes of war appear to change with arbitrary swiftness. It could be argued that it eventually gives out to a monism as metaphysical at base as the dualism is materialist at base. This seems inescapable when we consider that Shelley's politics were more weighted against the survival of evil than not. The battle might, metaphysically speaking, be equally joined; but the political reinforcement had to be on the side of the good. I am speaking here of Shelley's temperament as well as of the various strands of his thought.

Yet the evolution toward a monistic view of the universe involves no contradiction. Instead it exhibits an intensification of early convictions to the point where they are compelled to take account of forces which the early poetry had ignored. On this point it is necessary to emphasize at some length the strong affinity which exists between Shelley and one of the traditions of the French Enlightenment. Holbach's importance for him is known; but La Mettrie's anticipation of much that we find in Shelley and the absorption of some important elements in Cabanis need to be equally acknowledged if Shelley's radicalism is to be understood in its full context. Like Godwin and Madame de Staël he was deeply concerned with problems of human behavior once it is relieved of the weight of conventional religious and social imperatives. Unlike them he sought justification for his views in a philosophy of revolution which did not shirk the problem of evil in its attempt to affirm the primacy of love. Perhaps it was here that he was able to recognize the profound shock of the Revolution making itself felt in the heritage of Enlightenment thought. Evil was even less easily dismissed after 1793 than before, largely because it revealed itself then in the renovators as well as in the oppressors. Shelley is in the end the only English philosopher of the Revolution who seriously questions the existence of evil; in this respect his only follower of note is George Bernard Shaw.[20] Of course Shelley was above all else a poet, and his poems are the texts in which his thought most powerfully operates. It is to them that we must finally turn after an examination of some aspects of La Mettrie and Cabanis.

La Mettrie and the Attack on Remorse

La Mettrie's most famous work, *L'homme machine* (1748), was translated into English in 1749; three editions had been printed by 1750. His *Oeuvres philosophiques* appeared in eleven editions between 1751 and 1796. The notoriety of his major work, although exceeded later by that of Holbach's *Système de la nature,* was based largely on the misconception that he regarded the human being as nothing more than a machine. It has been pointed out often enough that this was not the case: to regard man as a machine was a purely heuristic device.[21] Yet there is a certain philosophical primitivism in La Mettrie which is in accord with his classic Enlightenment stance. He despised metaphysics and theology; he attempted, as did Helvétius, to import into ethics the methods of the physical sciences; and he gave special prominence to educational theory based on those methods.[22] He regarded happiness as an end in itself and spoke of it in terms of pleasure; and he expressed his devotion to the cause of humanity through the energy with which he developed and disseminated his ideas. He was in fact the philosophe par excellence, possessing all those attributes which Herbert Dieckmann describes in the commentary to his edition of *Le philosophe*.[23] La Mettrie's thought is more daring than subtle and is, despite its eccentricities, representative in its main preoccupations of much that was to follow in the next half-century.

Our main concern here is La Mettrie's attack on remorse, guilt, and regret. There is clearly a strong Epicurean strain in the attack. It is plain in the content as well as in the title of his *Système d'Epicure* and in the full title of the more important work *Anti-Sénèque; ou, Discours sur le bonheur*. But he plays some important variations on the *carpe diem* theme. Since, he claims, the ignorant and the prejudiced are happy, intelligence is no particular advantage. "The power to think is often almost a matter of regret."[24] If dreams give pleasure, we should avail ourselves of their deceit: "If Nature deceives us to our benefit, then may she always deceive us. Let us use reason itself to lead us astray, if we can, as a result, be happier. He who has found happiness, has found everything."[25] The pleasures of the present are preferable to the possibilities of the future: "If we have only imaginary roses to provide a pleasant dream, at least we avoid the real thorns that come with them. Ultimately, everything considered, it is an attitude worthy of the wise man to limit oneself to the present; for it alone is in our power. In this system, there are none of the disadvantages or anxieties which attend thinking about the future."[26] But this is a prelude, a sort of smiling manifesto to the real argument, which has of course to deal with man in society, not man in general. The central point is quickly made. Vices and virtues derive from the establishment of society; their foundation is political:

> But honour and glory, seductive phantoms, have been named to act as escorts to the virtue which they sponsor. Contempt, obloquy, fear, ignominy, remorse are associated with vice, in order to pursue, terrify and act as avenging fury towards it. Men's imaginations have been so stirred and part of their feelings so won over, that something essentially chimerical has come by association to be regarded as a positive good, excepting the self-esteem which derives from good actions, even when they are secret. When they are public, self-esteem is more enhanced. For it is in this that honour, glory, reputation, esteem, good name and all other such terms consist. They express nothing more than the judgements of others who are well-disposed to us and who please us thereby. For the rest, only convention, an arbitrary valuation, constitutes all there is of merit or demerit in what is generally called vice and virtue.[27]

Thus, although education can overcome it, remorse or regret is a constant threat to human happiness. It is created in man by his culture; and the more he is dominated by his culture, the deeper his anguish.

"Man, therefore carries within himself his worst enemy. It follows him everywhere."[28]

La Mettrie has so far touched on all those topics recurring in Holbach, Helvétius, and Godwin: crime, punishment, remorse, secrecy, self-esteem, reputation. The differentiating feature is his Epicureanism, because by virtue of it he can dismiss remorse on the simple ground that it does not contribute to our happiness. Nevertheless, since it exists and since it arises from social convention, it can be dismissed only along with the conventions which created it. La Mettrie's Epicureanism thus adds fuel to his radicalism. Moreover, his earlier distinction between the happy ignorant and the unhappy educated has a Rousseauistic implication. Society is seen as the enemy of nature when it should, properly speaking, be nature's expression. Since this is the case, the anxiety of the good man, artificially provoked by social pressure, contrasts unfavorably with the conscienceless happiness of the criminal, who ignores them. La Mettrie is at this point arguing tendentiously; but as long as everything is referred to an Epicurean base, the argument retains its force.

> Yet we have the spectacle of a model subject who, on an impulse, strikes a bad citizen, or gives himself over to a passion which he cannot control; this man, I say, of outstanding merit, is tormented by remorse which he would not have had, had he killed an enemy in open combat, or if he had been given the right to do so by a priest, legitimising what all nature does anyway. Ah! . . . how terrible are the rigours of the law. In my opinion, the most essential thing is to relieve man of remorse. Man, especially the honest man, was surely not made to be delivered into the hands of executioners; man whom nature has made to be in love with life, was surely not made to be destroyed by that depraved fate? No; I demand that he give to reason the same control over his life that criminals give to inured habit. For one waster who will escape unhappiness, . . . how many wise and virtuous people are there, miserable in the midst of our sweet and delicious, innocent existence, who, by relieving themselves of the yoke of an excessively onerous education, would not enjoy cloudless days and exchange a devouring boredom for delicious pleasure![29]

Remorse, he claims, is useless before, during, and after the commission of a crime. Those who most need it—the criminals—do not suffer it, so it is no restraint on vice. Since it makes criminals no better, being no more than a false prison, there is no danger in arguing for their release from it. As for the virtuous man, "we are therefore right to conclude that, if the pleasures derived from nature and reason are crimes, the happiness of man is the happiness of a criminal being."[30]

When we read this, the picture changes a good deal. Obviously La Mettrie, when he speaks of "remords," means what we would call guilt arising from the unconscious repression of instincts that have been frowned on by social mores. He is in this respect a more penetrating thinker than Holbach or Helvétius. The categories of virtue and vice, as he initially speaks of them, are social not moral categories. They describe only a man's capacity to conform or not to conform to a society's standards and demands; but these demands are unreasonable since they contradict man's nature, the proof of which is the unhappiness they cause. Therefore the happy criminal or ignoramus is better since he is in being happy more natural than the conscientious, educated citizen. Happiness is the end of man's existence. Therefore to be happy is to be more moral (in terms of that end, now subtly transforming itself into a criterion as well) than to be unhappy. Consequently the social categories of vice and virtue are reversed in the moral sphere, and the moral is identified with the natural. Epicureanism triumphs. Contemporary social convention is seen to be hostile to the organic nature of man. Materialism, so understood, thus supplies social revolution with a moral basis and makes the seductive association between the natural and the rational, opposing it to the artificial and the conventional. The argument is executed with more haste than elegance, and with a ruthlessly tendentious use of the key words *virtue* and *vice, l'honnête homme* and *le scélérat*. This becomes blatant when we see how they are used in a more relaxed and less aggressive work, *La volupté:*

> The wise man must therefore seek pleasure, since without it, he cannot be happy. Crime covers itself in shame; let it do so; love and pleasure are not of its sort. See joy's brilliant escort . . . probity goes with it; it is the symbol of purity of heart. But the criminal is sad, introspective; he is prey to the most bitter remorse; the natural law which he has violated, violates him in turn. The honest man laughs, opens his heart; he is so in love with pleasure and sensuality that, far from blushing because he has been made to feel so, he regards it as the most enduring reward of virtue and the highest dividend of reason.[31]

Finally, the *Discours sur le bonheur* admits to the radical egoism which underlies its polemical attack on remorse. In addition there is the recognition that the most natural and rational form of behavior is also the most selfish: "It is the same with all the wicked. They can be happy if they can be wicked without remorse. I dare say more; a man so habituated to crime that vices are for him virtues and who is completely without remorse, is happier than another who, after doing something fine and natural, repents of it and thereby loses all the benefit of it. Such is the wonderful sway of a tranquillity which nothing can disturb."[32] Or more briefly: "Each individual, in preferring himself above all others, does no more than follow the order of nature, in which one would have to be eccentric indeed and downright irrational not to believe that one can be happy."[33]

Egoism of this kind contrasts strongly with the luminous benevolence of Shelley. Yet it is based on an analysis of society and human nature which he shares to a large extent. It scarcely seems a sufficient basis for the dismissal of remorse, which would at least seem to act as a restraint on unbridled selfishness; but we misunderstand La Mettrie's position if we read it so. If pleasure is happiness and, as he claims, we have an organic inclination toward it, and since we become subject to neurosis if we stifle that tendency, then egoism is morally defensible and even admirable. Furthermore, he is speaking in a specific context—that of the penal code of the eighteenth century, which visited terrible punishment on wrongdoers without at the same time acknowledging that the crime had been thereby paid for in full. The general attitude was punitive in the extreme. If the crime was secret, the criminal suffered the torments of conscience; if it was discovered, he suffered the torments of the law. In each case torment contradicted the inclination of his nature; in each case torment, private or public, revealed something unnatural in the social system. Besides the torments of the law, there were those of religion. To La Mettrie the promise of eternal punishment seemed no more than a terror tactic. Men, he thought, are sufficiently punished by the remorse which nature visits upon them.[34]

The whole question of remorse must finally be understood against the background of a brutal penal code and the intransigent spirit of an unforgiving religion, which combined to create a social climate in which the concept of criminality had become, at the very least, ambiguous to enlightened minds. We can remind ourselves here of Shelley's hatred for the vengeful spirit of his society (which enormously increased, for instance, the number of crimes that carried with them a capital punishment) and for the psychic malformation of human nature which, in his opinion, it sanctioned. Shelley is in the same tradition as La Mettrie in his opposition to this spirit; and like La Mettrie he saw that the fundamentally religious concept of the tortured conscience strengthened rather than alleviated the law's acceptance of the torturing of the body as a punishment for what it considered to be crime. The prevalent notion of what crime was had to be questioned, along with the prevalent notion of what punishment should be, since neither seemed to have any connection with the natural inclinations of man. Instead, those inclinations were perverted precisely by being regarded not as natural but as themselves perverse.

Cabanis: Sympathy and the Nervous System

La Mettrie's discussion of remorse has a deep affinity with Shelley's exploration of that problem, but his defense of egoism separates him in many important ways from the poet's ideology. Pierre Cabanis, however, supplies an alternative to egoism without denying the physiological basis of human emotion and inclination which characterize La Mettrie's work. We know that Shelley ordered Cabanis's *Oeuvres* for his reading list in 1813. The notes to *Queen Mab* show that he had read at least some of the *Rapports*;[35] and the marks of Cabanis's influence are plainly visible in Shelley's writings, although this fact has never been sufficiently acknowledged.

Cabanis was one of the most favored members of that society of men attracted to the house at Auteuil where Helvétius's widow presided and where he lived from 1783 to 1800 "dans le petit pavillon au fond du jardin."[36] A physician and a philosophe, he gained a good deal of notoriety in his former role when, having attended Mirabeau in his last illness, he had to protect himself from dangerous accusations over his treatment of that famous patient (in the *Journal de la maladie et de la mort de Mirabeau* in 1791). He was a close friend of Condorcet, who also came to live in Auteuil before his arrest in 1794; Cabanis gave Condorcet the poison by which he died in prison. His closest friends, however, were the so-called Ideologues, particularly Fauriel, Volney, Dégerando, and Destutt de Tracy. Two months after his election to the Institut National in December 1795, Cabanis began to give readings there from the *Mémoirs* which later formed the substance of the *Rapports du physique et du moral*. Although, politically speaking, the Ideologues had distinct constitutionalist inclinations (Dégerando corresponded with James Mackintosh and was, with Constant and Madame de Staël, a leading and typical figure in the French Liberal groupings of that period), the brand of materialism Cabanis promoted had political implications which went far beyond constitutionalism. All were direct inheritors of the "sensationalist" tradition of the philosophes, priding themselves on an even greater precision of language and a more detailed medical knowledge of the human body. Physiology was for them the point of departure for the sciences of morality and legislation. Destutt de Tracy was completing a tendency which had been at work for more than half a century when, in his *Elémens d'idéologie*, he defined Ideology "comme une province de la phisiologie."[37] Lévesque de Pouilly, named along with Cabanis to the Institut National in 1795, had displayed this same conviction as early as 1747 in his *Théorie des sentimens agréables,* published a year before La Mettrie's *L'homme machine.* De Pouilly, like Cabanis, reduced pleasure to a physical basis, declaring: "Whatever exercises the bodily organs without weakening them, can contribute to their preservation and is accompanied by an agreeable feeling."[38] Cabanis gives such a suggestion the status of a philosophical position in the course of the eleven *Mémoirs* which compose the *Rapports* and in the *Lettre à Fauriel sur les causes premières* (1807).

There are three distinctive features in Cabanis which we find also in Shelley, although the emphasis given them is not, of course, identical. First there is a complete monism, which leads to the second element, a theory of universal sympathy; and third, there is a fusion of the moral and the physiological, which leads to that identification of nervous sensibility with moral sensitivity we find not only in Shelley but also in the sentimental movement before him and the Romantic movement after him.[39] These three features cohere well, and their relevance to Shelley is heightened by Cabanis's support for dieting and its moral effects, and for the idea of a presiding spirit of order in the physical and moral world which, despite conflict and contradiction, progressively exhibits itself in the social and political structure.

At the heart of Cabanis's thought is his doctrine of sympathy:

> Sympathy, in general, derives from the sense of the self, of the consciousness, at the least dim, of the will. It is even necessarily inseparable from that consciousness and this sense of self. We cannot participate in the feelings of someone else except to the degree that we attribute to that person the faculty of feeling as we do. To suppose that someone *feels,* we must lend to that person the sense we have of ourselves *[un moi].*[40]

This is a more elaborate idea than the widely sponsored benevolence of the period. When it is taken along with the *Lettre sur les causes premières,* we see that Cabanis has blended his physiological materialism with a form of Spinozaism—a blend that has its application to Shelley also, for the assumption basic to Cabanis's thought is that there exists a primary energy in the universe of which sympathy and order are emanations. The energy exists on a higher level, however, than order and sympathy. It is logically prior to its emanations in the physical and social worlds. The distinction recalls Spinoza's between *Natura naturans* and *Natura naturata;* and it is in this distinction, sanctioned and not contradicted by materialism, that Shelley's later Platonism takes root.[41] For Cabanis it is necessary to posit such an energetic principle in the world in order to give the physiological response to it by the individual endowed with nervous sensibility the status of a moral response. To give to another the status of a *moi* is to give to the *moi*, which recognizes the other, the status of a personality capable of reproducing in the world an image of himself and deriving this capacity from his sensitivity to the universal principle. This is a sublime form of egoism with its active principle nevertheless removed from the individual, given to the universe, and then electrically reconducted back to the individual through the receptivity of his nervous system. Inescapably, however, the individual sees others either in terms of himself or as versions of himself; and this egoistic aspect persists through the sympathetic doctrine which Cabanis attempts to expound.

The whole effort in such a theory is to find a physiological basis for an altruistic morality. It would be an exaggeration to say that Cabanis achieves this, but it is in the light of that ambition that his doctrine of sympathy must be understood. Its presence in the world is a logical prerequisite for its passage through the sensitized cells of the social circuit. The emphasis is on the human cell and its reactive capacity, which is a complicated matter of nerves, diet, illness, and sleep. If altruism depends on these, then medicine has a moral role—and the medical flavor is never absent from Cabanis's definitions of morality: "One must know the physical man to study with profit the moral man."[42]

The extraordinary quality in Cabanis is the force with which he can bring together so many elements and treat them all reductively, as physical only, before he then, in a backhanded manner, restores to them the moral or metaphysical dimension they initially had. Like La Mettrie, he has a polemical interest in locating imagination and emotion in the physical, in making the *sedes* of the human spirit the metabolism of the human body. But in order to do so he has to speak of the world as if it possessed a presiding spirit, and then agnostically to dismiss that spirit as such in demonstrating that for man it exists only insofar as his physical nature can express it. At times the fundamentalism of this position appears gross; but its ambition is revolutionary. For our purposes it is enough to recognize the image of man transmitted from Cabanis to Shelley—that of a complex nervous organism achieving morality by virtue of the sympathetic energy with which it, in recognizing its own existence, recognizes also the existence of others in a world which is potentially perfect. The metaphysical overtones of Spinoza and the Greek Stoics which are audible in certain passages seem to have reached Shelley's ear. His philosophy appears in comparison to have absorbed that of Cabanis without being limited, in the end, to its polemical and somewhat narrow intent.

Shelley: Remorse and Metaphysics

Of course Shelley had his own polemical intent. Evil takes one supreme form in his early poetry and fiction—that of kingship and priestcraft, the two institutional forms of an unrelenting egoism. But the lurid quality of this early verse owes much of its excess to an element of Gothic horror which provides the political passion with the scenarios of storm, mountain heights, moonlight, ruins, gibbets, and sinister hallucinatory figures which remain a feature of all his work. Poems such as *Henry and Luisa, Zeinab and Kathena, The Tombs, The Voyage,* and *A Retrospect of Times of Old*[43] exemplify that combination of radical political opinion and nightmare landscape which was so well equipped to express both horizonless utopian desires and scenes of cinemascope carnage, destruction, and disillusion. This unique blend in poetry of materials which had previously belonged mostly to the novel on the one hand and to political philosophy on the other was not useful for the purposes of melodrama and propaganda alone. It also involved a notion of human relationship (that of devotion through the individual to mankind) for which there was no social equivalent except in the Gothic novel's favorite version of illicit love—incest. Incest in Shelley is a form of political dedication to universal brother- and sisterhood at the expense of conventional social relations which merely express tyranny or egoism. It is intimacy defiantly parading itself before the world of distant relationships. Obviously a good deal of this can be seen to have biographical roots; but the flavor of Shelley's political and social convictions also depended to some degree on a literary and philosophical climate in which parents and the past could be rejected by innocents and orphans, who then between them inaugurate the period of universal benevolence, like a new Adam and Eve in a new Eden, bringing to a close the bloody record of Christianity, irrational custom, convention, and despotic rule. Incest is also a powerful synecdoche for all those feelings which, viewed conventionally, are criminal but, viewed rationally, are seen to be not only legitimate but necessary. The relation of crime to feeling and of individual passion to social norms is neatly encompassed in the incestuous relationship; and the implied critique of the convention of crime necessarily bred a critique of the convention of punishment. This led Shelley into that area previously traversed by La Mettrie, Holbach, and Godwin, in which human behavior is analyzed against the background of the contemporary (and antiquated) penal code and the most advanced contemporary knowledge. The code naturally suffers in the comparison; yet its replacement depends not on knowledge as such but on a conviction of the necessity of benevolence for the development of human values. This conviction expresses itself, as in Cabanis, in the hypothesis of a presiding spirit of goodness of which human sympathy is the primary emanation. Shelley brings other questions to bear here as well, among them the questions of the spiritual dimension of evil, of determinism, and, again remembering Cabanis, of the nature of the moral hero. Shelley's heroes and heroines have no psychology to speak of other than their capacity for sympathy or remorse. Otherwise their attributes are those of a prominent nervous sensibility which, in Cabanis and others, is a sign of moral worth.

Such sensitive heroes and heroines have their darker counterparts. The illicit atmosphere of incest helps to create in some of Shelley's Gothic fiction a moral climate in which the diabolic hero can also breathe. He is diabolic usually because he is a legendary victim of revenge, like Ahasuerus, the Wandering Jew, and as such attracts the fear and hatred of those whose God has condemned him.[44] He is also diabolic because he is ageless—a prophet, a symbol, and a nightmare— incarnating cruel punishment, endless remorse, and even, as in *Hellas*, wisdom through suffering. Like Milton's Satan he is the victim of an unequal struggle, a type of humanity suffering evil in the name of Christian goodness. Only as Prometheus does he finally develop as a figure of suffering who also becomes a revolutionary hero triumphing through the power of love. The last lines of *Hellas*, or much earlier those of *Zeinab and Kathena*, display what tremendous forces must be overcome before the Shelleyan hero, in his angelic or diabolic shape, can win:

> Thus, like its God, unjust and pityless,
> Crimes first are made and then avenged by man,
> For where's the tender heart, whose hope can bless
> Or man's, or God's, unprofitable plan—
> A universe of horror and decay,
> Gibbets, disease, and wars, and hearts as hard as they.[45]

That pessimism can nevertheless coexist with the simplistic optimism of *A Vindication of Natural Diet*, in which we are told that "crime is madness. Madness is disease. Whenever the cause of disease shall be discovered, the root from which all vice and misery have so long overshadowed the globe, will lay bare to the axe."[46]

The most immediately pertinent detail is Shelley's constant reference to crime in his attempt to elaborate an ethics which would replace revenge, remorse, and egoism—that trinity of conventional opinion—with forgiveness, clear conscience, and benevolence. The early Gothic fiction can give this effort an unwittingly comic emphasis, but Zastrozzi is not, after all, a freakish character. He has his counterparts in Byron and in Godwin; and most important, he has later incarnations in the Jupiter of *Prometheus Unbound* and in Count Cenci. In Zastrozzi we glimpse the Shelleyan villain-hero in a typical crisis of internal anguish; a pleasant moonlight scene, we are told,

> ill-accorded with the ferocious soul of Zastrozzi, which at one time agitated by revenge, at another by agonising remorse, or contending passions, could derive no pleasure from the past—anticipate no happiness in futurity.
>
> Zastrozzi sat for some time immersed in heart-rending contemplations; but though conscience for awhile reflected his past life in images of horror, again was his heart steeled by fiercest vengeance; and aroused by images of insatiate revenge, he hastily arose, and, waking Ugo and Bernardo, pursued his course.[47]

Zastrozzi and Wolfstein, the protagonist of *St. Irvyne,* are more literary-Gothic creations than Beatrice or Prometheus, both of whom nevertheless owe much of their presence to the occult systems to which they belong and to which the Gothic figures also have an important kinship. Yet all ask the same kind of question: " 'And what so horrible crimes have I committed,' exclaimed Wolfstein, driven to impiety by desperation, 'what crimes which merit punishment like this?' " They all experience the same punishment: isolation tortured by conscience. After Wolfstein has murdered Cavigni, he becomes "an isolated wicked wanderer; not a being on earth whom he could call a friend, and carrying with him that never-dying tormentor—conscience."[48]

Nevertheless, it is not entirely helpful simply to note this obsession with conscience and remorse in Shelley's work. The real importance lies in the fact that it was via these disputes over crime, its nature, and its punishment that Shelley developed that strange dialogue between Revolutionary Enlightenment principle and occult Gnostic belief which gives his work such an opaque and contradictory appearance to so many readers. There is evident in much of his writing a recrudescence of the conspiracy theory of the French Revolution and of history in general, stemming in part from the fulminations of the Abbé Barruel. For Shelley the notion of conspiracy had a certain attraction. He regarded the renovation of society as the work of an elite which, by gradually disseminating its ideas, overthrows a system of society which would otherwise try to deny its truth. Not only is such an elite an underground group; its ideas also belong to an underground religion. Enlightened Gnostics, Rosicrucians, Freemasons—these emerge in Shelley's thought as the carriers of the ideas of the philosophes into a dark world in which the magic seed of revolution has been planted. Barruel and Volney had, each in his own way, supplied the outlines of such a religion of the underworld, which is simultaneously a religion of renovation and revolt against a society darkened by the influence and cruelty of perverted priests.[49] The most powerful agents of this secret army of *illuminati* turn out in the end to be poets. This is perhaps Shelley's most ambitious claim—that the poet is the philosophe raised to a higher power; the harbinger of a revolution which will bring not blood and ruin but peace and love; the priest of truth, not the lackey of Frederick II or the unwitting dupe of Napoleon.

His attitude toward the philosophes, of whatever generation, was of course bound to be affected by his view of the course taken by the Revolution. He makes his position clear on a number of occasions, although nowhere more precisely than in *Proposals for an Association.* Among the many lessons Shelley learned from France was the need to organize men for the sake of diffusing certain basic principles concerning human nature and human rights. Diffusing, not discovering: the discoveries were already made; the truths were self-evident. "The analysis that we can draw from physical to moral topics are of all others the most striking. Does anyone yet question the possibility of inducing radical reform of moral and political evil?"[50]

The real shadow falling on this, as on other Shelley pamphlets, is not that of Malthus but that of the evident failure of the French Revolution to achieve the aims of the French Enlightenment. Shelley readily admits that his own principles "have their origin from the discoveries in the sciences of politics and morals, which preceded and occasioned the revolutions of America and France. It is with openness that I confess, nay with pride that I assert, that they are so."[51] The failure, however, is in many respects that of the individual thinkers themselves. While he does not wish to say outright "whether D'Alembert, Boulanger, Condorcet and other celebrated characters, were the causes of the overthrow of the ancient monarchy of France,"[52] he does accept a connection. Yet it was not sufficiently intimate. Because its writers had not prepared the state of society for a revolution free of revenge, France was not ready when the cataclysm came:

> The murders during the period of the French Revolution and the despotism which has since been established, prove that the doctrines of Philanthropy and Freedom, were but shallowly understood. Nor was it

until after that period, that their principles became clearly to be explained, and unanswerably to be established. Voltaire was the flatterer of Kings, though in his heart he despised them:—so far has he been instrumental in the present slavery of his country. Rousseau gave licence by his writings, to passions that only incapacitate and contract the human heart:—so far hath he prepared the necks of his fellow-beings for that yoke of galling and dishonourable servitude, which at this moment, it bears. Helvétius and Condorcet established principles, but if they drew conclusions, their conclusions were unsystematical and devoid of the luminousness and energy of method:—they were little understood in the Revolution. But this age of ours is not stationary. Philosophers have not developed the great principles of the human mind, that conclusions from them should be unprofitable and impracticable. We are in a state of continually progressive improvement . . . Godwin wrote during the Revolution of France, and certainly his writings were totally devoid of influence, with regard to its purposes. Oh! that they had not!—In the Revolution of France, were engaged men, whose names are inerasible from the records of Liberty. Their genius penetrated with a glance the gloom and glare which Church-craft and State-craft had spread before the imposture and villainy of their establishments . . . Had there been more of those men France would not now be a beacon to warn us of the hazard and horror of Revolutions, but a pattern of society, rapidly advancing to a state of perfection, and holding out an example for the gradual and peaceful regeneration of the world.[53]

For the young Shelley, Godwin was clearly the perfect philosophe. It is also evident that he regarded the state of feeling, first in Ireland, then in England, as particularly favorable for the progress of enlightenment. The move for Catholic Emancipation in Ireland had, in his view, made that country particularly susceptible to change. As for England he could declare:

That our country is on the point of submitting to some momentous change in its internal government, is a fact which few who observe and compare the state of human society will dispute. The distribution of wealth, no less than the spirit by which it is upheld and that by which it is assailed, render the event inevitable. Call it reform or revolution, as you will, a change must take place; one of the consequences of which will be, the wresting of political power from those who are at present the depositaries of it.[54]

He then goes on to warn against the dangers of revenge and the subsequent possibility of revolutionaries becoming tyrants—again.

The so-called utopianism of Shelley is not at issue here. He is not guilty of misreading either the Irish or the English situation any more than he later misreads the Spanish and the Greek situations. Instead what he consistently does is to see them all in terms of pre-Revolutionary France, acknowledging that each of them has in its own particular way an affinity with that period in which enlightenment had partly cleared the way for reform and revolution. As in France failure is a possibility in the short term, for the progress of the mass of the people must, in Shelley's view, be carefully promoted by the elite groups of philosophers so that, in the absence of the uncivilized emotions of revenge and hate, a revolution can take place without becoming a tyranny. Shelley, in other words, saw all the revolutions of his time against the model of revolutionary achievement which he had constructed in his mind. In measuring them against it he could see their faults; in retaining the model he asserted the permanence of the moral principles for which it stood.

The crux of the problem was that there seemed to be no way in which the emotions of hatred and revenge could be exorcised. Shelley often gives the standard response to this problem when he demands that the civil and criminal code—the areas in which revenge and hatred are most consistently practiced—be reformed in accordance with the principle of "the good of the whole."[55] In *A System of Government by Juries* he returns to the subject of legal vengeance with his usual clarity and passion:

> The author of these pages ought not to suppress his conviction, that the principles on which punishment is usually inflicted are essentially erroneous; and that, in general, ten times more is apportioned to the victims of law, than is demanded by the welfare of society, under the shape of reformation or example. He believes that, although universally disowned, the execrable passion of vengeance, exasperated by fear, exists as a chief source among the causes of this exercise of criminal justice.[56]

This, however, is only a partial answer. The criminal code is not the source but the expression of vengeance in society. The source is in man himself; but this also raises a difficulty.

If the springs of revenge are in the human heart, then man is by nature evil, since revenge is evil. Shelley does not, however, rest on this assumption. Like La Mettrie he finds a way of explaining evil as a cultural phenomenon rather than accept it (at this point anyway) as an abiding metaphysical fact. Poems such as *Queen Mab* and *Laon and Cythna* have frequent recourse to the idea of man as his own enemy, taking revenge on himself for his own blamable imperfections, as in the recurrent image of the scorpion that stings himself to death in fury and fear inside his own ring of fire. This is the Godwinian and Holbachian criminal turning remorsefully upon himself

> like a scorpion stung
> By his own rage upon his burning bier
> Of circling coals of fire . . .[57]

In *Queen Mab* the Fairy comforts Ianthe's troubled spirit with the thought that crime, misery, falsehood, and lust can be cured by the appearance of virtuous men who

> shall start up
> Even in perversest time:
> The truths of their pure lips, that never die,
> Shall bind the scorpion falsehood with a wreath
> Of ever-lasting flame,
> Until the monster sting itself to death.[58]

So error destroys itself; crime takes its revenge on the criminal. This is very close to Godwin but even closer to La Mettrie in that the self-poisoning (remorse) is understood as a by-product of a faulty social system in which criminality is inevitable—more so indeed for some than for others. In the notes to *Queen Mab* Shelley cites the example of the prostitute as the typical victim of defective social organization:

> Prostitution is the legitimate offspring of marriage and its accompanying errors. Women, for no other crime than having followed the dictates of a natural appetite, are driven with fury from the comforts and sympathies of society . . . Has a woman obeyed the impulse of unerring nature;— society declares war against her, pitiless and eternal war: . . . theirs is the right of persecution, hers the duty of endurance . . . She dies of long and lingering disease: yet *she* is in fault, *she* is the criminal, *she* the forward and untameable child,—and society, forsooth the pure and virtuous matron, who casts her as an abortion from her undefiled bosom! Society avenges herself on the criminals of her own creation; she is employed in anathematising the vice today, which yesterday she was most zealous to teach.[59]

The oppositions here are as clearly defined as those in La Mettrie or Cabanis. On one side we have convention, on the other natural appetites. To satisfy the latter is natural; but to be natural is to be anticonventional, which is to become criminal. Convention makes the natural criminal. It is therefore virtuous to be "criminal" if it is right to be "natural." The scales are even more heavily weighted if we add to them the mass of Holbachian necessity which compels us to be natural—that is, criminal. Shelley's polemic is complete. By treating remorse as the poisonous deposit of exploitation after La Mettrie and "natural appetite" as a source of pleasure and therefore of happiness, as Cabanis would have said, and by overlaying both with Holbach's notion of necessity and "blindly-working will,"[60] Shelley avoids attributing to human nature any radical inclination toward evil. Instead evil is regarded as a form of ignorance leading in the end to neurosis and self-destruction. Since "yet every heart contains perfection's germ," the ideal may be attained by all, rich and poor alike, who, in their perversion turn to crime as a stimulant; and this ideal every slave

> Pining with famine, swoln with luxury,
> Blunting the keeness of his spiritual sense
> With narrow schemings and unworthy cares,
> Or madly rushing through all violent crime,
> To move the deep stagnation of his soul,—
> Might imitate and equal.[61]

The power of Shelley's writings up to 1819 owes a good deal to their political ambition and their consequent polemical force. He was not at all unaware (as has now been sufficiently shown) of "the difficult and unbending realities of actual life."[62] But he also knew the value of retaining in the mind as an ideal a model civilization in which morals and politics would not suffer their normal and damaging separation: "Morals and politics can only be considered as portions of the same science, with relation to a system of such absolute perfection as Christ and Plato and Rousseau and other reasoners have asserted, and as Godwin has, with irresistible eloquence, systematised and developed."[63] Despite this realism he was nonetheless inclined to be vague about the nature of the transformation of society which would extirpate revenge and remorse, inaugurate the reign of benevolence, and knit the fracture in human nature between political and moral behavior.[64] His *Speculations on Morals*, written between 1815 and 1819, is a relatively undistinguished tract on benevolence, justice, and virtue, offering trite definitions, any one of which could have come from the pages of Helvétius, Godwin, or Holbach. There is, however, an important and typically Shelleyan variation on these themes which points toward new developments in his thought and makes it qualitatively different from theirs. He declares:

> He who shall have cultivated his intellectual powers by familiarity with the finest specimens of poetry and philosophy will, usually, sympathise more than one engaged in the less refined functions of manual labour.
> The imagination thus acquires by exercise a habit as it were of perceiving and abhorring evil, however remote from the immediate sphere of sensations with which that individual mind is conversant. Imagination or mind employed in prophetically imaging forth its objects is that faculty

of human nature on which every gradation of its progress, nay, every, the minutest change depends. Pain or pleasure, if subtly analysed, will be found to consist entirely in prospect. The only distinction between the selfish man, and the virtuous man, is that the imagination of the former is confined within a narrow limit, whilst that of the latter embraces a comprehensive circumference. In this sense, wisdom and virtue may be said to be inseparable, and criteria of each other. Selfishness is thus the offspring of ignorance and mistake; it is the portion of unreflecting infancy, and savage solitude, or of those whom toil and evil preoccupations have blunted and rendered torpid; disinterested benevolence is the product of a cultivated imagination, and has an intimate connection with all the arts which add ornament, or dignity, or power, or stability to the social state of man. Virtue is thus entirely a refinement of civilised life; a creation of the human mind or rather a combination which it has made, according to elementary rules contained within itself, of the feelings suggested by the relations established between man and man.[65]

I have quoted this passage at such length because it heralds so much of what is to come in Shelley's prose and poetry. Here we may see Shelley releasing himself from the doctrine of egoism, which had been so dominant in the French materialist school of thought, and developing in its stead the doctrine of sympathy, which he found in both Ideologues (Cabanis) and Dissenters (Godwin, Price, and Holcroft). It is a passage in which he is seen to digest his intellectual inheritance from the previous century and then transmute it into something which will in the end indeed appear "rich and strange" by comparison, for Shelley brings out here a number of hitherto subdued or missing elements. One is obviously the importance of the imagination and its connection with disinterestedness; a second is the relationship between the development of disinterestedness and the development of culture, a word used here in specific relation to the arts and the social sciences; and a third is the new relationship established between ignorance and selfishness. Ignorance is here regarded as more than a failure of the reason; it is defined as something brutish and isolating, something which cannot coexist with the social life. The effects in Shelley's poetry of these variations on the hardened crust of conventional materialist thinking is seismic. From the appearance of *Rosalind and Helen* in 1819 (finished in 1818) to that of the *Posthumous Poems* in 1824, the poetry exhibits these most clearly in the renewed concentration on and development of the themes of guilt, remorse, crime, and punishment—especially in *Rosalind and Helen* itself, in *The Cenci*, and in *Prometheus Unbound*. These themes become involved with others, and they especially become involved with that mystery which worried most of those thinkers who accepted in one form or another the materialist conception of thought as the sum of sensation. In a passage which characteristically fuses a Gothic with a Platonic image, a castle with a cave, a darkness with a light, Shelley speaks of the nature of thought itself and its mysterious relationship to sensation. Without denying its physical basis he gives it a metaphysical extension:

> But thought can with difficulty visit the intricate and winding chambers which it inhabits. It is like a river whose rapid and perpetual stream flows outwards;—like one in dread who speeds through the recesses of some haunted pile, and dares not look behind. The caverns of the mind are obscure and shadowy; or pervaded with a lustre, beautifully bright indeed, but shining not beyond their portals. If it were possible to be where we have been, vitally and indeed—if, at the moment of our presence there, we could define the results of our experience,—if the passage from sensation to reflection—from a state of passive perception to voluntary contemplation, were not so dizzying and tumultuous, this attempt would be less difficult.[66]

In the earlier essay *On Life* he summarizes this more cryptically in the sentence "Nothing exists but as it is perceived."[67]

In developing the "intellectual philosophy" Shelley rescues himself from "the shocking absurdities of the popular philosophy of mind and matter";[68] yet he does not in any sense cease to be a believer in the objective nature of the world. Just as in *A Philosophical View of Reform* he had spoken of the necessity for an ideal system like that of Christ or Plato or Godwin, so in the essay *On Life* he speaks of an ideal system like that of William Drummond's *Academical Questions*, in which we are urged to make men virtuous by seeking "to elevate the mind to the contemplation of divine perfection, in which alone is assembled whatever is most excellent in intellectual nature."[69] Similarly, in the essay *On Love* Shelley speaks of our seeing

> within our intellectual nature a miniature as it were of our entire self, yet deprived of all that we condemn or despise, the ideal prototype of every thing excellent or lovely that we are capable of conceiving as belonging to the nature of man . . . a mirror whose surface reflects only the forms of purity and brightness; a soul within our soul that describes a circle around its proper paradise, which pain, and sorrow, and evil dare not overlap.[70]

In each case a political or moral ideal is given in order that we may have something specific to aspire toward. The ideal is not unreal; neither is it actual. It is the potentiality of all that is actual realized in thought. The "intellectual philosophy" is a system of possibility which is also a possible system. It has utopian and idealist elements, but it is fundamentally devoted to the improvement of human conduct in the actual world.[71] The inevitable collision between these worlds is not avoided. Shelley's typical philosophe-poet would not be welcome in the debased world, entering it as he does from the serene realm where the intellectual philosophy holds sway. In his fragment *The Assassins* Shelley describes the conflict:

> Against their predilections and distastes an Assassin, accidentally the inhabitant of a civilised community, would wage unremitting hostility from principle. He would find himself compelled to adopt means which they would abhor, for the sake of an object which they could not conceive that he should propose to himself. Secure and self-enshrined in the magnificence and pre-eminence of his conceptions, spotless as the light of heaven, he would be the victim among men of calumny and perse-cution. Incapable of distinguishing his motives, they would rank him among the vilest and most atrocious criminals. Great, beyond all com-parison with them, they would despise him in the presumption of their ignorance. Because his spirit burned with an unquenchable passion for their welfare, they would lead him, like his illustrious master, amidst scoffs, and mockery, and insult, to the remuneration of an ignominious death.[72]

This Gnostic hero, a combination of Christ and Caleb Williams, is Shelley's version of the philosophe abroad in the world, assuming martyrdom for the sake of mankind with the serenity of a man who knows that his truth is great and will prevail. He is in fact Prometheus. He is also, it is worth saying, "among the vilest and most atrocious criminals" in the eyes of the society which he would die to redeem.

The fallen world of society is one in which tyranny and revenge flourish and create as their neurotic by-product remorse. For Shelley all three create a hell on earth in their attempt to satisfy or compensate for desires which, being self-centered, are brutishly unnatural. In *Ros-alind and Helen*, a poem "in no degree calculated to excite profound meditation" but hoping to awaken "a certain ideal melancholy,"[73] Rosalind describes her own and her children's reaction to the death of her tyrannical, gold-worshipping husband:

> They laughed, for he was dead: but I
> Sate with a hard and tearless eye,
> And with a heart which would deny
> The secret joy it could not quell,
> Low muttering o'er his loathed name;
> Till from that self-contention came
> Remorse where sin was none; a hell
> Which in pure spirits should not dwell.[74]

Rosalind's unwittingly incestuous love for her brother (her "soul's soul") has led to their final separation, his death, the death of her parents, and her socially sanctioned marriage to this tyrant, whose death she guiltily cannot mourn. Helen loved the very Shelleyan Lionel, an aristocrat who supported the Revolution, was shattered by its defeat, imprisoned by the priests, and died in a strange Temple of Love in the arms of his mistress; she has by him a son, who eventually marries Rosalind's restored daughter. Then Rosalind dies. The tale is unabashedly Gothic and naively comic in many ways; but we can appreciate its importance in Shelley's poetry if we recognize that it is a story of crimes and punishments, the two social crimes being incest and Revolutionary sentiments, the punishment being death. The moral crimes are of course tyranny, marital and political; the psychological crimes are money worship and power lust. Only in the wedding of the son and daughter of each marriage is there any hope for the future. The main point, though, is that the poem, slight as it is, draws its strength from that ethical nucleus which no particle of Shelleyan benevolence had yet been powerful enough to split.

Mary Shelley's version of her husband's theory of evil hardly takes into account his preoccupation with crime and remorse. For her it seems simple:

> The prominent feature of Shelley's theory of the destiny of the human species was, that evil is not inherent in the system of creation, but an accident that might be expelled . . . Shelley believed that mankind had only to will that there should be no evil, and there would be none . . . That man could be so perfectionized as to be able to expel evil from his own nature, and from the greater part of creation, was the cardinal point of his system. And the subject he loved best to dwell on was the image of One warring with the Evil Principle, oppressed not only by it, but by all, even the good, who were deluded into considering evil a necessary portion of humanity. A victim full of fortitude and hope, and the spirit of triumph emanating from a reliance in the ultimate omnipotence of good.[75]

This is inaccurate because it is incomplete. The whole force of such an attitude depends on the kind of reform sponsored by the hope that "man could be so perfectionized as to be able to expel evil from his own nature." For Shelley, as we have seen, practical reform can be generated by the exemplary spectacle of ideal systems—Christian, Platonic, and Godwinian utopias. But the instrument of such reform has to be the faculty with which "the beautiful idealisms of moral excellence" may be perceived. That faculty is the imagination; and it is characterized by its capacity for disinterestedness. This concept is not new with Shelley. Cabanis's doctrine of sympathy is very similar. But its chief virtue for Shelley is that it releases man from the short circuit of sensational materialism, since it allows him to feel without compelling him to admit a prior sensation as the source of his feeling. Disinterestedness is the living proof that man is not merely a creature of sensation. He is rather a creature of imagination: "He is not a moral, and an intellectual,—but also, and pre-eminently, an imaginative being."[76] Disinterestedness therefore is not identical with benevolence, since the latter derives from a moral sense which is itself the creation of the disinterested imagination. Benevolence is what disinterestedness becomes in action; its end is virtue. Disinterestedness is not itself a virtue; it is a capacity awakened in an imagination which contemplates the beautiful. Obviously the man most distinguished by disinterestedness is the most civilized of his kind, the least subject to gross error and selfishness. He is not bound by the conventions of his time or place; he does not presume to teach specific lessons. Instead he widens the circumference of human consciousness by bringing it into contact with the universal spirit; and this intimacy is an index of beauty as well as a condition of moral effectiveness. The text for this hero is of course *A Defence of Poetry*. Where beauty exists, love is born; and with love, true morality.

> The great secret of morals is love; or a going out of our own nature, and an identification of ourselves with the beautiful which exists in thought, action, or person, not our own. A man, to be greatly good, must imagine intensely and comprehensively; he must put himself in the place of another and of many others; the pains and pleasures of his species must become his own. The great instrument of moral good is the imagination; and poetry administers to the effect by acting upon the cause. Poetry enlarges the circumference of the imagination.[77]

Poetry therefore increases the imagination's capacity for disinterestedness and thus also for love. It is the antithesis of all those systems which preach the necessity of egoism. Shelley is the only important English poet to have made the traditional Romantic claims for the poet by changing to another key the standard claims made for the philosophe by French and English alike. He retains the structure of thought we find in Cabanis on sympathy and the need to attune oneself to the spirit of the world by going out of the self into the feelings of another. He divorces himself from crude egoism and crude materialism without rejecting the more substantial claims each can make in a more complete context. Nevertheless, his theory is vivified for us primarily by its dramatization in two of his greatest works, *The*

Cenci and *Prometheus Unbound,* and the antagonistic forces which test it there are, again, the forces of tyranny, revenge, and remorse.

Remorse haunts all the characters of *The Cenci,* except Beatrice. But it is not a play about the effects of remorse; it is a play about its nature and utility. It would be easy and not entirely wrong to say that remorse is shown to be an emotion which we would not feel were we not so addicted to revenge and treachery. Of course Count Cenci himself, on his own admission, feels no remorse:

> And I have no remorse, and little fear,
> Which are, I think, the checks of other men.[78]

Shelley makes it clear in his preface that Beatrice would not be so tragic were she more enlightened: "Revenge, retaliation, atonement, are pernicious mistakes. If Beatrice had thought in this manner she would have been wiser and better; but she would never have been a tragic character."[79]

In the light of such statements it would seem that Beatrice is more to blame than her father. He sins in the name of sin, she in the name of virtue. As has been pointed out before, she is, like Satan, a rebel against tyranny who, by allowing her actions to be governed by the moral climate of the tyranny she suffers, becomes corrupt herself. The affinity between her situation and that of the French revolutionaries is also clear and has been noted.[80] The dilemma at the center of the play, however, is not entirely clarified by reading it in these contexts, even though Earl Wasserman's arguments, based on Beatrice's "pernicious casuistry" and Shelley's "sublime casuistry," dispel much previous confusion.[81] Beatrice is like the Shelleyan scorpion caught in a ring of fire and obliged by her own nature to sting herself to death; but she does not die by the sting of remorse. She is superior to all others who take part in the crime because she will not submit to remorse. When the judge declares, "She is convicted, but has not confessed,"[82] he makes the proper distinction. Beatrice does not refuse to admit her part in the death of her father. She simply refuses to admit that it was a crime to have him killed. In violating her, Cenci shattered the moral structure which up to that point had compelled her to accept his tyranny. But just as incest had been in other poems a relationship of genuine love opposed to the tyranny of conventional relationship, so here it becomes an ultimate perversion of the genuine and intimate, so profound that conventional morality cannot even supply a name for it. Incest is a perversion of something natural; tyranny is a perversion of something artificial. Tyranny is a social crime. Incest is a crime against the very assumptions on which the defective

social structure is based. Beatrice therefore demands that the pope
recognize that the conventions of crime and punishment are incompetent to deal with her situation, just as she demands of her fellow
conspirators that they not feel a conventional remorse for a crime
which, in its uniqueness, should not even be called by that name.
The judge might as well ask God as ask Beatrice who is guilty of her
father's death. The problem for her is metaphysical; for her accusers
and for the other accused it is judicial:

> Or wilt thou rather tax high-judging God
> That he permitted such an act as that
> Which I have suffered, and which he beheld;
> All refuge, all revenge, all consequence,
> But that which thou hast called my father's death?
> Which is or is not what men call a crime,
> Which either I have done, or have not done;
> Say what ye will.[83]

She is, naturally, condemned on conventional judicial grounds that
have nothing to do with the nature of her particular case. Had Paolo
Santa Croce not killed his mother the day before, the pope might
have relented; the inconsequence of the judgment is emphasized by
that fact. The problem is not the rise in the parricide rate, but that,
judicially speaking, is how it is conceived and solved.

The fact that the conventional bounds of morality have been passed
makes the emotions which that morality promotes irrelevant. Beatrice
tells her mother:

> And, honoured Lady, while I speak, I pray
> That you put off, as garments overworn,
> Forbearance and respect, remorse and fear,
> And all the fit restraints of daily life.[84]

Even Giacomo, Beatrice's brother, briefly sees how unjustified remorse
is when, just as his fellow conspirator Orsino tells him that Cenci has
escaped death, the lamp goes out:

> If no remorse is ours when the dim air
> Has drank this innocent flame, why should we quail
> When Cenci's life, that light by which ill spirits
> See the worst deeds they prompt, shall sink for ever?
> No, I am hardened.
>   *Orsino:* Why, what need of this?
> Who feared the pale intrusion of remorse
> In a just deed?[85]

Both Giacomo and Orsino become prey to remorse in the end, but only because of falsifying what has happened. Like the judges, Giacomo sees the crime as an evil act of parricide; but it is hard to reconcile the actual Count Cenci with the victim of the following speech:

> Do evil deeds thus quickly come to end?
> O, that the vain remorse which must chastise
> Crimes done, had but as loud a voice to warn
> As its keen sting is mortal to avenge:
> O, that the hour when present had cast off
> The mantle of its mystery, and shown
> The ghastly form with which it now returns
> When its scared game is roused, cheering the hounds
> Of conscience to their prey! Alas! Alas!
> It was a wicked thought, a piteous deed,
> To kill an old and hoary-headed father.[86]

Orsino, resolving to flee in disguise, is the typical victim of secret crime—the crime against conscience—whom we meet in Holbach and Godwin:

> Have I not the power to fly
> My own reproaches? . . .
>   Where shall I
> Find the disguise to hide me from myself
> As now I skulk from every other eye?[87]

He has lost self-esteem. Giacomo has lost his true perception of the "crime" and returns to the judicial notion of its nature. Each, bound by the conventional morality, suffers the pangs of remorse. In doing so they and Lucretia impugn the "eternal honour"[88] of Beatrice. They confess guilt under torture, either of the rack or of conscience. As Orsino says to Giacomo,

> Confess, 'tis fear disguised
> From its own shame that takes the mantle now
> Of thin remorse.[89]

Of course their conception of the crime can never be Beatrice's, since they did not suffer the violation which for her robbed her act of its conventional criminality. They belong to the moral world from which she has been expelled. Her expulsion reveals to her the nature of that world; shows how in its structure crime, punishment, and remorse are so interwoven that those who suffer punishment accept it as justified, even though it is no more than a legalized form of revenge. The setting of the play emphasizes the subjection of its characters to their local circumstances and their acceptance of these as universal principles. In judicial terms revenge gains its justification in the minds of its victims through the operation of remorse; but remorse is clearly shown to be a culturally determined emotion, deriving its power from the distorted nature of the social system. Like La Mettrie, Shelley is finally opposed to its power, since he too regards it as a neurotic inheritance of exploitation. In *The Cenci* Beatrice is the vehicle of that perception. The others are closer to the Holbach-Godwin notion of remorse as an internal surrogate for physical punishment. Shelley as usual brings the moral radicalism of Godwin to a more subtle and flexible stage.

Yet the attack on remorse in *The Cenci* is not a defense of revenge. Beatrice recognizes the limits of her society's morality, but she does not realize (is indeed puzzled by) the blind strength of the convictions which impose them. She suffers the illusion that her action will alter society's moral evolution by bringing upon it a violent revolutionary crisis. The action of killing her father has for her a falsely liberating quality, since she conceives herself to be free from its consequences:

> The deed is done,
> And what may follow now regards not me.
> I am as universal as the light;
> Free as the earth-surrounding air; as firm
> As the world's centre. Consequence, to me,
> Is as the wind which strikes the solid rock,
> But shakes it not.[90]

She attributes to herself a freedom she cannot have, because she makes the mistake of the French philosophes and of the French revolutionaries in demanding that the mass of society, which is still in moral darkness, appreciate her action in the light of a morality which is available only to her. Her action does have consequences, and, given the state of her society, they are inevitable and bloody. The world is not subject to fundamental change by violence because the practice of violence is precisely what retards its advancement. Her enlightenment is greater than that of those around her, but it is not sufficient in itself, since it is expressed by an act of personal will only. Insofar as that will is out of accord with the spirit of necessity which rules the world, it is self-defeating. It pretends to a freedom which it does not possess. It does not allow for a liberating action so much as it submits to an outraged but imprisoning reaction. Beatrice is not a true necessarian, described in the *Notes to Queen Mab* as inconsequent to his own principles, if he indulges in hatred or contempt; the compassion which he feels for the criminal is unmixed with a desire for injuring him: he looks with an elevated and dreadless composure upon the links of the universal chain as they pass before his eyes; whilst cowardice, curiosity and inconsistency only assail him in proportion to the feebleness, and indistinctness with which he has perceived and rejected the delusions of free will.[91]

She is insensitive to the energy which controls the universe and can thus achieve neither disinterestedness nor benevolence, even though her sensitivity to the injustices of her society exposes to her the nullity of remorse. By itself that is not enough, since it brings destruction in its train. Revenge is the action of those imprisoned by their own will and subject to its exclusive authority and to its false appearance as freedom.

The Cenci was written between May and August 1820, after the third act of *Prometheus Unbound* had been completed and before the fourth was begun. The two works are obviously closely related, and much comment has been devoted to their intimacy.[92] They both, in containing a theodicy, also analyze the nature of liberty. Each complements the other. They also, more unfortunately, share the fate of being open to crude misinterpretation, largely because their ethical terminology is that of the late eighteenth century, colored by its close alliance with sensationalist thought, much of it French. There is a sense in which this tradition can supply a critique which helps us to understand Shelley's debt to it and his important variations on it. The fairly primitive notion of necessity which informs Holbach's work, for instance, was attacked on various occasions in terms which have a certain, if limited, relevance to *The Cenci* and *Prometheus Unbound*. Frederick II of Prussia, in his *Examen critique du système de la nature*, summarizes one aspect of his argument against Holbach: "When we allow ourselves to be carried away by the strength of our passions, fate triumphs over our freedom; and when reason conquers passion, freedom prevails."[93] This could be a gloss for Shelley's poems if for Frederick's "passions" we substituted the human will "that thus enchains us to permitted ill"[94] and for his "reason" the human will in submission to necessity. Yet, although there is a similarity in the structure of thought, the terminological change is vital. Shelley's concentration is on "evil, the immedicable plague,"[95] and the nature and extent of human bondage to it. Demogorgon defines these and their limitations when he says, "All spirits are enslaved which serve things evil,"[96] and further, when he declares that it would avail nothing to bid speak

> Fate, Time, Occasion, Chance and Change[.] To these
> All things are subject but eternal love.[97]

In *Prometheus Unbound*, then, Shelley aligns his Revolutionary faith with Enlightenment morality while confronting the problem of evil. It is this combination of elements which makes him unique in the history of the European Enlightenment, to which he belongs as much as he does to the history of English poetry.

Prometheus Unbound differs most from *The Cenci* in that the ethical system it promotes has no place for remorse. The vultures which tear at the hero's heart are not "the hounds of conscience" of which Giacomo spoke. They are, more straightforwardly, the ministers of Jupiter's revenge:

> Heaven's winged hound, polluting from thy lips
> His beak in poison not his own, tears up
> My heart.[98]

Only Jupiter, who later sees himself as a vulture "twisted in inextricable fight"[99] with the serpent of necessity, can suffer the pangs of conscience. The point is that he and they become defunct. The new age has arrived. Prometheus, Jupiter's better self, has broken the vicious circle of crime, revenge, remorse, torture, and crime again by his great act of forgiveness. When we first hear from the Phantasm of Jupiter what Prometheus' curse had been, we are treading on familiar ground, but Shelley makes it clear that this territory of moral anguish has by now been crossed and left behind forever:

> I curse thee! let a sufferer's curse
> Clasp thee, his torturer, like remorse!
> Till thy Infinity shall be
> A robe of envenomed agony;
> And thine Omnipotence a crown of pain
> To cling like burning gold round thy dissolving brain.[100]

Jupiter's "self-torturing solitude"[101] is that of the remorseful criminal who is suffering the neurosis which tyranny produces in the human psyche. Through Prometheus, Shelley finally offers the defining comment on tyranny and on violent revolution. Inevitably the terminology is again that of crime, but not, on this occasion, of punishment as well:

> Let others flatter Crime, where it sits throned
> In brief Omnipotence: secure are they:
> For Justice, when triumphant, will weep down
> Pity, not punishment, on her own wrongs,
> Too much avenged by those who err.[102]

The ethics of remorse, which found their culminating expression in *The Cenci*, receives cursory treatment in *Prometheus Unbound* because there they have been transcended by the spirit of love. The disinterested imagination finally rules over the tortured conscience; utopia replaces history.

I have discussed only particular aspects of Shelley's work; others have been ignored or treated in a peremptory manner. But some important features do retain their prominence or gain a new salience: Shelley's conception of the poet-philosophe; his doctrine of benevolence and its relation to necessity; the relation of his early materialism to its later incorporation into a more elaborate and subtler philosophy, including a new and more powerful role for the imagination; and of course his intricately developed theory of evil, in which the ratio of cause and effect between crime, punishment, and remorse undergoes a relentless scrutiny, much of it impelled by the failure of the French Revolution and much of it governed by the categories of thought he inherited from a group of thinkers closely associated in his mind with it—Godwin, Rousseau, Holbach, Cabanis, and La Mettrie. In *The Triumph of Life* new forces emerge. Rousseau and Napoleon dominate as examples of man's tyranny over himself. By then the ethical system which Shelley had developed and which I have been trying to describe had begun to be undermined by a deep skepticism.[103] *Prometheus Unbound* brings to a crisis one long phase of development which had begun in the Gothic fiction and had undergone variation and persistent extension since then; *The Triumph of Life* belongs to a different phase, and to its beginnings only. Yet the famous and final question "Then, what is life?" addressed to Rousseau reminds us how deeply Shelley was indebted to the thought of pre-Revolutionary France, just as his disillusion reminds us of the effect of the failure of the Revolution on the group of radical thinkers whom Shelley dominated. He was not only an English poet. He was also, in the European sense, a philosophe; and he was also, perhaps on account of that combination, a revolutionary moral thinker.

7 Hazlitt and the French: A Jacobin Profile

Throughout his career William Hazlitt devoted to the French a fascinated attention and a polemical energy which allowed for no glib or slipshod description of their qualities and achievements. This alone distinguished him from most of his contemporaries. Voltaire and Rousseau, Condillac and Helvétius, Holbach and Mirabeau, Napoleon and Mme. de Staël consume between them a respectably large proportion of his writings. If we add to this the extent of his commentary on the French Enlightenment and Revolution, the Napoleonic era, and the Restoration, it becomes quickly apparent that the history of the relationship between France and England during this period forms an important part of Hazlitt's thought, just as his thought forms part of that relationship.

Despite various and important reservations, it is clear that Rousseau was the French writer (or more precisely the writer of French) whom Hazlitt most admired, whereas for Condillac and Helvétius he had little but an insistent scorn and contempt. His attitudes have a complex basis. They are not simply (or simple) expressions of a "Romantic" preference for the "emotive" over standard eighteenth-century rational empiricism. Few writers are less amenable to that kind of categorization in their responses than Hazlitt. He is not a man given to the expression of superficial opinions on any subject, least of all on what he called "that enigma, the French character"[1] and its most representative figures.

The coherence of Hazlitt's aesthetic and philosophical opinions has been widely acknowledged and brilliantly analyzed;[2] but the consistency of his political opinions and the extent to which they agree with his other positions has not yet received attention. Nor can it until Hazlitt's view of the French, of contemporary politics, of the "modern philosophy," and of particular French authors and politicians has been clearly established,[3] for Hazlitt's attitude toward France is the most pronounced version of his attitude toward his age and the spirit which he perceived to be its informing principle. The French incorporated both the radiance of hope and the darkness of disillusion in their Revolution, in their writings, and in their national character. Without ever claiming to understand them entirely, Hazlitt was fascinated by them as by a symbol which remained meaningful even while most perplexing. Conscious at all times of his Englishness, he nevertheless looked to the French as the defenders of liberty, sentiment, and reason in an age characterized by its betrayal of them all.

Hazlitt, as his biographer Herschel Baker has remarked, belongs to the tradition of the Dissenting Radicals.[4] That does not necessarily mean he represents a tradition of radical dissent. In intellectual terms the Unitarians were the most formidable group within the ranks of the Dissenters. From its founding in 1791, the Unitarian Society emerged in the public eye as an ominous group, led by Joseph Priestley, tainted by the Revolution, and seeking radical change in England.[5] The riots in Birmingham in 1791 and Manchester in 1792, when added to the failure of the campaign for the repeal of the Test Acts, revealed a disposition on the part of loyalist mobs and the British government to make a much more direct and sinister connection between Dissent and the French Revolution than the Dissenters themselves would have wished to acknowledge. The Birmingham mob had two slogans: one was "Church and King," the other "No Philosophes!"[6] In fact the aims of the Dissenters were far more limited than their rhetoric would lead one to believe. They wanted civil and religious liberty for themselves, but not necessarily for Roman Catholics.[7] They wished for no transformation in society as a whole, merely in its attitude toward them. The progressive, utilitarian element in their thinking found its most perfect expression not in Priestley, Godwin, Paine, or Hazlitt but in the career and achievement of William Smith, the Dissenting politician, who was to cause Hazlitt some pleasure and Robert Southey some embarrassment in 1817, during the dispute over the pirated publication of Southey's *Wat Tyler*.[8] The Dissenters' natural alliance was with the Westminster Reformers and Benthamism. They were extremely reluctant, especially during the repression stimulated in England by the French Revolution, to ally themselves with the Jacobinism which the government press so execrated. Yet their finest minds were Jacobin minds. Paine, Godwin, and Hazlitt left the sectarian and provincial origins of Dissent for the cosmopolitan ambitions of the Revolution.[9] In doing so they suffered severe disillusion. Hazlitt attributed this to a variety of interacting causes, the definition of which constitutes the most complete analysis in this period of Jacobinism, seen from an English point of view.[10] Between Bentham, who made man less than he was, and Godwin, who made him more than he could be, Hazlitt sought a deeper perception of the human condition as such and of its capacity for realization in the existing political conditions of the time.

Jacobinism, according to Hazlitt, began with Rousseau in France and was almost destroyed by Burke in England:

> He [Rousseau] was the founder of Jacobinism, which disclaims the division of the species into two classes, the one the property of the others. It was of the disciples of *his* school, where a principle is converted into a passion, that Mr. Burke said and said truly,—"Once a Jacobin, and always a Jacobin!" The adept in this school does not so much consider the political injury as the personal insult. This is the way to put the case to set the true revolutionary leaven, the self-love which is at the bottom of every heart, at work, and this was the way in which Rousseau puts it.[11]

It is remarkable to find such a view of Rousseau's political philosophy at this early stage. Hazlitt recognized the importance of the feeling as well as of the fact of being degraded or insulted by the insolence of rank. The individual whose self-love was damaged could only compensate by allying himself with the cause of the equality of mankind. His passion became a principle. It was for Hazlitt no abstract principle. It was rooted in human feeling. Rousseau was the political philosopher whose ideas of social and political renovation arose out of a true perception of the oppressed state of feeling and its desire for liberation. This was the essence of Jacobinism.

Even as late as 1817, when his essay *On the Character of Rousseau* was published, Hazlitt took it for granted that Rousseau and Voltaire "caused" the Revolution, not by conspiracy but by the power of their genius in altering the political and cultural climate of the ancien régime. This at first sight seems an odd position for Hazlitt to adopt because it was then and had been for years a commonplace among his political opponents.[12] The question of the responsibility of the philosophes for the Revolution was by its nature complicated; but Hazlitt read it straightforwardly. The originality of his approach can be appreciated, however, if we note the grounds on which he chose to disagree with Madame de Staël's opinion of Rousseau and the bearing of this disagreement on his conception of Rousseau's contribution to the Revolution. Rousseau was extraordinary, declares Hazlitt, solely because the only quality he possessed in an eminent degree, which alone raised him above ordinary men, and which gave to his writings and opinions an influence greater, perhaps, than has been exerted by any individual in modern times, was extreme sensibility, or an acute and even morbid feeling of all that related to his own impressions, to the objects and events of his life. He had the most intense consciousness of his own existence.[13]

In the same essay Rousseau is ranked with Wordsworth and Benvenuto Cellini as "the three greatest egotists that we know of."[14] Yet it is this very egotism, this "most intense consciousness of his own existence," that is invoked to convince us that, among other things, Rousseau was the great apostle of humanity, the Jacobin behind the Revolution. In other words egotism, evidently by virtue of its intensity, becomes universal in its benevolent effects. The paradox is more apparent than real. Hazlitt is delving for something other than the conventional calculus of selfishness and altruism. Rousseau "did more towards the French Revolution than any other man. Voltaire, by his wit and penetration, had rendered superstition contemptible, and tyranny odious: but it was Rousseau who brought the feeling of irreconcilable enmity to rank and privileges, ABOVE HUMANITY, home to the bosom of every man,—identified it with all the pride of intellect, and with the deepest yearnings of the human heart."[15] There is not, therefore, any authentic connection between self-love (as Hobbes, La Rochefoucauld, Locke, Mandeville, and Helvétius, the members of Hazlitt's enemy tradition, would define it) and universal benevolence. For Hazlitt that is a vapid generalization, a clever piece of dialectic construed by social engineers who take everything into account but the common nature of man. The authentic connection for him is that between self-consciousness and consciousness of others, a connection characterized by intensity and achieved by sympathy. When he speaks of Rousseau, he is not only speaking of a French author. He is also speaking of a period in his own life with which this author is indissolubly connected—not simply because Hazlitt read him when he was young but because his youthful sympathies found in Rousseau an enduring response and an unforgettable analysis. He can say of *La nouvelle Heloise*, and above all of *Les confessions*, "We spent two whole years in reading these two works; . . . They were the happiest years of our life."[16] Rousseau, in making the young Hazlitt more self-aware, made him more complete. By his self-analysis he transmitted to his young reader a sense of what was basic to human nature; and that sense found itself thereafter in opposition to all that conspired to oppress it in the name of law, order, or any other shibboleth of politicians

and writers whose view of human nature was more limited and therefore distorted.

Hazlitt thus elaborates a defense of Rousseau and of the Revolution
which is of a piece with his philosophy of mind and the later development of his aesthetic. The final sentence of his early essay *Remarks
on the Systems of Hartley and Helvétius* (1805) gives us one formulation:
"The love of others has the same necessary foundation in the human
mind as the love of ourselves."[17] His *Preface to an Abridgment of Abraham
Tucker's Light of Nature Pursued* gives us a more complete view:

> I know but two sorts of philosophy; that of those who believe what they
> feel, and endeavour to account for it, and those who only believe what
> they understand, and have already accounted for. The one is the phi-
> losophy of consciousness, the other that of experiment; the one may be
> called the intellectual, the other the material philosophy. The one rests
> mainly on the general notions and conscious perceptions of mankind,
> and endeavours to discover what the mind is, by looking into the mind
> itself; the other denies the existence of everything in the mind, of which
> it cannot find some rubbishy archetype, and visible image in its crucibles
> and furnaces, or in the distinct forms of verbal analysis. The first of these
> is the only philosophy that is fit for men of sense, the other should be
> left to chymists and logicians. Of this last kind is the philosophy of Locke;
> though I would be understood to speak of him rather as having laid the
> foundation, on which others have built absurd conclusions, than of what
> he was in himself.[18]

Among those builders of absurd conclusions, Condillac is given a
prominent place.

Hazlitt makes an important distinction, however, between selfishness and self-consciousness which needs to be seen more clearly than
the preceding remarks would permit. Selfishness is not for him the
embodiment of self-consciousness. It is its ghost. It is self-consciousness robbed of its concrete and specific nature and rendered an abstraction of the intellect. To refer all action to the principle of self-love
inevitably entails the view that human happiness is merely a matter
of selfish pleasure and pleasure merely a matter of pleasing physical
sensations, with pain, its opposite, simply understood as unpleasant
physical sensation. From this basis, building on the association principle, one could understand man as an amalgam of sensory impulses
fed into his sensorium by a world of objects. Thought in such a case
could be no more than sensation—even though, as Hazlitt and others
were to remark, how could a mind so constituted find the power to
define itself as physical? A model of the mind remarkable for its peculiar combination of poverty, philosophically speaking, and power,

practically speaking, had come to replace actual experience. Furthermore, the tendency had been long visible and had, in Hazlitt's view,
reached a culmination in his own time.

Like Coleridge, he saw this philosophy as having Bacon and Hobbes
for parents. Since them it had gained wide acceptance through the
unwitting Locke and had become more drastically systematic when
it reached France, particularly in thinkers such as Condillac and Helvétius, before returning again to England in Bentham and, in a different form, in Godwin. For Hazlitt not only was this view of the
mind the most damaging and characteristic feature of the "modern
philosophy"; it also contradicted the whole bias of the native English
character. He is again like Coleridge in his claim that since Hobbes
there had been what we would now call a "dissociation of sensibility"
which had, as far as Hazlitt was concerned, led to the impoverishment
of the old English feeling for liberty and its replacement by the repression of Pitt and the inhuman organization of Bentham. But Hazlitt
goes farther than this when he claims that this philosophy is as naturally attractive to the French as it is repulsive to the English.[19] This
is an important conviction, although its crudeness is equaled only by
its popularity. That is to say, insofar as this reading of a philosophical
development is referred to a set of national characteristics, French
and English, it now seems more than faintly ridiculous—but we must
at the same time remember the general acceptance given to these distinctions at the time. Wordsworth, Southey, Croker, Coleridge, Mme.
de Staël, Mackintosh, and even Godwin, as well as a host of reviewers,
journalists, pamphleteers, politicians, and clergymen, dwelt on this
distinction with a steadiness that owed as much to genuine conviction
as it did to political hatred and chauvinism.[20]

Hazlitt admits, for instance, in his "Critical Notes to Bulstrode Whit-
locke" in *The Eloquence of the British Senate* that "one object that I have
chiefly had in view in this work, has been to select such examples as
might serve to mark the successive changes that have taken place in
the minds and characters of Englishmen within the last 200 years,"
and then goes on to summarize them:

> The distinctive character of the period of which we are now speaking
> was, I think, that men's minds were stored with facts and images, almost
> to excess; there was a tenacity and firmness in them that kept fast hold
> of the impressions of things as they were first stamped upon the mind;
> and "their ideas seemed to lie like substances in the brain." Facts and
> feeling went in hand; the one naturally implied the other; and our ideas,
> not yet exorcised and squeezed and tortured out of their natural objects,
> into a subtle essence of pure intellect, did not fly about like ghosts without

a body, tossed up and down, or upborne only by the ELEGANT FORMS of words, through the vacuum of abstract reasoning, and sentimental refinement.[21]

The inescapable fact was that, protest as Hazlitt might, the new philosophy had become dominant. He pointed out, for example, that the emergence and the reputation of Malthus, who decried the possibility of perfectibility in the world, actually depended on the prevalence of the speculative opinions of Godwin and Condorcet. Only those who believed in perfectibility could be upset by the demonstration that it could not be achieved.[22] Malthus was thus, like Mackintosh, Horne Tooke, and Bentham, a symptom of the spirit of an age which had been a long time in preparation. Now that it had appeared wearing "the terrible mask of modern philosophy,"[23] it maintained the dominance of its shallow opinions by making them fashionable, by taking them out of the severe context of philosophical dispute and bringing them into the laxer atmosphere of the salon or the review. In achieving this transition the French had, in his opinion, played a dominant role. Not only were they notoriously fond of the combination of philosophy and the salon; they were also by nature incapable of philosophical profundity, which would be incongruous in such a glittering social milieu. An attack on Helvétius is buttressed by the following exemplary disquisition in the form of a note:

> This is all the proof he brings, and perhaps, considering the language and country in which this celebrated author wrote, it is reasoning good enough. Do I say this with any view to throw contempt on that lively, ingenious, gay, social, and polished people? No; but philosophy is not their forte: they are not in earnest in these remote speculations. In order duly to appreciate their writings, we must consider them not as the dictates of the understanding, but as the effects of constitution. Otherwise we shall do them great injustice. They pursue truth, like all other things, as far as it is agreeable; they reason for their amusement; they engage in abstruse questions to vary the topics of conversation. Whatever does not answer this purpose is banished out of books and society as a morose and cynical philosophy. To obtrude the dark and difficult parts of a question, or to enter into elaborate investigation of them, is considered as a piece of ill manners. Those writers, therefore, have been the most popular among the French who have supplied their readers with the greatest number of dazzling conclusions founded on the most slight and superficial evidence, whose reasonings could be applied to everything, because they explained nothing, and who most effectually kept out of sight every thing true or profound or interesting in a question. Who would ever think of plunging into abstruse, metaphysical inquiries concerning the nature of the understanding, when he may with entire ease

to himself and satisfaction to others solve all the phenomena of the mind by repeating the three words, juger est sentir. As it was the object of the school-philosophy, by a jargon of technical distinctions, to sharpen the eagerness of debate and give birth to endless verbal controversies, so the modern system transferring philosophy from the cloistered hall to the toilette and the drawing-room, is calculated by a set of portable phrases, as familiar and as current as the forms of salutation, to silence every difference of opinion, and to produce an euthanasia of all thought.[24]

It is difficult not to sense the influence of Burke in such a passage. Hazlitt's view of France would have been unremarkable had it stopped there; but the counteracting influence of Rousseau is even more impressive, and we can see the friction between the two in the repeated charge that Burke attacked the Revolution because he was jealous of Rousseau's part in bringing it about.[25] There is no evidence I know of on which Hazlitt could have made such an accusation—yet his disposition to do so indicates the friction in his thought between these two men who represented so perfectly for him the spirit of the Revolution and its denial. Hazlitt's various and often brilliant, if unsparing, attacks on Burke are an integral part of his ceaseless attempt to understand the nature of the perversion to which French Jacobinism had been subjected in England in the long war between the two countries during this period.

Leaving aside that quarrel, the main point at issue becomes the degree to which, in Hazlitt's mind, Rousseau represents something both authentic in itself and typically French, something not to be found in Condillac or in Helvétius. In order to make this distinction Hazlitt performed the valuable service for the England of his day of making the otherwise faintly acknowledged hostility between Voltaire, the Encyclopedists, and Rousseau a central feature of his reading of the pre-Revolutionary situation in France. It was important to him that Rousseau, while never entirely free of the taint of being French, should be recognized as a writer who, in the profundity of the emotions he provoked, was entirely removed from the vapid spirit of shallow abstraction which afflicted his salon-haunting contemporaries. Instead he was to be allied with the solidity and fullness of apprehension which Hazlitt granted preeminently to Shakespeare and Milton—and, with more qualification, to Wordsworth. Rousseau is in fact seen as a figure in the world of imaginative literature, not in the world of modern philosophy, with the implication always present that philosophy needed to rediscover the concreteness of literature in order to regain its stature. For as philosophy had grown to love abstraction, literature in Rousseau and Wordsworth had learned to cling to the actual and specific. In abstraction, feeling either vanishes or becomes attenuated; in adhering to the actual, feeling becomes refreshed and strengthened. It indeed becomes part of intellect and not the ghostly opposite of mind. We can therefore see the difference between Rousseau and the French people as a whole:

> The general clue to that enigma, the character of the French, seems to be that their feelings are very imperfectly modified by the objects exciting them . . . They want neither feeling nor ideas in the abstract; but there seems to be no connection in their minds between the one and the other. Consequently their feelings want compass and variety, and whatever else must depend on the "building up of our feelings through the imagination" . . . They do not give the object time to be *thoroughly* impressed on their minds, their feelings are roused at the first notice of its approach, and . . . fairly run away from the object. Their feelings do not grapple with the object. The least stimulus is sufficient to excite them and more is superfluous, for they do not wait for the impression, or stop to inquire what degree or kind it is of. There is not resistance sufficient in the matter to receive those sharp incisions, those deep, marked, and strangely rooted impressions, the traces of which remain for ever. From whatever cause it proceeds, the sensitive principle in them does not seem to be susceptible of the same modification and variety of action as it does in others; and certainly the outward forms of things do not adhere to, do not wind themselves round their feelings in the same manner.[26]

The vocabulary of this passage demonstrates with a marvelous precision how Hazlitt was able to take the stereotyped notion of French volatility, instability, and so forth and convert it into an aesthetic dominated by directly opposite terms. Heavy emphasis is placed on retentiveness, on a prehensile and loving grasp of the object, its incorporation into the sensibility; and yet what we have here is initially little more than the commonplace eighteenth-century description of national characteristics. In reading Hazlitt on Wordsworth we find the same stress on Wordsworth's ability to give his reflection that full-bodied presence which for Hazlitt distinguished it above all other contemporary writing. Egoism of this kind is the supreme form of consciousness. Insofar as it is retentive in its appreciation of the world, it is also closely allied with memory and the pristine responses of childhood. For him Rousseau has this quality too, French though he may be. Although the French have great facility with words, they are not attentive to feeling. The more somber English are "in the habit of retaining individual images and of brooding over the feelings connected with them," and they are therefore not prone to classifying things in that spirit of abstraction so typical of the French. Therefore the French prefer Racine to Shakespeare; but, Hazlitt goes on: "Rousseau is the only French writer I am acquainted with (though he by the bye was not a Frenchman) who from the depth of his feelings without many distinct images, produces the same kind of interest in the mind that is excited by the events and recollections of our own lives. If he had not true genius, he had at least something which was a very good substitute for it."[27] Fidelity to the actual is for Hazlitt the abiding law of the marriage between the mind and the universe. Both Rousseau and Wordsworth "wind their own being round whatever object occurs to them."[28] The ratio of the relationship between the self and the object may differ, but in both writers the power of feeling depends on the existence of such a relationship. What Hazlitt sought in literature was a rebuttal of the epistemology of the sensationalist school of thought, in which Condillac and Helvétius were so prominent. In literature we see that the intensity of feeling, a form of commitment to the object, provides the transience of merely physical sensation with an endurance which belongs not to the sensation itself but to the human experience of which sensation is only an ingredient. The feeling inheres in the object, and the object is transfigured by the feeling. He cites as proof of this the power of memory to cast a glow of feeling on past objects of perception. Great literature, in casting such an aura of significance around the otherwise meaningless sequence of our physical sensations, touches closely on our own lives.[29]

If this is true, though, the French cannot really have a body of poetic literature, since they are by nature radically incapable of any intimate alliance between feeling and perceiving. Hazlitt's aesthetic and his politics come into critical contact on this issue. In denying the French this spirit, he can, for instance, play Shakespeare off against Racine in a manner which was by then almost routine, and which led directly to a conclusion that was always implicit in the premise.[30] Yet the noticeably democratic appeal of the new literature, exemplified by Rousseau in France and by the Lake Poets in England, compelled him to acknowledge the existence in literature of a Jacobin spirit which displayed itself in the promotion, through particular instances drawn from common life, of a universal love. To put it in terms perhaps more suitable to Hazlitt, the preoccupation with the self-as-such (that is, the self liberated from the categories of rank and class) bred a consciousness of others-as-such. Romantic egoism, "the egotistical sublime" spirit of Wordsworth, had Jacobin (or, if this was thought to be opprobrious at the time, Jacobinical) consequences, since it abolished artificial distinctions between men and fostered instead a consciousness of our common inheritance as Man. The greatest egotists

were those who could perceive in what sense they were represen-
tatively human. In this way Hazlitt rescues Rousseau from Burke's
charge that Rousseau's self-consciousness was no more than a mere
concentration on his own eccentricities. Such reasoning had, however,
important political consequences for Hazlitt, especially in the matter
of his attitude toward the French Revolution; for if Rousseau had
helped more than any other to bring about the Revolution, and if he
represented a more profound sense of human experience than the
abstractions of the modern philosophy could do, then the French,
who philosophically had taken the Hobbes-Locke tradition to absurdly
systematic lengths, were politically now taking the Rousseauistic revolution in feeling to its proper conclusion. The superficial and volatile
nation had produced the most astonishing revolution in modern European history, and the solid and profound English were doing all in
their power to have it suppressed. The only explanation for this state
of affairs—one forced on Hazlitt by the nature of his position—was
that the English had betrayed, and the French had changed, their
national character.[31] The alternative—that the current prejudices about
national character might themselves be wrong—does not arise because
those prejudices were so deeply woven into the assumptions of Hazlitt
and his contemporaries.

Hazlitt took the conventional view that the French Revolution was
primarily a repetition of England's Glorious Revolution of 1688.[32] But
he also saw it in a less constrictingly provincial sense, as an extension
to Europe of what had been achieved in America, with this difference:
in France the feelings of mankind had been roused from the concussion
given them by the "petrific mace" of the Hobbes-Mandeville-Helvétius
tradition, to assert not only the principles of political liberty but also
the resumption of an authentic philosophy which would place (or
replace) the heart at the center of its allied theories of moral conduct.[33]
Like Mme. de Staël he saw literature as the realm in which this important resurgence of feeling was most clearly and comprehensively
manifest. It was the early warning system of coming political change.
In France Rousseau's writings were the Bible of this revelation; in
England the Lake School of poets had been, in its early stages, Rousseau's echo and counterpart; and in Germany the new drama and the
critical writings of A. W. Schlegel (especially on Shakespeare) embodied this new spirit.[34] For Hazlitt the most significant body of new
literature in Europe was a Jacobin literature. As such it was as open
to betrayal as Jacobin politics. Its fresh self-consciousness could be
degraded into the selfishness of institutional poetry. The Lake School,
he claimed in the seventh lecture of his *Lectures on the English Poets*,

"had its origin in the French Revolution, or rather in those sentiments and opinions which produced that revolution; and which sentiments and opinions were directly imported into this country in translations from the German about that period."[35]

On this basis he could therefore attack the Lake Poets for a political betrayal of feeling which was thus coincident, or said to be coincident, with a decline in literary quality. He so construed the situation that Jacobinism became a literary and political characteristic by means of which the commitment of any given author to true feeling and to true philosophy could be judged. The loss of Jacobin principle led to a loss in creative power. On this he was as logical as he was straightforward and savage. Southey, Coleridge, and Wordsworth all wrote their best poetry before they changed their political opinions: "Their Jacobin principles indeed gave rise to their Jacobin poetry. Since they gave up the first, their poetical powers have flagged . . . Their poetical innovations unhappily did not answer any more than the French Revolution . . . as they could not change their style, they changed their principles; and instead of writing popular poetry, fell to scribbling venal prose."[36] This comment appeared on the occasion of the *Wat Tyler* dispute in 1817 and was followed by the three articles on Southey's *Letter to William Smith M.P.*[37] Southey, the Jacobin turned Tory, was caught between the fury of the Dissenter turned Jacobin and the guile of the Dissenter turned Reformer.

Two months earlier Hazlitt had written what amounts to the manifesto of a Jacobin reviewer in a period of betrayal: "To be a true Jacobin, a man must be a good hater; . . . The love of liberty consists in the hatred of tyrants. The true Jacobin hates the enemies of liberty as they hate liberty, with all his strength and with all his might, and with all his heart and with all his soul."[38] So by 1826 we read of Hazlitt at Vevey remembering his Rousseau with deep affection, despite the fulminations of Burke, the Lake Poets, and Thomas Moore against his memory.[39] The vision of Rousseau strengthens in Hazlitt as the sense of betrayal deepens. Seeing the place where Rousseau had stopped on his way to Paris "when he went to overturn the French monarchy by the force of his style," Hazlitt bitterly imagines what the forces of reaction would have done to prevent that famous arrival: "What couriers posting to all parts of Europe, what manifestoes from Armies, what a hubbub of Holy Alliances, and all for what? To prevent one man from speaking what he and every other man felt, and whose only fault was that the beatings of the human heart had found an echo in his pen!"[40]

What we witness in Hazlitt's Rousseau is the spectacle of a very complex English response to France, which finds in the French writer a beautifully appropriate focus for a sense of betrayal involving the literary, political, and philosophical worlds of both countries. It is so well achieved that we are allowed to see Rousseau as the French parallel to Hazlitt and Hazlitt as the English parallel to Rousseau; for Rousseau, as philosopher and as imaginative writer, ran athwart certain tendencies of the Enlightenment and its sensationalist philosophy, just as Hazlitt in those same roles contradicted the prevalent Benthamite philosophy in England. So too Rousseau's legacy, the Revolution, in its Jacobin purity, was equally defended by Hazlitt in the political arena against the prevailing Pittite and Eldonian reaction, which retained its ascendancy beyond the death of Napoleon up to the death of Hazlitt himself. Such, at all events, was Hazlitt's own view of British developments in these years. The French Revolution of 1830 and the Catholic Emancipation Bill of 1829 as well as the Reform Bill of 1832 came too late to give Hazlitt any sense of that reaction's retreat or of his possible misreading of its nature.

In this curious intimacy which Hazlitt created between himself and Rousseau, we see the cult of the Revolutionary writer, which had begun harmlessly enough in English travel literature, reach its first important culmination in England.[41] The new kinds of complex associations between the cultures of England and France are caught here in a relationship between two writers in which one uses the other as a metaphor or symbol of whatever values of his own he feels to have been betrayed.

Betrayal is the basic motif of Hazlitt's writings. England betrays itself and France; France betrays itself and the Revolution; the Lake Poets betray their Jacobin principles; the English politicians betray the spirit of the British Constitution and the tradition of liberty; France betrays Napoleon; the Holy Alliance betrays Europe; Burke betrays his American principles and Mackintosh mimics him; Bentham betrays human possibility and Malthus and Godwin betray human experience; the Revolution betrays itself. One could multiply the instances. Yet even as they accumulate, the consistency of Hazlitt's position becomes more apparent. If there is a paranoid element in his bitterness, it scarcely seems excessive, given the degrees of disillusion through which he had progressively to pass. Fundamentally he believed that he had witnessed the defeat of the Jacobin principle of the natural disinterestedness of the human mind by the principle of its natural selfishness just at a time when the reversal of the latter belief had become gloriously possible. Rousseau went down before Helvétius, Hazlitt before Bentham. To put it another way, the "intellectual philosophy" had been superseded by the "material philosophy." Genius had been overwhelmed by Legitimacy. The Spirit of the Age of Revolution had been crushed by the Spirit of the Age of Reaction:

> It was a misfortune to any man of talent to be born in the latter end of the last century. Genius stopped the way of Legitimacy, and therefore it was to be abated, crushed, or set aside as a nuisance. The spirit of the monarchy was at variance with the spirit of the age. The flame of liberty, the light of intellect, was to be extinguished with the sword,—or with slander, whose edge is sharper than the sword. The war between power and reason was carried on by the first of these abroad—by the last at home. No quarter was given (then or now), by the Government critics, the authorised censors of the press, to those who followed the dictates of independence, who listened to the voice of the tempter, Fancy.[42]

That was the general betrayal, but it held within itself other forms of treachery which accumulated to "convert the fairest prospects into a scene of devastation and blood."[43] The coalitions of the allied powers against Revolutionary France had yielded temporarily at the Peace of Amiens in 1802. This gave those who had been opposed to Pitt's war the opportunity they had sought. This "hollow, peevish truce" gave "those who had hitherto disapproved the attempt to overturn the French Republic as an unprincipled aggression on the rights and liberties of mankind, but who were grown lukewarm in the cause, or were tired out with opposition, a plausible pretext to change sides, and to come over, with loud clamour and tardy repentance, to the views of their King and Country."[44] Chief among these culprits were the poets who had betrayed Jacobinism, not the philosophers who had retained their faith in reform throughout the whole long period of repression. But since these philosophers represented anyway what the Revolution had been most profoundly opposed to—the mechanical philosophy—the desertion of the poets was especially open to condemnation and sarcasm: "The philosophers, the dry abstract reasoners, submitted to this reverse pretty well, and armed themselves with patience 'as with triple steel' to bear discomfiture, persecution and disgrace. But the poets, the creatures of sympathy, could not stand the frowns both of king and people."[45] Southey seemed to Hazlitt the worst instance of a man who, in withdrawing from the humanity of his earlier opinions, left himself bereft of general principle and subject only to the demands of party. The terms of this attack repay attention, since they exemplify the venal selfishness which Hazlitt saw as the end product of the separation of the self from the feelings and principles of Jacobinism:

He has too little sympathy with the common pursuits, the follies, the vices, and even the virtues of the rest of mankind, to have any tact or depth of insight into the actual characters or manners of men . . . As to general principles of any sort, we see no traces of any thing like them in any of his writings. He shows the same contempt for abstract reasoning that Mr. Coleridge has for "history and particular facts." Even his intimacy with the metaphysical author of "The Friend," with whom he has chimed in both poetry and politics, in verse and prose, in Jacobinism and Antijacobinism, any time these twenty years has never inoculated him with the most distant admiration of Hartley, or Berkeley, or Jacob Behmen, or Spinosa, or Kant, or Fichte, or Schelling. His essays are in fact the contents of his commonplace-book, strung together with little thought or judgment, and rendered marketable by their petulant adaptation to party purposes.[46]

Here we have the typical combination of poetry, politics, and philosophy driven under the lash of treachery to the security of a venal respectability.

There were, then, for Hazlitt three types of English betrayal. On the political level Burke and Pitt were the architects of reaction, with Mackintosh one of their most notable assistants. In the literary world the Lake Poets were the chief culprits, although Walter Scott's role in encouraging "the lowest panders of a venal press"[47] and Byron's shutting "himself up in the Bastille of his own ruling passions"[48] were further examples of the alienation of genius from the cause of truth. In philosophy Bentham and his cohorts ruled, extending the sway of the Lockean abstractions which had been deprived even more systematically of all real content by Condillac, Helvétius, and the Godwin of *Political Justice*. Moreover, the political recanter Mackintosh revealed in his Lincoln's Inn lectures, the natural alliance between that Lockean philosophical tradition (from which Mackintosh extracted the political sting) and anti-Revolutionary sentiment.

The English conducted two kinds of war on the Revolution. One was military, the other was the warfare of propaganda. The latter was violently unprincipled and blunt. It relied on the intensification of anti-French feeling and, as Hazlitt put it, aimed "to rouse the national prejudices of John Bull against the French, as if this were the old vulgar quarrel, instead of being the great cause of mankind. The two noblest impulses of our nature, the love of country and the love of kind, were to be set in hostile array, and armed with inextinguishable fury against each other."[49] Yet, although Hazlitt could say as late as 1828 that he saw no prospect of improvement in the European situation "while the Englishman with his notions of solid beef and pudding holds fast by his substantial identity, and the Frenchman with his lighter food and air mistakes every shadowy impulse for himself,"[50] he was involved in a serious contradiction. His opinion of the French as a race was in no important sense different from the opinion broadcast by the English propaganda press to which he objected so violently. His opinion of the Revolution was indeed different from theirs, but as long as his opinion of the French national characteristics was the same, his attempts to separate his definition of Jacobinism from theirs was liable to a certain degree of blurring and distortion. It is clear that Hazlitt at no time regarded France as the nation best equipped to inaugurate a new era of democratic liberty. Its traditions and national psychology seemed to indicate that France had quite a different and lesser role. Complex as the French were, full of paradox and extremes, they were suited to precisely that spirit of abstraction which was for Hazlitt the most damaging and characteristic feature of the modern philosophy. Even though that philosophy had arisen and taken root in England, its more vulgarized forms seemed eminently suited to the occluding egoism of the French: "The French, indeed, can conceive of nothing that is not French. There is something that prevents them from entering into any views which do not perfectly fall in with their habitual prejudices. In a word, they are not a people of imagination . . . They are the creatures of sensation or abstraction."[51] It was prejudice of this nature that had to be stretched by what Hazlitt was fond of calling "the Ulysses' bow of the French Revolution."[52]

It helped that many of the extraordinary developments in recent French culture could be attributed to Rousseau, Mme. de Staël, and Napoleon—two Swiss and a Corsican. The typical Frenchman was still Voltaire or Helvétius—Voltaire in his omnicompetence encompassing all the French qualities and Helvétius representing only one, the tendency to glib and shallow philosophizing. Hazlitt's bitterness toward the French is evident throughout *The Life of Napoleon* (1828–1830). He notes that after the Peace of Amiens the speeches in the French Senate "substituted the effervescence of French conceit for the old leaven of Jacobinism,"[53] but the same attitude prevails in his writings of 1814 and 1815. No nation was less fit by its nature for a revolution involving such important principles. The French had produced that Revolution because of Rousseau, whose dream of liberty lifted them out of their customary egoism, and they had sustained it because Bonaparte stiffened their customary fickleness: "Both of these gave an energy and consistency to their character, by concentrating their natural volatility on one great object. But when both of these causes failed, the Allies found that France consisted of nothing but ladies' toilettes."[54] (It would be an interesting exercise to note the correlation between English notions of French effeminacy and their use of the epithets *manly* and *moral* to describe English national character and English liberty during this period.)

It must therefore be recognized, according to Hazlitt, that the excesses of the Revolution were inevitable, given two things: the brittleness of the French character and the pressure brought to bear on it by the allied coalition.

> The French were very hardly dealt with in this case which was an *experimentum crucis* upon the national character. They are a people extremely susceptible of provocation. Like women, forced out of their natural character, they become furies. Naturally light and quick, good sense and good temper are their undeniable and enviable characteristics: but if events occur to stagger or supersede these habitual qualities, there then seems no end of the extravagances of opinion, or cruelties in practice, of which they are capable, as it were from the mere impression of novelty and contrast. They are the creatures of impulse, whether good or bad. Their very thoughtlessness and indifference prevent them from being shocked at the irregularities which the passion of the moment leads them to commit; and from the nicest sense of the ridiculous and the justest tact in common things, there is no absurdity of speculation, no disgusting rodomontade or wildness of abstraction, into which they will not run when thrown off their guard. They excel in the trifling and familiar, and have not the strength of character or solidity of judgment to cope with great questions or trying occasions. When they attempt the grand and striking, they fail from too much presumption and from too much fickleness. In a word, from that eternal smile on the cheek to a massacre, there is but one step: for those who are delighted with everything, will be shocked at nothing. Vanity strives in general to please and make itself amiable; but if it is the fashion to do mischief, it will take the lead in mischief, and is, therefore, a dangerous principle in times of crisis and convulsion. A revolution was the Ulysses' bow of the French philosophers and politicians.[55]

The great cause of Jacobinism was obviously too much for the French to bear in the circumstances of European politics at that time. It was the French after all who in their volatile ferocity "made the tree of liberty spout nothing but blood."[56]

It would of course be wrong to imply that Hazlitt launched this kind of attack on the French alone. He also devotes a good deal of space and sarcasm to the defects of the John Bullish national character, and especially to the brainwashed attitude of the average Englishman toward the wars with the French.[57] Nevertheless the question naturally arises at this point, what *was* Jacobinism if both its French and English adherents, each group possessing an entirely different set of national characteristics, were so prone to betray its principles? Part of Hazlitt's answer is of course that special circumstances obtained temporarily in France and England to make the first promote Jacobinism and the other to suppress it; and farther back he points to the dominance of a demeaning philosophy which made the French circumstances no more than temporary and the English ones no less than permanent. But the puzzle increases when we consider that Hazlitt named Rousseau as Jacobinism's progenitor and Napoleon as its "child and champion."[58] The grounds of his admiration for Rousseau are not those of his admiration for Napoleon. There is no question of his seeing Napoleon as the fulfillment of a totalitarian (or, less anachronistically, a despotic) tendency in Rousseau's thought.[59] Surely, however, Robespierre or St. Just would have been more likely candidates even then for the mantle of Jacobin martyrdom. Yet such an attribution would have been impossible, given Hazlitt's attitudes. Robespierre and the bloody sequence of events with which his name was sometimes extravagantly associated was more an expression of volatile ferocity than a hero of liberty. If Rousseau raised the French from their constitutional weaknesses on the one hand, only one figure could be given the credit for saving them from the pressures of external military pressure on the other. Napoleon had to be Hazlitt's hero since only he fit the interpretation which Hazlitt gave to the Revolution, its relation to the French national character, and the disgraceful vindictiveness and hypocrisy of British and Allied foreign policy. His reading of the whole situation left him with Napoleon as the heroic counterweight to Rousseau. Between them these two bracketed the whole tragic story of betrayal.

Napoleon in his fight against Legitimacy preserved the great issue on which the Revolution had begun: "He kept off that last indignity and wrong offered to a whole people (and through them to the rest of the world) of being handed over, like a herd of cattle, to a particular family, and chained to the foot of a legitimate throne. This was the chief point at issue . . . Whether mankind were, from the beginning to the end of time, born slaves or not?"[60] Given Napoleon's military and political record, this sounds something less than rational; but this granted, we can nevertheless see that the force which linked Rousseau and Napoleon together in Hazlitt's mind was the same force which in his opinion differentiated the French Revolution from all others. It was not, as the propagandists would have it, a version of the old rivalry between England and France. It was a struggle for the principle of liberty itself. Had that principle prevailed, the national characteristics which finally emerged in its betrayal would have been transcended in the common cause of mankind. For Hazlitt this was the most disastrous and effective result of the propaganda war which had broken out between France and England. On both sides of the Channel the Revolution had been reduced to a war over the balance of power between two rival peoples. The rivalry was exhibited in their different characteristics; but it is precisely this difference which could have been overcome. He did not base his faith in the Revolution on the respective qualities of the English and the French. He described his disillusion in those terms.

Rousseau and Napoleon, the young Wordsworth and Coleridge, the efflorescence of German literature, the investigations of Sismondi and to a lesser degree of Mme. de Staël, the novels of Scott—all of these were signs of the spirit of humanity, not classifiable in terms of nationality but recognizable as great human achievements. Yet all of them were in the end reduced to the sectarian confines of a situation which the Revolution had tried to break open. Liberty had lost its proper language, the Jacobin language of man free not only of distinctions of rank and property but also of those of national character. In its place there remained the old eighteenth-century specter of Legitimacy: "Those who have deprived us of the natural language of liberty, and changed it to the fretful whine of the hunting-tygers of Legitimacy have much to answer for."[61] Or again, "It was a war of proscription against a great and powerful state, for having set the example of a people ridding itself of an odious and despicable tyranny. It was the question of the balance of power between kings and people; a question, compared with which the balance of power in Europe is petty and insignificant."[62]

This reading of the political evolution of Anglo-French relationships during this period has its aesthetic and philosophical resonances in Hazlitt's thinking. Rousseau and Napoleon had, each in his own way, galvanized the French out of their customary frivolity and paradoxical extremes to defend a moral issue—the issue of republican liberty and its hostility to monarchical despotism. This was itself bound up with the long-standing philosophical dispute between those who, like Hazlitt, defended the natural disinterestedness of the mind and those who argued for the primacy of self-love. One attitude was as native to the cosmopolitan as the other was to the nationalistic spirit. The affinities between Hazlitt's attitude and that of Mme. de Staël and Shelley are numerous, despite the notably different opinions those authors would have expressed on Napoleon. Mme. de Staël, like Hazlitt, identified liberty with republicanism and saw the impulse toward this new political form coming from the new Romantic literature, which in its passionate intensity (with Rousseau as its paradigm) would overcome the shallowness of a materialistic and specifically French tradition.[63] What in her work later became known as the cosmopolitan spirit was in Hazlitt "the flame of liberty, the light of intellect"[64] or "the abstract right of the human race to be free."[65]

Jacobinism was, then, the new form of patriotism. Its country was the world and its race mankind. Unlike the feelings of "local attachment,"[66] which had played such an important part in Burke's attack on the Revolution and was taken up in different ways thereafter by hack reviewers and great poets, Jacobinism devoted the whole strength of its feeling to a principle, not to a place. The patriotism Hazlitt expounds in the *Illustrations of Vetus*,[67] and to which he devotes an essay in *The Round Table*, is remarkably close in its disinterested nature to the loyalty to the cause of humanity which he would describe fourteen years later. As usual his consistency survives through the most formal and the most occasional of his writings. In *The Round Table* we read:

> Patriotism, in modern times, and in great states, is and must be the creature of reason and reflection, rather than the offspring of physical or local attachment. Our country is a complex abstract existence, recognised only by the understanding. It is an immense riddle, containing numberless modifications of reason and prejudice, of thought and passion. Patriotism is not, in a strict or exclusive sense, a natural or personal affection, but a law of our rational and moral nature, strengthened and determined by particular circumstances and associations, but not born of them, nor wholly nourished by them.[68]

And in 1828 he writes:

> It is not a blind, physical repugnance to pain, as affecting ourselves, but a rational or intelligible conception of it as existing out of ourselves, that prompts and sustains our exertions in behalf of humanity. Nor can it be otherwise while man is the creature of imagination and reason and has faculties that implicate him (whether he will or not) in the pleasures and pains of others, and bind up his fate with theirs.[69]

There we have Jacobinism defined as something greater than the pleasure-and-pain syndrome of the sensationalist philosophy. Republicanism, cosmopolitanism, the natural disinterestedness of the human mind, and eventually, as we shall see, the imagination all lead into one another in Hazlitt's analysis of the elements of the Jacobin spirit. It is this which Rousseau promoted and Napoleon defended; this which Burke attacked and the Lake Poets betrayed. Europe, robbed of the opportunity to exist on the high level of principle, sank to survive on the pap of the propaganda press, that mixture of nationalistic rivalry and monarchical despotism the success of which was most strikingly evinced for Hazlitt in the arrest of reform at home in England and in the restoration of the Bourbons by the Allies and their acceptance by the French. The republican spirit of liberty was so subdued on both sides of the Channel that Hazlitt could say in 1830:

> The word republic has a harsh and incongruous sound to ears bred under a constitutional monarchy; and we strove hard for many years to overturn the French republic, merely because we could not reconcile it to ourselves that such a thing should exist at all, notwithstanding the examples of Holland, Switzerland, and many others. The term has hardly yet performed quarantine: to the loyal and patriotic it has an ugly taint in it and is scarcely fit to be mentioned in good company.[70]

Nationalism had won over cosmopolitanism, selfish particularity over disinterested principle: "Such is the effect of our boasted nationality; it is active, fierce in doing mischief; dormant, lukewarm in doing good."[71]

Such an emphasis is important in reminding us that the radical strain in Romantic literature was as attached to principles of universal benevolence, as was the conservative reaction to notions of national and natural feeling.[72] Jacobinism as understood by Hazlitt was not merely a faith in the natural goodness of man *tout court*. It was a faith which contradicted notions of his natural selfishness and notions of his natural benevolence by introducing into the fairly barren debate between them the volitional element for which men such as Bishop Butler and more recently Richard Price had argued,[73] and which had previously been a dominant feature of English moral thought: "The truth is, that the affectation of philosophy and fine taste has spoiled every thing; and instead of the honest seriousness and simplicity of old English reasoning in law, in politics, in morality, in all the grave concerns of life, we have nothing left but a mixed species of bastard sophistry, got between ignorance and vanity, and generating nothing."[74] That philosophical sophistry had its political equivalent. Hazlitt demonstrated time and again that the survival or extinction of liberty and the Jacobin spirit was a matter of deliberate choice on the part of those who had pledged themselves to one side or the other. This explains the element of personal rancor in his writings. All those responsible for treachery could have been other than they were. When he spoke of the Spirit of the Age he was not referring to a Zeitgeist before which the individual will crumpled; he was speaking of a spirit composed of the general direction taken by individual wills in an age when the very concept of will was itself being denied by the mechanical, sensationalist philosophy on the one hand and by the subtler prevarications of the poets on the other. To understand his concept of the will, we need to investigate, however briefly, his concept of the imagination.

Sympathy and Will

Hazlitt claimed that, according to the pure sensationalism expounded by Condillac in his *Logic,* "that favourite manual of the modern sciolist,"[75] physical response to a given stimulus dictates moral response to a given issue. This seemed to him philosophically indefensible and contrary to the common experience of mankind.[76] He wished to restore to the mind the freedom of moral discrimination which the doctrine of selfishness and the pain-pleasure calculus denied: "The human mind differs from an inanimate substance or an automaton, inasmuch as it is actuated by sympathy as well as by necessity."[77] Sympathy is superior to sensibility because it survives the immediate stimulus of the moment. Through sympathy the mind apprehends the object; it is not simply receptive to it as though it were a galvanic charge. As in the writings of Rousseau and Wordsworth, the mind becomes entwined with the objects it perceives, until the object ceases to matter in itself but comes to have importance for itself. Its importance is in the sympathetic power which the object has been instrumental in creating. The mind lends to the object a symbolism not intrinsic to the object's nature but intrinsic to the manner in which it is perceived by the particular human observer at a given time. The operation of this kind of sympathy is in fact the operation of self-consciousness, a consciousness mediated through the world of objects. It is in this sense that what Hazlitt refers to as egotism in Rousseau and Wordsworth is inseparable from what he refers to as sympathy when he speaks of the imagination. Feeling rises in the self but can be transmitted to others. It is thereby generalized or rendered universal. This is the definition of the work of the imagination. Thought so generalized is reason.[78] Feeling and reason are complementary to each other, not opposites. Each entails a communication from the self to others; each is a mode of finding that which is basically human in the writer and in his audience. The sharing of this common humanity is a mark of the radical and inescapable Jacobinism of all great art.

The capacity of the mind to achieve morality is not, however, merely resident in its capacity to feel, although in his early work *Remarks on the System of Hartley and Helvétius* Hazlitt refuses to distinguish between feeling and thinking, citing Rousseau against Helvétius and Condillac on this point.[79] Morality is also a matter of choosing, and the will which operates on this level is influenced not by physical stimulus but by imagination and reason. Morality is thereby moved safely out of the thrall of the pleasure principle into the freedom of the regions of sympathy, where imagination and reason dwell in contact with humankind and not merely, like physical sensibility, in contact with the self: "The will is amenable not to our immediate sensibility but to reason and imagination, which point out and enforce a line of duty very different from that prescribed by self-love."[80] There is no Romantic titanism of the will here of the kind that we find in Byron. Instead Hazlitt is seeking more simply to rehabilitate the older moral theories of Butler and Price and to annihilate as irrelevant to any evaluation of human conduct the endless calculation of consequence which utilitarian ethics proposed to indulge instead. He vaguely sensed that this tradition of ethical freedom had reached some kind of culmination in Kant, but his knowledge extended no further than that.[81]

The effect of this effort to reemphasize the primacy of the will on Hazlitt's attitude toward France and the French was considerable. The moral tradition he supported was in his view fundamentally English in the "old," pre-Hobbesian sense, even though it had obviously survived healthily enough in various writers (Bishop Butler, David Hume, Samuel Clarke, Francis Hutcheson, Adam Smith) since Hobbes. Like Coleridge he made much of the difference between seventeenth-century England and the England of his own day. As we have seen, he insisted on the inconsistency of this modern philosophy with the English national character and its suitability for the French, a suitability enhanced by the popularity among them of Helvétius. Although Helvétius was not the first to have "conceived the hypothesis" of self-love as the basis of all our actions, "(for I do not think he had wit enough to invent even an ingenious absurdity) but it was through him I believe that this notion has attained its present popularity, and in France particularly it has had, I am certain, a very general influence on the national character."[82]

What is extraordinary in Hazlitt is his persistence in incorporating the contrast between two philosophical traditions, the "modern" and the "old," into his contrast between the two national characters as he conceived them and then making the crucial point of difference between them the volitional element. The English, out of the depth of their sympathetic attachment to the actual, chose liberty; the French, out of the shallowness of their sensibility, helplessly lost it. This is the literary argument between Racine and Shakespeare, between English naturalness and French artificiality, in political dress. From this springs the supposed French tendency to abstraction and the accusation that they prefer "words" to "things."[83] French Jacobinism withered because of the constitutional inability of the French to fix their fidelity on the great issues beneath it. It is impossible in the end to say whether French instability helped create the modern philosophy or vice versa. For all the consistency of his attitude, for all its internal coherence, its external validity is, to say the least, questionable, since it rests on his description of the indigenous characteristics of two races. Hazlitt's opinion of the French undergoes no notable change between 1805 and *The Notes of a Journey through France and Italy* (1826) or *The Life of Napoleon (1828–1830).* "The inconsequentiality in the French character, from extreme facility and buoyancy of impression is a matter of astonishment to the English."[84] Or again, "In whatever relates to the flutter and caprice of fashion, where there is no impulse but vanity, no limit but extravagance, no rule but want of meaning, they are in their element and quite at home. Beyond that, they have no style of their own, and are a nation of second-hand artists, poets and philosophers."[85] Or from *The Life of Napoleon:*

> Perhaps a reformation in religion ought always to precede a revolution in the government. Catholics may make good subjects, but bad rebels. They are so used to the trammels of authority, that they do not immediately know how to do without them; or, like manumitted slaves, only feel assured of their liberty in committing some Saturnalian license. A revolution, to give it stability and soundness, should first be conducted down to a Protestant ground.[86]

There the English Dissenter and the admirer of the events of 1688 appear more strongly than the Jacobin with his theory of cosmopolitanism. Increasingly after the defeat of Napoleon, the Bourbon restoration, and the triumph of the Holy Alliance in Europe and of repression at home in England, Hazlitt became more and more bitter toward those who he felt had betrayed the cause. The French had to take a great deal of the blame, given his reading of the situation; in his reaction against them his John Bullish prejudices toward France became more openly exposed. It required an effort of the imagination to cross the boundaries of national cliché, especially in a time of great hostility. Although he was aware of this, he was not equally capable of it: "The prejudice we entertain against foreigners is not in the first instance owing to any ill-will we bear them, so much as to the intractableness of the imagination, which cannot admit two standards of moral value according to circumstances, but is puzzled by the diversity of manners and character it observes, and made uneasy in its estimate of the propriety and excellence of its own."[87]

In this hinterland of anti-French prejudice which Hazlitt occupied with his contemporaries, we can see more incisively the profile of his Jacobinism. It had cosmopolitan ambitions but nationalistic, even chauvinistic loyalties at its heart. Just as it could be argued that Mme. de Staël in her campaign for constitutional liberty and republicanism reserved a special place for the French contribution, so too Hazlitt, especially toward the end of his life, and certainly in the last five years, gave England a special role to play also, entirely abandoning the French to the whimsicality of their innate character. England of course embittered him too, since it had the character for liberty and the historical and philosophical traditions to go with it but in its present state was denying both. Hence his bitterness against the utilitarian philosophers and Romantic poets, both of whom, in different ways, were contributing to this denial.

Jacobinism was, then, defeated not only in France but more precisely in and by England. Although its source was in Rousseau and its most dramatic expression in the Revolution, Hazlitt regarded it as fundamentally the irruption into the political arena of feelings which had first made themselves felt in literature. It had two enemies. One was Tory reaction, with which the English poets who had brought Jacobinism into English poetry had joined, and had thereby extinguished liberty. The apparatus of military repression had been almost defeated by Napoleon, for whom, however, Hazlitt's admiration was not unqualified—he recognized that dictatorship, although it might defend a principle, could not preserve it.[88] The other enemy was the prevalent philosophy of self-love and all its variations in the work of Condillac, Helvétius, Destutt de Tracy, Adam Smith, Godwin, Malthus, Mackintosh, Bentham, and the Westminster Reformers.[89] Like Horne Tooke they all had "a hard dry materialism in the very texture of their understanding,"[90] and in the spectacle of Mackintosh's subjugation to Burke, Hazlitt perceived the affinity of both these enemies—Tory reaction and the philosophy of self-love—to each other. The combination of the first-rate talents of one group with the second-rate philosophy of the other, of political venality and malice with philosophical and moral poverty, was for him the outstanding feature of the degraded English scene.[91]

Both Hazlitt's discipleship to Rousseau and his loyalty to his own vision of French Jacobinism rest on his doctrine of the sympathetic imagination. It alone was capable of defining and retaining the close intimacy between concrete experience and general principle, which was for Hazlitt the only sane and proper mode of acknowledging the richness and diversity of the human situation. He opposed it to the philistine John Bullish rejection of all things intellectual and to the equally philistine vaporization of all experience into theory which lusted for symmetry at the expense of truth.[92] Although his own position crumbled under the pressure of events, although he was finally indistinguishable in his general attitude to the French from people of quite different political and philosophical principles, Hazlitt remains nevertheless the only figure comparable to Shelley and Blake in his analysis of the Revolution and its significance for the evolution of both society and the imagination in a period of almost unprecedented hostility to any formulation of an attitude toward France which was not dismissive. The spectacle of the Revolution was unforgettable. Hazlitt's imagination cast about it that aura of nostalgia and significance which was not dimmed by the subsequent disillusion:

> The dawn of that day was suddenly overcast; that season of hope is past; it is fled with the other dreams of our youth, which we cannot recall, but has left behind it traces, which are not to be affected by Birth-day and Thanksgiving odes, or the chaunting of Te Deums in all the Churches of Christendom. To those hopes eternal regrets are due; to those who maliciously and wilfully blasted them, in the fear that they might be accomplished, we feel no less what we owe—"hatred and scorn as lasting."[93]

Hazlitt, the Criminal Mind, and Godwin's Jacobinism

The portrait of Bentham in *The Spirit of the Age* contains some remarkable passages on the impossibility of effecting criminal reform. The code, says Hazlitt, could be altered, made more consistent, softened; but the criminal could not. This is a striking instance of his Jacobinism operating in a field which drew the attention of all who boasted radical or reforming opinions. In his review for the *Edinburgh* of the *Report of the Select Committee on Criminal Laws* in 1821 Hazlitt pays tribute to Cesare Beccaria for contributing to the problem of the reform of the criminal code by his demonstration "that the efficacy of the law is very frequently in the *inverse* ratio of its *severity*."[94] Hazlitt's interest in this problem began, on his own testimony, in 1792, when he was fourteen and when he began his *Project for a New Theory of Civil and Criminal Legislation*.[95] He could not accept the kind of reform achieved by Sir Samuel Romilly, Mackintosh, and Peel. Because of the very structure of society, because of its demarcation into privileged and underprivileged classes, neither Bentham nor the Parliamentarians could have any conception of what went on in the mind of the criminal for whom they were legislating. It follows that:

the laws of the country are, therefore, ineffectual and abortive, because they are made by the rich for the poor; by the wise for the ignorant, by the respectable and exalted in situation for the very scum and refuse of the community. If Newgate would resolve itself into a committee of the whole Pressyard, with Jack Ketch at its head, aided by confidential persons from the county prisons or the Hulks, and would make a clean breast, some data might be found out to proceed upon; but as it is, the criminal mind of the country is a book sealed, no one has been able to penetrate to the inside![96]

Besides, since in Hazlitt's opinion the only restraint on criminality is public opinion, reform is a hopeless dream: once reputation is publicly lost, all is lost. The only force, therefore, which "keeps the machine" of society together is "not punishment or discipline, but sympathy."[97]

Hazlitt was not attacking the notion of reform itself. He was attacking the ineffectual nature of piecemeal reform, even while he was demonstrating that the artificial divisions of society made the piecemeal and ineffectual nature of reform inevitable. The weary implication is that criminal reform is attainable only in a restructured society, where a man's self-respect depends not on the preservation of reputation but on the recognition of his needs. These opinions are remarkably close to the theory of criminality, punishment, and reputation which we meet in Godwin's fiction. Hazlitt was Godwin's most perceptive reviewer. Equally, Godwin represented for him, more than anyone else, the summit of Jacobin feeling in England. Nor had anyone except Bentham paid a more concentrated attention to the problem of crime. In his portraits of Godwin and Bentham in *The Spirit of the Age* Hazlitt evokes from the vantage point of 1825 that period of the 1790s in which Godwin could be associated with Jacobinism and Bentham by subtle innuendo with Milton. In each case the association is shown to be satiric. Hazlitt blends his autobiographical excursions with a critical perception for the sake of establishing a moral perspective from which these men can be viewed. Crime stems from passions not accessible to a remote theorist like Bentham or to a purist intellectual like the Godwin of *Political Justice*.

In their portrayal we see the critique of the Jacobin taking shape. The hostility of the modern philosophy to the actual is epitomized in the distance of these two thinkers from the passions with which they were attempting to deal. Godwin was no more than the sun of the false dawn of Jacobinism now "sunk below the horizon."[98] The issue of criminal reform, so integral to the spirit of the Enlightenment, which Godwin and Bentham both exemplified, was soluble not in the frigidities of a philosophical or legal treatise but in literature, the only written form in which principle and concrete recognition of lived experience were conjoined. Again we recognize how, for Hazlitt, the Jacobin spirit had a permanent career in great writing. This is why he admired Godwin's novels more than his philosophical work (and why the implicit contrast between the spirit of Milton and that of Bentham has such force). Godwin's *Caleb Williams* would never lead one to suspect that its author "had ever dabbled in logic or metaphysics."[99] Only in the novel, where the Godwinian model of mind finds itself collapsing under the pressure of the demonic passions associated with crime, does Hazlitt see that author gaining his full stature. *Caleb Williams* is a Jacobin work because of its investigation of the psychic disturbances provoked in men by social distinctions and the consequences of these in the form of crime, internal remorse, and anguish.

It seems appropriate that Hazlitt should have chosen the subject of the criminal mind and its relation to the writings of Bentham and Godwin and to the efforts of the Westminister Reformers as one of the objects of his attack and sarcasm: in microcosm this was a version of the impulse of his age. A theory taken from the Enlightenment is deprived of its force of application because it is removed from the common experience of mankind. It is deprived of its passion and its radicalism simultaneously. In this context it is easier perhaps to appreciate the rather savage irony of his maxim, "I believe in the theoretical benevolence and practical malignity of man."[100] In such a statement Hazlitt's Jacobinism admits a bitter defeat.

8 English Dissent and the Philosophes: The Exercise of Reason

For more than forty years after the outbreak of the French Revolution, Britain, in order to define its own sense of what it was, had to create in France its opposite. There was a growing awareness of serious changes taking place in many fields at once which did not cohere with the views into which most people had been born. The blame for this incoherence rested, in the eyes of many English commentators, with France and with its disciples and admirers in England, even though the changes independently taking place in England were even more remarkable.[1] Security from such incoherence was discovered in the assertion of the superiority of English social and political traditions, which, having allegedly stood the test of so many previous crises, could also stand the test of this one.

One would expect that the Dissenters would be the only group which would feel out of sympathy with the conservative assertion of national uniqueness and identity, predicated as it was on the identity of English church and state and on resistance to any substantial reform of the existing constitutional system. They were indeed the most vociferous of all those who welcomed the Revolution, and their demand for civil liberty would seem to have found in French political doctrine its most powerful and universal expression. Yet when we look more closely, we find that the affinities of English Dissent with the thought of the French Enlightenment and, even more, with the activities of the French revolutionaries are superficial, while the antipathies to both are deep-seated. An exemplary instance of this set of attitudes is found in the writings of Joseph Priestley, the great Unitarian scientist, one of the victims of the Church and King mobs in Birmingham in 1791, and one of the most prolific writers on the social and political issues of the day.

Priestley and the Dissenters

The great Dissenting academies of eighteenth-century England were subject to severe pressures from a hostile public and from their own incorrigible tendency to disagree and break up into splinter groups. Warrington closed in 1786, Hackney in 1796.[2] The intellectual wing known as the Rational Dissenters, most of them Unitarians, included many famous names, some loyal to their Dissenting faith, some ultimately apostates. Only the apostates retained a substantial sympathy for the French Revolution. This fact alone indicates how strongly the mainstream tradition of Dissent was attached to the idea of the English national spirit. Among the outstanding Dissenting authors and preachers were Price and Priestley, Godwin, Gilbert Wakefield, Robert Hall, William Fox, Robert Robinson, Benjamin Flower, Theophilus Lindsay, Joseph Towers, and Andrew Kippis. Hazlitt and Paine, and briefly Coleridge, also belonged to their ranks. Holcroft was their outstanding novelist and playwright, William Taylor their best modern scholar. The general positions of this group on education, tolerance, the doctrine of necessity, and the relation of the individual conscience to church or state do not radically differ from those we would find in Voltaire, Helvétius, or even Holbach. Yet the Dissenters developed their positions on these issues from a specifically English inheritance going back to Locke and owing a particular debt to David Hartley.[3] Since this is also true in some measure of the French thinkers, the coincidence between the two groups is not altogether surprising. But there were essential differences which were exaggerated by the political situation created in England by the Revolution. The Dissenters were in general willing to defend the reputation of the philosophes against the more extreme attacks of the time; they were nevertheless insistent on the purity and independence of their own nonconformist tradition and were uniformly hostile to the possible damaging effects of foreign influence on English culture. Godwin was the outstanding exception to this rule, but Priestley exemplified it.

Mackintosh, on reading Priestley's autobiography, was struck by its resemblance to himself: "The theological character of our first metaphysical studies; our Hartleianism; the great singularity of having studied physiology and law; great power in him, and some little perhaps, in me, wasted and scattered; and finally, our exiles in countries where we cannot have a neighbour to understand us."[4] Had he added unpopularity to this list of similarities, he would have made it complete. Priestley, like Mackintosh, was made a French citizen by the

National Assembly; this made him a target for attack in England. Mackintosh in India, in government pay, and Priestley in America, a victim of government policy, make a nice contrast between the fate of the recanter of political principle and the martyr to it. Had Mackintosh known it, there was yet another point of resemblance, although it had all but vanished by the last decade of the century. Priestley too had come under the influence of Montesquieu at one point and had delivered a series of lectures at Warrington in 1761 in which this influence was evident.[5] But this phase of being, in his own description, a Unitarian in religion and a Trinitarian in politics soon passed. Priestley abandoned the theory of the tripartite balance of powers which Montesquieu had perceived in the British and fathered upon the American Constitution. It seemed to him finally that a government was the better for being simple in its structure; in America he supported the idea of a unicameral legislature.[6] In his view government fulfilled all of its useful functions in administration. Any extension beyond that role appeared to him to be an infringement of the natural liberty of the individual. If representation in government and personal security were achieved, the only restraint to be condoned thereafter was the inner one of conscience.[7] During his years in England he had found this basic and radical freedom of the individual conscience to be increasingly threatened and even denied. On that ground he came to accept the need for revolution.[8]

Priestley's separation of the private and public spheres of conscience and government was quite in accord with the general Dissenting position on the relationship of the individual to the church and to the secular power. For them religion was an affair of solitude; Burke's marriage of church and state was scripturally unjustifiable and politically dangerous. Priestley did not follow this line of thought to its logical conclusion—that government was as such unnecessary, indeed an evil. He shied away from this anarchist position, which Godwin and Holcroft both accepted, and restricted himself to a philosophy of individualism whereby action in the private sphere remained free from public interference but contributed to public happiness by conforming to the requirements of Christian morality. This could be achieved by nothing less than providential design or cosmic coincidence. This is Benthamism in Dissenting Christian dress.

Government, then, would have its actions measured by the standard of public utility, but the individual would rely on the criterion of his own conscience. We find here that characteristic division of the Dissenter between the private and the public worlds which has as one of its consequences a peremptory demand that the effectiveness of the private conscience as an agent of social good be ratified. It is here that the issue of secret crime, so troublesome to Godwin and to others, had its origin. Priestley avoids the problem, or simply does not see it. Instead he preaches a belief in the inevitability of progressive improvement in accord with the increasing freedom of the individual from official and artificial constraints. The day of the millennium will be the day when the state in its executive, governmental form withers away: "Government, we may now expect to see . . . in actual practice, calculated for the general good, and taking no more upon it than the general good requires; leaving all men the enjoyment of as many of their 'natural' rights as possible, and no more interfering with matters of religion, with men's notions concerning God, and a future state, than with philosophy or medicine."[9] This is not French Enlightenment doctrine, but it is very close to the positions espoused by Voltaire and Helvétius, to name but two. Yet despite this affinity with the French, deriving from a common English ancestry in the seventeenth-century political tradition, Priestley delivered to the philosophes some of the sternest rebukes they received in this period.

The reason for this apparent contradiction is easily discovered. Priestley was writing in the English tradition of Radical Dissent, which was cast in a fundamentally (even fundamentalist) biblical mold.[10] The philosophes wrote in the quite different French classical tradition. Hedonistic libertinism was as integral to their background as was religious, even sectarian fervor to his. Their "Infidelity" and their "Licence" alienated him and many of his coreligionists. Furthermore, the extreme form of necessitarianism which a writer like Holbach developed had a too dangerously atheistic implication. Instead of envisioning a world which developed progressively to unfold the divine scheme of revelation, Holbach and his like portrayed a strictly godless world, governed by purely physical laws. Writing of Holbach's *Système de la nature*, Priestley tries to deify Holbach's idea of nature: "If what this writer here calls *nature* be really capable of all that he ascribes to it; if it be thus powerful and industrious, if it does nothing at random and produces beings of such intelligence as men & c . . . it is indeed no bad substitute for a deity."[11] This was true. But instead of being ironic about it, Priestley might as well have admitted the similarity more fully and recognized that his God, like Holbach's nature, was a hypothesis from which anything could be derived. The whole point was in the naming of the hypothesis. In the difference between these names lay the vast difference between the French philosophe and the English Dissenter.

It is therefore quite appropriate and not at all contradictory that

Priestley should be among the most severe critics of the "irreligion" of the philosophes. His *Letters to the French Philosophers* is an attempt to explain to contemporary ideologues such as Lequinio and Volney the kind of reforms an English Dissenter would have liked to see them suggest for France.[12] This is a rather tame pamphlet, however, compared to his *Observations on the Increase of Infidelity* (1797), which he wrote after reading the recently published correspondence between Frederick II, Voltaire, and D'Alembert, about which the conservative press had made such a fuss. He flinched before the levity of Voltaire's address of issues such as death, the Christian religion, belief. He was shocked to the core by Voltaire's hatred of the Christian churches. As for Rousseau, he could do no better than mimic Burke's ferocious denunciation.[13] As in Burke and so many others we find that the relationship between Infidelity and sexual license is thought to be indisputable and entirely typical of the French national character. Despite the coolness of his style and the self-conscious differentiation between it and that of Burke—which he abhorred[14]—he is in no substantial disagreement with him over the danger, the extremism, and the essential foreignness of French philosophy. In the end Priestley saw the Revolution as a disaster of biblical proportions. Ancient prophecies of doom fill his footnotes, apocalypse is a recurrent theme, and the promise of the millenium fades into the distant future. The Revolution becomes the standard image of threat in the Bible: at first it had "resembled Elijah's cloud, appearing no bigger than a *man's hand*; but now it covers, and darkens, the whole European hemisphere."[15]

Other Dissenters followed Priestley in blaming the excesses of the Revolution on the spirit of atheism which informed it, and for which the philosophes were ultimately responsible.[16] Even when they retained some hope for the Revolution, they were defending a visionary English Dissenting notion of what it might yet be against the French origins of what it in fact was. Yet some were willing to state openly what others wished to forget—that the French doctrines had their roots in England. William Fox makes this quite clear in his pamphlet *On Jacobinism* (1794), in which he writes of 1789 as an opportunity to improve on rather than to emulate 1688. His most popular pamphlet, *The Interest of Great Britain Respecting the French War*, is unusually plainspoken about the French Revolutionary ideas:

> It is not the principles themselves, but it is those principles becoming *French*, which constitutes the danger; while they were confined to this foggy island, while they were locked up in a language almost unknown on the continent, the monarchs of Europe were either strangers to their existence, or fearless of their effects. But when these principles are

adopted by a nation, situated in the midst of happy, despotic monarchies; by a nation whose language is the universal language of Europe; and whose writers, by their genius, their wit, their learning, and their taste, had almost monopolized the literature of Europe; then it was that these principles excited their alarm, and threatened danger.[17]

If atheism was not a sufficient explanation in itself for the nature of the Revolution, then Catholicism could be introduced to explain the nature of the atheism. The infidelity of the philosophes could be understood in such a light as a necessary physic administered by God to a nation sick with popery in the cause of startling it back to a Protestant kind of vigor.[18] Events did not deal kindly with this diagnosis; William Fox was amused at the various forecasts of the horrible fate which awaited infidels, many of them issuing from Dissenters.[19] In the decade between 1790 and 1800, however, such amusement seemed misplaced to many Dissenters, for there was along with their anxieties about atheism and Catholicism the problem of the conspiracy thesis of the French Revolution.

The *Eclectic Review*, the most orthodox of the Dissenting magazines of the time, announced its program and purpose in unequivocally national terms: "Had not the supporters of the *Eclectic Review* perceived that the great engine of the press, as far as related to periodical publications, was, with a few honourable exceptions, engaged on the side of a sophistical philosophy, exerting itself in sapping the foundations of religious and moral principles in their beloved country, their humble labours would never have obtruded on public opinion."[20] This was more a response to the conspiracy panic than to any sudden appearance of pro-French or antiestablishment periodicals—of which there were few indeed. Perhaps the founders of the *Eclectic* imagined that the supporters of false doctrine were to be found in the columns of the *Analytical Review*, the *Critical Review*, the *Monthly Review*, and *The Monthly Magazine and British Register*. All of these had a distinctly more Continental bias than their Tory counterparts,[21] so much so that the *Anti-Jacobin Review* decided in 1798 to restore the balance by including a foreign appendix which would deprive their opponents of the exclusive opportunity to comment on foreign literature—by which the journal meant "the views of the French 'Economists' and other 'Philosophists' of modern times [who] have facilitated the propagation of principles, subversive of social order, and, consequently, destructive of social happiness."[22]

There was therefore little to distinguish between the chief journal of the Dissenters and that of the establishment on the issue of French philosophy. In fact the *Edinburgh Review* was far more scathing about the so-called conspiracy, and far more ready to deal with the philosophes directly—by reading them, for instance—than was any Dissenting journal. Of the reviewers themselves it can be said, however, that one of the best and most effective was William Taylor of Norwich, who did so much to introduce German thought and literature to England in this period. He was also one of those who helped to diminish the mindless hostility to the French Enlightenment. In speaking of the Barruel-Robison thesis, he pointed out that its absurdity had not prevented its having serious and retarding social and political consequences.

> That brain-phantoms so vapourish as those exhibited by the Scotch professor and the emigrant priest, should ever have had the power to frighten a nation out of their senses, might now excite a smile, had we still not to deplore the injurious effects of the delusion, in improvements retarded till error became inveterate and almost irretrievable, and in reforms delayed, till abuses and corruption have insinuated themselves almost inextricably into every accessible department of our polity.[23]

In effect the Radical Dissenters were in a permanently compromised position. They could explain to some degree why English principles had undergone such a transformation at the hands of the formerly popish, now atheistic, French; but they could not at the same time join with full enthusiasm in the anti-French crusade, since it was so bound up with a preservation of the very system which it was in their interest to see reformed. They made their Dissenting Christianity a badge of English patriotism and argued for the uniqueness of the national tradition in those terms. Still it was difficult to keep the distinction between the Burkean and the Dissenting notions of Englishness alive when the debate was centered on the topics of Infidelity, licentiousness, and French power. When they had to choose, they chose patriotism and remained English Dissenters by keeping the tone as biblical and evangelical as possible. It was only when Dissent turned toward a secular view, when it became essentially Benthamite, that it was able to make a clear and decisive distinction. For this to happen, the *Westminster Review* had to appear.

Paine and the Radicals

In 1791 the *Monthly Review* described Paine's style as "desultory, uncouth and inelegant. His wit is coarse and sometimes disgraced by wretched puns; and his language, though energetic, is awkward, ungrammatical, and often debased by vulgar phraseology."[24] In 1820 his

Rights of Man was said to be "nothing more than a repetition of all the trash and nonsense of the French Revolutionary School, applied to the circumstances and to the institutions of the British nation."[25] These remarks fairly summarize the aesthetic and political objections to Paine in this period. He was both inelegant and subversive. Scores of pamphleteers (the majority of them Whigs or Dissenters) attacked his coarseness and jargon,[26] while others, even more numerous, attacked his exemplary blend of radical politics and Infidelity. The combination was perfectly represented by *The Rights of Man* and *The Age of Reason.*[27] The campaign against him was waged to such good effect that William Cobbett could say in 1804 that Paine's writings "had been suppressed by brute force" before 1796, since which time "he had, unfortunately, rendered himself unpopular amongst the very best part of the people by his gratuitous and rude assault on the Christian religion."[28] Like Burke, Godwin, and Cobbett himself, Paine was and still is regarded as a writer whose style is to a remarkable degree a function of his political attitudes.

Despite his obvious debts to the Enlightenment in France, it is impossible to say upon which specific author he drew most heavily. Traces of Montesquieu, Voltaire, and Rousseau are discernible in much of his work. The Abbé de St. Pierre left his mark, as did his Parisian friends Condorcet, Brissot, and Bonneville. He simplified and popularized many of the ideas of these authors, aiming to construct a social and political philosophy which would in its clarity and elegance match the symmetries of the mechanical sciences.[29] The abstract individualism of Helvétius is linked with Rousseau's primitivism, thus providing the fiction of the average man existing in a primitive environment as the basic image of the ideal political condition which it was the purpose of revolution to restore. As in Priestley and Godwin the role of government is minimized. A species of Quaker individualism is crossed with French theory. The result for political philosophy was essentially barren, but the propaganda effect was enormous.[30]

Paine's writings are a compendium of Enlightenment ideas. He brought these to the mass of the English people by his skill in the art of distilling complex matters and by his recognition of the need for widespread distribution to the largest possible audience. No carefully argued octavo volume was needed to display his passionate distrust of government;[31] his sense of the opposition between it and society;[32] his belief in the naturally altruistic character of man and its role in the general harmony of the universe;[33] his rejection of Christianity and the Middle Ages;[34] his deism;[35] his reading of political situations on the model of mechanical systems;[36] his dislike of hereditary rights, monarchy, discrimination, and intolerance;[37] and his nostalgia for a simply organized social system and his distrust of arguments which endow the political world with a mystery and a complexity not native to it.[38] All of these features existed in French political thought before him. Only Paine attempted to bring them within one systematic program of action.[39]

Probably the most inspiring of Paine's beliefs is his conviction that three great republics could be created in America, France, and England, in that order, by the force of persuasive propaganda and with the help of the uniformity of attitude which the spread of scientific technology would bring with it, necessarily involving the reduction of national and cultural differences.[40] He took the philosophes as the most outstanding example of the effects which organized campaigning on behalf of human progress could achieve. Because of Montesquieu, Rousseau, Voltaire, and Raynal, "readers of every class met with something to their taste, and a spirit of rational inquiry began to diffuse itself through the nation at the time the dispute between England and the then colonies of America broke out."[41] For all that, Paine is still recognizably English in some of his responses to the French. Most particularly he objects to Voltaire's scurrility and licentiousness. But he is also very much in the Dissenting tradition in his millenial beliefs, his hostility to government, his distrust of religious establishments, and his belief that religion is a personal and solitary affair, not an institutional and coercive force. He universalized these notions or inherited attitudes and was one of the first English writers to project the cosmopolitan ideal which was later to be developed in a quite different direction by Mme. de Staël. By the success of his campaign he became both a martyr to Pitt's repression and an emblem of the power and presence of French influence in England.[42] After his sojourn in jail in Revolutionary Paris, however, he also became a reminder of the dangerous difference between political theories and revolutionary practice.

Paine, Holcroft, Godwin, Bage, and many other radicals of lesser note did help confirm one of the most cherished of counter-Revolutionary beliefs: that the French Revolution had been the result of an organized conspiracy of *some* kind, if not necessarily of the sort described by Barruel. It was indeed, they claimed, the result of the diffusion of opinion and ideas through the new and mighty engine of the press, a favorite phrase. It was for their mastery of this that they praised the philosophes as much as for the actual opinions they disseminated. All sides in the dispute were conscious of the new importance of the reading audience. It is inevitable, therefore, that the reviews and magazines should play such a governing part in the formation of both public opinion and individual theories. Paine, Cobbett, Southey, Coleridge, and Hazlitt were journalists; after Burke everybody was a pamphleteer. But in the great pamphlet war only Paine matched Burke in influence, although in every other respect he was Burke's antithesis. The dispute over the Revolution, the Enlightenment, and the French national character was finally brought to a kind of conclusion on the radical side when Radical Dissent finally found its voice in a review of prestige and importance comparable to that of the *Edinburgh* and the *Quarterly*. As Paine's immediate influence waned, the more potent force of Benthamism emerged to dominate and to alter the main lines of the long dispute.

The Appearance of the Westminster Review

Perhaps it could justifiably be said of the *Edinburgh Review* that it sought to find in the French Enlightenment, in men like Montesquieu and Turgot, figures who could be compared with Whig heroes of the past. In doing so the *Edinburgh* was attempting to redeem something of the Enlightenment spirit from the fervid anti-French reaction of the time. It did nevertheless give substantial support to the idea of the uniquely English quality of anti-Revolutionary politics, and it published so many reviews which had conflicting attitudes toward these issues that it might be accused of being at least hesitant and indecisive.[43] But in 1824, when the *Westminster Review*, the journal of the utilitarians, appeared, it gave no quarter to the *Edinburgh* for its uncertain attitudes toward the philosophes or the whole question of France, the Revolution, or the national character.

The opening numbers of the *Westminster* carried surveys by James Mill of the achievements of the *Edinburgh* and the *Quarterly* over the preceding twenty years. The verdict on the *Quarterly* was predictably severe; but the *Edinburgh* came in for more sustained criticism. Its tendency to "see-saw" (in Mill's words) between aristocratic prejudice and philosophically grounded opinion was epitomized for him in the first review of the first number, in which Francis Jeffrey had commented on Mounier's rejection of Barruel. This is an attractive conjunction. The defeat of the conspiracy theory is analyzed, then the analysis is itself reanalyzed, each commentary marking the shift in the prevailing attitude toward France. Mill dismisses Jeffrey's review as an exercise in trimming. This is for him an accurate definition of Whig doctrine anyway: "Observe, however, the real doctrine. It is laudable to put forth such writings as those of Montesquieu, Turgot, and Raynal: this is for the philosophers. It is wicked to put forth such writings as those of Rousseau, Mably, and Condorcet: this is for the aristocrats."[44] But it was John Stuart Mill, taking up the running from his father, who attacked the whole nationalistic ideology on which the contemporary attitude toward France was founded. British self-congratulation had become a habit, but, he goes on: "On the other hand, the prejudices which prevail in this country against the French, are carefully nourished and fostered. Every opportunity is taken of showing how much the habits and character of that nation differ from excellence; meaning, of course, by excellence, the English habits and character. Sometimes, indeed, a torrent of mere abuse is poured out against the French, for the sole purpose of gratifying national antipathy."[45] Mill goes on to identify with great accuracy the accusations most frequently made against the French, among them those specifically made against the philosophes. Licentiousness and atheism are the "horrid ideas"[46] which justify to the English their hatred of the French; but these, says Mill, are mere slogans of government propaganda. To apply them to the philosophes is no more than an admission of ignorance. He cites Sir Walter Scott's *Life of Napoleon* as an example: "Here we may be sure that the opportunity is eagerly seized, of recommending himself to our moral public, by an invective against the French philosophers as they are termed; principally upon the two points of licentiousness and irreligion. In the course of this diatribe, our author manifests no very accurate knowledge of the writings or lives of these objects of his undiscriminating dislike."[47] This passage could stand as an epigraph to much of the review literature of the whole period.

Mill expands the point in greater detail thereafter, demonstrating that he, unlike so many others, *had* read the philosophes and appreciated the distinctions which had to be made between them—distinctions not amenable to the fury and prejudice of the preceding forty years. He also points out the importance of the fact that Montesquieu and Mme. de Staël were praised because of their support for the British Constitution. In effect he demolishes a whole structure of hostility toward France by analyzing the political reasons for its construction and by exposing the sheer ignorance which had sustained it.

The position was more complex than he allowed; yet his perception of its nature is essentially true. After the appearance of the *Westminster* the word *philosophe* lost a great deal of the pejorative force which it had previously carried. Writers began to use the term *the French*, but not like Horace Walpole as a shorthand term of abuse for every species of corruption, terror, and immorality imaginable. In Mill's early writings on this issue the pro-French and pro-Enlightenment whisperings of the previous two generations finally found a voice. Although the battle had not been won, it entered a new stage after 1824 which was even more marked and important than that after 1802. French thought and French culture resumed their place in English life in an atmosphere far removed from that in which the conspiracy thesis had first arisen to agitate English nationalism into an ugly state of xenophobia. The Enlightenment had finally reemerged in England. If we remember Barruel and the strong clerical reactions of the 1790s in particular, it seems appropriate to leave the final word with the *Westminster:* "It is all too late now, to get up a religious opposition to the exercise of reason on any subject connected with the welfare of mankind."[48]

It is clear that the French Enlightenment and Revolution, as they were understood in England in this period, initiated an unprecedented historical crisis of which these were the first two phases. There was a very real fear that the next phase would develop in England. As a consequence both the Enlightenment and the Revolution were rejected, and the determined effort to stifle their effects stimulated many writers to generate a more vivid and powerful awareness of the English past and the English national character and destiny than had previously been thought necessary. This heightened patriotism claimed the need to preserve certain forms of loyalty, fidelity, and humanity of feeling against the modern French attack on them; the emphasis on the past, on precedent, and on the intricacies of a long historical evolution was itself a sign of a culture's essential vigor. A fascination with theory, doctrines of abstract right, and systematic philosophies which were internally coherent but externally invalid was deemed to be a symptom of the decline which in France, because of its inherited traditions, had led inexorably toward tyranny and despotism and away from the proclaimed goal of liberty. The deficiencies of the French national character were as much the product of history as were the countervailing virtues of the English. This opinion was modified on occasion to indicate that the French degeneracy was comparatively recent—the years of the Regency being the most favored date of origin—and that a nobler France, represented, say, by Montesquieu, had succumbed to the attritional internecine warfare of the philosophes. The breaking of established codes of sexual morality had been among the most effective successes of the radical intellectuals; this too was more readily achieved among a people who were notoriously volatile and unstable in both their public and private affections.

Nevertheless the ominous achievement of the philosophes was an example of the new power of the press and of the organization of the intellectuals as a separate but powerful influence within the state. The idea that all of these influences were the result of a long-nourished conspiracy, of which the Revolution was the direct result, had an immediate appeal for those who recognized that a cataclysm of unprecedented proportions had taken place. Burke was the leading analyst and propagandist of these views. It would be difficult to underestimate his success in making them prevail as the basis of the counter-Revolutionary reaction.

Even when the conspiracy theory of the Revolution was discredited, it lingered on as a proximate version of the truth. The government was willing to nurture this notion because it kept anti-French feeling alive and because it was a useful weapon in its own battle against Jacobins in England, Scotland, and Ireland.[49] The fears of Infidelity, of internal revolution, and of Napoleonic dictatorship were easily worked on by the conspiracy alarm. Infidelity was an especially potent catchphrase; it became indissolubly connected with loose sexual morals and with a peculiar cold-hearted and cold-blooded attitude toward the pieties of family life and the affections binding one to the place and associations of one's birth and upbringing. An evangelical religious fervor cooperated with this new kind of regional loyalty to combat both doctrinal politics and the international, cosmopolitan spirit which were believed to be their natural accompaniment. This moral patrotism, profoundly emotional in its appeal, was to survive late into the century in Wordsworth's poetry and in the religious revival of the 1830s. National character was thought to be a moral achievement dependent on the retention of fundamental affections and through them the tradition of political liberty. It was to remain hostile to the influence of intellectuals and their schemes for renovating traditional society.

It is against this background that the examples of specific intellectual influence or rejection need to be viewed. Mackintosh, although he was not a man of first-rate abilities, is an outstanding example of the victimization to which a writer could be subjected by the pressures of the dispute on the Revolution, especially by the charge of betrayal visited on so many because of their early attachment to and later disillusion with the French cause. Coleridge, at least equally guilty in this respect, had the intellectual capacity to offer both a coherent interpretation of the Revolution and a political philosophy to oppose it. His engagement with Rousseau is one of the most telling if flawed analyses of the time. He is so far superior to Mackintosh, Southey, and Croker that their common adherence to Burke's thought would at first seem to be their only substantial point of contact. Yet much of Southey was incorporated into Coleridge—anti-French feeling, emphasis on local patriotism, fear of revolution and of utilitarian commercialism in England, respect for the church and for the "old England" of the preindustrial era. Part of Coleridge's greatness lies in his transformation of these elements into a philosophy which is informed by a vision of culture and civilization not confined in its range to the particular English conditions of the period. He does go beyond Burke, and in that he is unique among the anti-Revolutionaries.

Godwin and Shelley were attracted to the so-called materialist thinkers of the French Enlightenment. Godwin found it possible to retain the utilitarianism of Helvétius along with the anarchist implications he derived from the Radical Dissenting convictions of his youth. Shelley by contrast transformed French materialism beyond all recognition into a theory of the sympathetic imagination which only Hazlitt (and through him Keats) developed in any comparable manner. The stress on sympathy was a consequence of the reaction on the part of both Hazlitt and Shelley to the various philosophies of egoism which had been so popular in the eighteenth century. It is odd that the hostility of two of the most radical of the English sympathizers with the French Revolution should have been directed at some of the more radical thinkers of the French Enlightenment, such as Helvétius. But each was concerned to find an explanation for the failure and the significance of the Revolution; and while their answers were very different, they did at least share the belief that selfish egoism, translated into political behavior, was one of the characteristic responses of reactionary Europe and England to the generous hopes and possibilities of 1789. Therefore it was important to each of them that a doctrine of sympathy should be the basis for that renovating spirit which, in private and in public concerns, would rescue mankind from the post-Revolutionary gloom.

As with the opponents of revolution, it was standard doctrine among its supporters that the capacity for a genuine human sympathy differentiated the true from the false patriot. Since Burke had inveighed against Rousseau and his gospel of benevolence, this issue—as well as that of Rousseau himself—had become central to the dispute. The old battle between reason and feeling was thus refought; but now it was politicized. It is central to all of Shelley's and Hazlitt's writings, and the rather maladroit handling of it by Godwin, especially in the first edition of *Political Justice*, gave his opponents the opportunity to portray the typical Revolutionary intellectual as seriously deficient in the emotional sphere. Shelley and Hazlitt did much to counteract this characterization, but it remained part of the popular conception of the intellectual and, as always, was associated with infidelity of the sexual as well as the religious variety. The memoirs of the women of the French Enlightenment confirmed this view, although the fact that they were women made their attitude appear even more scandalous. Even Mme. de Staël, despite her popularity among the English Whigs, was regarded as a rather dubious person because of her candor about sexual matters. Not even her admiration for the British Constitution, nor Napoleon's dislike of her, wholly outweighed this consideration. She revived the cause of French constitutional liberalism in England by projecting for it a splendid career in a new cosmopolitan Europe, which would witness a post-Revolutionary fusion of Nordic and Mediterranean national characteristics, which the new Rousseauistic literature would help to bring about through the agency of what she called *enthousiasme*. She is close to Hazlitt in her admiration for Rousseau and in her belief in the power of the new literature, although her eagerness to introduce Europe to German philosophy and literature is matched, for very different reasons, by Coleridge, William Taylor of Norwich, and later Carlyle. Still, even in her we see how privileged a position was assigned to the new concept of feeling in the course of the debate on the political as well as literary issues of the day.

Godwin and Shelley revived other issues which had been discussed earlier by Holbach and La Mettrie. Most important was the problem of secret crime and its attendant punishment by the afflicted conscience of the criminal, who knew that he had violated the principle of human solidarity. At one level their fascination with the problem is perfectly easy to explain. They wished to demonstrate that there is a binding moral principle which brings punishment on the heads of those who act in contravention of it. At least in a negative way this proved the existence of a moral ground for the idea of universal brotherhood. Equally it gave some kind of explanation for the failure of the French Revolution. To the degree that it had been violent and vengeful, it had done no more than imitate the evils of the regime it had displaced. To ascribe to the conscience an inescapable power of punishment was to relieve society of the need to practice it. It was at this point that complications arose.

English Dissent was in general terms less friendly to the French Revolution than might have been expected. Although some of its leading lights, especially the Unitarians Price and Priestley, welcomed it, and although some of the most influential pamphleteers (such as Paine) and reviewers who supported the French cause were of Dissenting stock, there was a marked hostility toward France among this group which was not entirely part of the national feeling released by the outbreak of war in 1793. In part the explanation lies in the unease with which the Dissenters, like many members of the established church, viewed the attacks of the philosophes on Christianity as such rather than on Catholicism only. They also believed that the French were, like most Catholics, acclimatized to authoritarian political systems and to the corruption of private morals. They were therefore eager to dissociate themselves from the sexual laxity and despotic tendencies of the French and to assert that principles of civil liberty were essentially English. This inevitably involved them in arguments about the relationship between the events of 1688 and 1789; ultimately they were forced to agree with Burke that the French Revolution had been informed by a spirit quite foreign to that of 1688. If they sought a parallel for 1688, they found it more readily in the American Revolution. But this did not in any way distinguish them from those who, like Southey, opposed the repeal of the Test and Corporation Acts. The problem of differentiating between 1688 and 1789 was disputed by people as various as Priestley, Burke, Croker, Mackintosh, Godwin, and Mme. de Staël. It was not a definitive issue for the Dissenters, although in 1788, the centenary year, it must have appeared as though it might be. What *was* definitive was the Dissenters' repudiation of France on the grounds that French doctrines, although derived from English sources, had lost their appeal because they had been torn out of the Christian context which had given them such millennial power in England. Given the biblical nature of the Dissenting tradition and the prominent role it gave to the private conscience, it is not altogether unexpected that the rejection of French political doctrines should be accompanied by an acceptance of those aspects of French thinking which permitted conscience to play its dominant role in matters of public as well as private importance. Secret crime was one of those matters.

The right of the state to punish offenders was a famous subject of controversy in the heyday of the Enlightenment. The great crusades, begun by Beccaria, Voltaire, and others on the Continent, were carried on in England by Bentham and the parliamentary battles to reform the penal code. The discussion of secret crime in the literature of this period is part of the history of that dispute. It is not confined to Godwin and Shelley. Mackintosh was one of the sturdiest supporters of the parliamentary campaign to bring about penal reform. Hazlitt's interest in the problem began, as we have seen, in 1792, when at the age of fourteen he embarked on his *Project for a New Theory of Civil and Criminal Legislation.*[50] He did not believe that the efforts of the Westminster Reformers—men like Mackintosh, Romilly, and Peel— had much significance because society needed to be restructured before any substantial improvements in the penal code could be effected. In his review for the *Edinburgh* of the *Report of the Select Committee on Criminal Laws* (1821) he praised Beccaria, but his essays on Godwin and Bentham in *The Spirit of the Age* show his contempt for theoreticians who seek to solve a problem which demands a radical sympathy. Yet he also praised Godwin's *Caleb Williams* as an unexpected example of that feeling for others which, as a political theorist, Godwin so conspicuously lacked.[51] Characteristically Hazlitt saw the criminal reform issue as another demonstration of the failure of sympathetic feeling, fading from the high point of the 1790s to the nadir of the mid 1820s, when all genuine hope, all the high benevolence of early Jacobinism had disappeared.

All those who dealt with the problem of secret crime saw its punishment as a form of remorse which isolates the sufferer and makes him an outcast from mankind. The young Wordsworth, in *A Letter to the Bishop of Llandaff* (1793)—its proper title is *Apology for the French Revolution*—wrote bitterly of the penal code which would make a "conscientious man" sacrifice "his respect for the laws to the common feelings of humanity."[52] Although it is clear that he had changed his mind by the time he composed the fourteen *Sonnets upon the Punishment of Death* (1839–40), he had been very much of Godwin's opinion on the issue until 1798. *The Borderers* is well known as a Godwinian work, most especially in its emphasis on remorse and the internalization of the issue of crime and its punishment. Coleridge's play *Remorse* (or in its earlier form *Osorio*) dwells on similar issues. Both poets saw the commission of crime as a fatal step in the direction of a gloomy and isolating misanthropy. The man who betrays human solidarity is enclosed within his own suffering. He may be seen as a victim of circumstance or of society; he may be mysteriously disaffected; but he is certainly a tragic if sometimes glamorous Romantic hero, a man plagued by guilt, a traitor to common feelings even if a connoisseur of his own. It is therefore a sensitive issue. Remorse is a subject which has much to do with Romantic isolation, political betrayal, the dissenting conscience, and the history of penal reform from Beccaria and Holbach to Hazlitt, Shelley, and the Westminster Reformers. But it is also one more topic recruited for the resolution of the political dispute about the authenticity of feeling and the guarantee of political worth presumed to go with it.

In a sense this has been no more than an account of the debate on the French Revolution. But in its course that debate generated questions and attitudes which were to affect English political and literary life for much of the nineteenth century. The greatest and the most anonymous writers contributed to the discussions in ways which show the mutual interaction of one on the other. In seeing part of the process of that interaction, we can see the extent of the impact of the Revolution and of the French Enlightenment on English thought and letters during that first hectic period of reaction and response.

Notes

1. Burke and the Enlightenment

1. See *The Debate on the French Revolution*, ed. A. Cobban, 2d ed. (London, 1960), p. 13; F. O'Gorman, *The Whig Party and the French Revolution* (London, 1967), pp. 48–69; F. P. Canavan, "The Burke-Paine Controversy," *Political Science Review* 6 (1976), 389–420; C. B. Cone, "Pamphlet Replies to Burke's *Reflections, Southwestern Social Science Quarterly* 26 (1945), 22–34; R. R. Fennessy, *Burke, Paine, and the Rights of Man: A Difference of Political Opinion* (The Hague, 1963); A. Goodwin, *The Friends of Liberty: The English Democratic Movement in the Age of the French Revolution* (London, 1979), pp. 99–268; G. T. Pendleton, "The English Pamphlet Literature of the Age of the French Revolution Anatomized," *Eighteenth-Century Life* 5 (1978), 29–37.
2. Burke was himself the first to be so accused. Later Sir James Mackintosh and Dr. Samuel Parr became notorious for renouncing their former sympathies. The disillusion of the poets Wordsworth, Coleridge, and Southey is, of course, a commonplace.
3. Cf. S. Maccoby, *English Radicalism* (London, 1954–55), Vol. II, *1787–1832: From Paine to Cobbett*, pp. 57–58.
4. Sir B. Boothby, *Observations on the Appeal from the New to the Old Whigs and on Mr. Paine's Rights of Man* (London, 1792), p. 77: "But what if the Whigs . . . find the puritan cant of the *Rights of Man*, and the episcopal cant of the *Reflections* equally uninviting?"
5. See P. A. Brown, *The French Revolution in English History* (London, 1918), pp. 75–99, 160.
6. K. G. Feiling, *The Second Tory Party, 1714–1832* (London, 1938), p. 192; W. T. Laprade, *England and the French Revolution, 1789–1798* (Baltimore, 1909), takes the view that Pitt used Burke's hostility to the Revolution to divide the Whigs and secure his own supremacy.
7. Cf. C. B. Cone, *Burke and the Nature of Politics: The Age of the French Revolution* (Lexington, Ky., 1964), p. 299.
8. For an extension of this, see S. Deane, "The Reputation of the French 'Philosophes' in the Whig Reviews between 1802 and 1824," *The Modern Language Review* 70 (April 1978), 271–290; "John Bull and Voltaire: The Emergence of

a Cultural Cliché," *Revue de littérature comparée* 45 (Oct.–Dec. 1971), 582–594. See also *Annual Register* 2 (1758), 238–239, on the character of Voltaire: "He is a politician, a naturalist, a geometrician, or whatever else he pleases; but he is always superficial because he is not able to be deep."

9. *The Works of the Right Honourable Edmund Burke*, 8 vols. (London, 1881), II, 31.

10. Burke, *Works*, I, 8.

11. Ibid., V, 397.

12. Among many, see D. N. Archibald, "Edmund Burke and the Conservative Imagination," *Colby Library Quarterly* 12 (1976), 191–204, and 13 (1977), 19–41; H. Barth, *The Idea of Order: Contributions to a Philosophy of Politics*, trans. E. W. Hankamer and W. M. Newell (Dordrecht, 1960); R. A. Bevan, *Marx and Burke: A Revisionist View* (La Salle, Ill., 1973); F. P. Canavan, *The Political Reason of Edmund Burke* (Durham, N.C., 1960); G. W. Chapman, *Edmund Burke: The Practical Imagination* (Cambridge, Mass., 1967); A. Cobban, *Edmund Burke and the Revolt against the Eighteenth Century*, 2d ed. (London, 1960); C. P. Courtney, *Montesquieu and Burke* (Oxford, 1963); C. P. Courtney, "Edmund Burke and the Enlightenment," in *Statesmen, Scholars, and Merchants: Essays in Eighteenth-Century History Presented to Dame Lucy Sutherland*, ed. A. Whiteman, J. S. Bromley, and P. G. M. Dickson (Oxford, 1973), pp. 304–322; F. A. Dreyer, *Burke's Politics: A Study in Whig Orthodoxy* (Waterloo, Ontario, 1979); M. Freeman, *Edmund Burke and the Critique of Political Radicalism* (Chicago, 1980); J. MacCunn, *The Political Philosophy of Burke* (London, 1913); F. O'Gorman, *Edmund Burke: His Political Philosophy* (Bloomington, Ind., 1973); A. M. Osborn, *Rousseau and Burke: A Study of the Idea of Liberty in Eighteenth-Century Thought* (London, 1940); C. Parkin, *The Moral Basis of Burke's Political Thought* (Cambridge, 1956); P. Stanlis, *Edmund Burke and the Natural Law* (Ann Arbor, 1958); P. Stanlis, ed., *Edmund Burke: The Enlightenment and the Modern World* (Detroit, 1967); L. Strauss, *Natural Right and History* (Chicago, 1953); B. T. Wilkins, *The Problem of Burke's Political Philosophy* (Oxford, 1967).

13. J. T. Boulton, *The Language of Politics in the Age of Wilkes and Burke* (London, 1963); M. Hodgart, "Radical Prose in the Late Eighteenth Century," in *The English Mind*, ed. H. S. Davies and G. Watson (Cambridge, 1964), pp. 146–152.

14. Cf. R. Weaver, *The Ethics of Rhetoric* (Chicago, 1953), pp. 55–84; D. K. Weiser, "The Imagery of Burke's *Reflections*," *Studies in Burke and His Time* 16 (1975), 213–233; J. A. Campbell, "Edmund Burke: Argument from Circumstance in *Reflections on the Revolution in France*," *Studies in Burke and His Time* 12 (1970–71), 1764–1783; S. Deane, "Burke and the French *Philosophes*," *Studies in Burke and His Time* 10 (1968–69), 1113–1137.

15. See, for example, Burke, *Works*, I, 501; II, 30, 327, 335, 404–405, 443–445, 452, 455; III, 16; V, 73.

16. Burke, *Works*, II, 441–442.

17. Ibid., II, 540–541.

18. Ibid., II, 536.

19. Ibid., II, 537. *Letter to a Member of the National Assembly* also contains the picture of disgraced parenthood in the person of Louis XVI, an echo of the vision of Marie Antoinette in *Reflections*.

20. Burke, *Works*, II, 542.
21. Ibid., II, 539–540.
22. Ibid., II, 307.
23. Ibid., II, 344.
24. Ibid., VI, 112. Cf. *The Parliamentary History of England*, ed. W. Cobbett and J. Wright, 36 vols. (London, 1806–1820), XVIII, 432.
25. Burke, *Works*, II, 439.
26. Ibid., II, 325.
27. Ibid., II, 357. For other references to the "cabal," see pp. 360, 383, 448, 460.
28. Ibid., III, 350, 352.
29. Ibid., II, 382. See also pp. 424–426.
30. See B. N. Schilling, *Conservative England and the Case against Voltaire* (New York, 1950), pp. 218–277.
31. L. Werkmeister, *The London Daily Press, 1772–1792* (Lincoln, Neb., 1963), p. 344.
32. *The Correspondence of Edmund Burke*, ed. T. Copeland et al., 10 vols. (Cambridge, 1958–1978), VII, 426.
33. A. Barruel, *Memoirs Illustrating the History of Jacobinism*, 4 vols. (London, 1797–1798), I, 166; II, 98–136. For further comment on Barruel's *Memoirs*, see D. Mornet, *Les origines intellectuelles de la revolution française* (Paris, 1933), pp. 363–364; F. Baldensperger, *Le mouvement des idées dans l'émigration française (1789–1815)*, 2 vols. (Paris, 1925), II, 19–20. See also R. R. Palmer, "World Revolution of the West, 1763–1801," *Political Science Quarterly* 69 (1954), 6–7.
34. Barruel, *Memoirs*, I, v.
35. *Application of Barruel's "Memoirs of Jacobinism" to the Secret Societies of Ireland and Great Britain* (London, 1798), advertisement.
36. *Proofs of a Conspiracy against All the Religions and Governments of Europe*, 2d ed. (London, 1797), pp. 41, 52–53, 366, 433.
37. *On the Influence Attributed to Philosophers, Freemasons, and to the Illuminati on the Revolution in France*, trans. J. Walker (London, 1801).
38. See Chapter 2. A quite different view obtained in France, where the Revolution was associated with an outburst of particularly intense feeling and of theories which gave feeling priority over all else. See P. Trahard, *La sensibilité révolutionnaire (1789–1794)* (Paris, 1936).
39. Cf. Burke, *Works*, II, 357–363.
40. Ibid., II, 361–362.
41. Brown's book (2 vols., 1757) was reviewed favorably in the *Annual Register*, 2 (1758), 445–450. Brown claimed that the English national character had recently changed to a frivolous effeminacy.
42. Cf. Goodwin, *The Friends of Liberty*, pp. 264–267.
43. Burke, *Works*, V, 79.
44. Ibid., V, 207.
45. Ibid., II, 382, 537.
46. Ibid., II, 465–466.
47. Ibid., II, 352, 466–467, 513.
48. Ibid., V, 79.
49. Ibid., II, 324.
50. Ibid., V, 425.

51. Burke, *Correspondence*, II, 221; Burke, *Works*, III, 110; I, 257.
52. The myth of the balance of powers, said Burke, was "a contrivance full of danger." *Works*, II, 259. See R. Caillois, ed., *Oeuvres de Montesquieu*, 2 vols. (Paris, 1956–1958), II, 405 (*L'esprit des lois*, XI, chap. 6); Courtney, *Montesquieu and Burke*, pp. 122–123.
53. C. B. Cone, *The English Jacobins: Reformers in Late Eighteenth-Century England* (New York, 1968).
54. See C. C. O'Brien, ed., *Reflections on the Revolution in France* (Harmondsworth, 1970), introduction, pp. 27–41; T. H. D. Mahoney, *Edmund Burke and Ireland* (Cambridge, Mass., 1960); I. Kramnick, *The Rage of Edmund Burke: Portrait of an Ambivalent Conservative* (New York, 1977); S. Deane, "Edmund Burke and the Ideology of Irish Liberalism," in *The Irish Mind: Exploring Intellectual Traditions*, ed. R. Kearney (Dublin, 1985), pp. 141–156.
55. *A Tale of a Tub: With Other Early Works, 1696–1707*, ed. H. Davis (Oxford, 1957), p. 108: "For, the Brain, in its natural Position and State of Serenity, disposeth its Owner to pass his Life in the common Forms, without any Thought of subduing Multitudes to his own *Power*, his *Reasons* or his *Visions*."
56. See S. Deane, "The Anglo-Irish Intellect: Hutcheson, Swift, and Burke," in *Eighteenth-Century Ireland* 1 (1986), 7–21.
57. P. Harth, *Swift and Anglican Rationalism: The Religious Background of* A Tale of a Tub (Chicago, 1961).
58. *An Inquiry into the Original of Our Ideas of Beauty and Virtue* (London, 1725), pp. 164–165.
59. Burke, *Works*, II, 320.
60. *An Inquiry*, p. 165.
61. See B. O'Connell, "Edmund Burke: Gaps in the Family Record," *Studies in Burke and His Time* 9 (1968), 714–715, for information on the judicial murder of his father's Catholic employer; on that of Father Nicholas Sheehy in 1766, see Burke, *Correspondence*, I, 337, 249, 255–256. Burke also refers to this event in *Letter to a Peer of Ireland on the Penal Laws* (1782), *Letter to Sir Hercules Langrishe* (1790), and *Letter to William Smith* (1792).
62. Burke, *Works*, VI, 27.
63. Ibid., III, 296.
64. Ibid., III, 304–305.
65. Ibid., VI, 58.
66. Ibid., II, 494.
67. J. A. Lester, Jr., "An Analysis of the Conservative Thought of Edmund Burke" (Ph.D. diss., Harvard University, 1942), 102.
68. *An Essay on the Nature and Immutability of Truth*, in *The Works of James Beattie, LL.D.*, 5 vols. (Philadelphia, 1809), V, 3; on abstraction and theory, see pp. 124–125; on atheism and hard-heartedness, see pp. 72–76, 117, 119–120; on the term *metaphysical*, see p. 38.
69. D. Berman, "The Jacobitism of Berkeley's *Passive Obedience*," *Journal of the History of Ideas* 47, no. 2 (April–June 1986), 309–319; and "The Irish Counter-Enlightenment," in Kearney, *The Irish Mind*, pp. 119–140.
70. Burke, *Works*, V, 220; cf. V, 364, and III, 334.
71. Ibid., III, 334.

72. See *Oeuvres de Montesquieu*, II, 717 (*Lois*, XXIV, chap. 3); I, 108 (*Considérations sur les causes de la grandeur des Romains et de leur décadence*, chap. 6); II, 24, 34 (*Réflexions sur la monarchie universelle*).
73. "Extracts from Mr. Burke's Table Talk," *Miscellanies of the Philobiblion Society* 7, no. 3 (1862–63); Burke, *Correspondence*, VI, 36.
74. Burke, *Correspondence*, VI, 215.
75. E. Carcassonne, *Montesquieu et la problème de la constitution française au XVIIIᵉ siècle* (Paris, 1927).
76. See *Oeuvres de Montesquieu*, II, 39–69 (*Lois*, XI, chaps. 5, 6).
77. Burke, *Correspondence*, VI, 215.

2. National Character and the Conspiracy

1. *The Correspondence of Horace Walpole*, ed. W. S. Lewis (New Haven, 1961), XXXI, 329.
2. See M. Kallich, "Horace Walpole against Edmund Burke: A Study in Antagonism," *Studies in Burke and His Time* 9 (1967–68), 834–863, and 9 (1968), 927–945; J. W. Johnson, "Walpole against Burke: Some Ancillary Speculations," *Studies in Burke and His Time* 10 (1969), 1022–1034.
3. Walpole, *Correspondence*, XXXI, 377.
4. *Brief Reflections Relative to the Emigrant French Clergy: Earnestly Submitted to the Humane Consideration of the Ladies of Great Britain* (London, 1793), p. 11.
5. *Domestic Anecdotes of the French Nation during the Last Thirty Years, Indicative of the French Revolution* (London, 1793), p. 307.
6. *Vaurien; or, Sketches of the Times*, 2 vols. (London, 1793), I, 179.
7. Cf. K. G. Feiling, *The Second Tory Party, 1714–1832* (London, 1938), p. 187.
8. *Vaurien*, I, viii.
9. Burke, for instance, pleaded that the émigré aristocrat the Chevalier de La Bintinaye be officially acknowledged as the representative of the legitimate government of France. See *The Correspondence of Edmund Burke*, ed. T. Copeland et al., 10 vols. (Cambridge, 1958–1978), VI, xix.
10. *Proofs of a Conspiracy against All the Religions and Governments of Europe*, 2d ed. (London, 1797), p. 425.
11. Cf. F. Plowden, *A Short History of the British Empire during the Year 1794* (London, 1795), p. 265. Plowden argues that the conspiracy thesis was used as an excuse to prevent parliamentary reform. See also F. Baldensperger, *Le mouvement des idées dans l'émigration française, 1789–1815*, 2 vols. (Paris, 1925), as well as the works of Schilling, Mornet, and Palmer cited in Chapter 1.
12. *The Letters of Edward Gibbon*, ed. J. E. Norton, 3 vols. (London, 1956), III, 265.
13. B. Mallet, *Mallet du Pan and the French Revolution* (London, 1902), pp. 291–295. See also J. Farington, *The Farington Diary*, ed. J. Grieg, 8 vols. (London, 1922–1928), I, 255, where we learn that the "periodical work" in which Du Pan was engaged had "19,000 subscribers." For a full account, see F. Acomb, *Mallet du Pan (1749–1800): A Career in Political Journalism* (Durham, N.C., 1973).
14. On the anglomania of the French Constitutionalists, see G. Bonno, *La Constitution britannique devant l'opinion française de Montesquieu à Bonaparte* (Paris, 1932), esp. pp. 189–272; F. T. H. Fletcher, *Montesquieu and English Politics,*

1750–1800 (London, 1939); D. P. Heatley, "Fox, Montesquieu, and Blackstone," *Law Quarterly Review* 35, no. 140 (October 1919), 339–343.

15. *Vie de la reine de France, Marie Lecksinska* (Brussels, 1794), p. 311.

16. J. B. Duvoisin, *An Examination of the Principles of the French Revolution* (London, 1796), pp. 12, 25.

17. *Des principes et des causes de la révolution en France* (London, 1790), pp. 14, 27–28.

18. *Le nouveau Paris,* 6 vols. (Paris, 1799), II, 123.

19. *Memoirs of a Traveller, Now in Retirement,* 5 vols. (London, 1805), IV, 198.

20. *Historical and Political Memoirs of the Reign of Louis XVI,* 6 vols. (London, 1802), IV, 366.

21. J. Mallet du Pan, "Du degré d'influence qu'a eu la philosophie française sur la révolution," *Mercure Britannique* 16 (Feb. 25, 1799), 358 (my translation).

22. F. Gentz, "De la marche de l'opinion publique en Europe relativement à la révolution française," *Mercure Britannique* 23 (April 25, 1799), 3–34.

23. *On the Influence Attributed to the Philosophers, Freemasons, and to the Illuminati on the Revolution of France* (London, 1821), pp. 18–28.

24. *Historical and Political Memoirs,* V, 370.

25. *Histoire de France pendant le dix-huitième siècle,* 8 vols. (Paris, 1808–1821), III, 46, 131–132; IV, 128.

26. *Monthly Review* 103 (February 1824), 192–193, admired Lacretelle because, unlike Voltaire, he had "a temperate, moral Protestant sort of feeling which loves liberty, abhors infidelity and reproves libertinism." See also *Quarterly* 11 (April 1814), 177; *Critical Review* 20, 3d ser. (1810), 482–494; *Eclectic Review* 4, n. ser. (August 1815), 107; and *Knight's Quarterly Magazine* 3 (November 1824), 65.

27. *British Review* 5 (February 1814), 311.

28. *Edinburgh Review* 24 (February 1815), 530; 1 (January 1803), 365; 15 (January 1810), 464; and *Quarterly* 8 (December 1812), 292–293.

29. *Letters to Burke* (London, 1790), p. 44n.

30. *Edinburgh Review* 43 (October 1813), 201.

31. Mme. de Staël, *Correspondance générale,* ed. B. W. Jasinski (Paris, 1960), I, pt. 2, p. 493.

32. *Oeuvres complètes de Madame la Baronne de Staël-Holstein,* 2 vols. (Paris, 1836), I, 255. She attributes British political and German literary achievements to Protestantism. See *De la littérature,* ed. P. Van Tieghem, 2 vols. (Geneva, 1959), I, 187–188.

33. See I. A. Henning, *L'Allemagne de Mme. de Staël et la polémique romantique* (Paris, 1921), p. 21, where he claims that Sismondi's *De la littérature du midi de l'Europe* and August Schlegel's *Cours de littérature dramatique* "forment l'avant-garde immédiate du livre *De l'Allemagne.*"

34. Mme. de Staël, *Oeuvres complètes,* I, 701 (my translation).

35. *De la littérature,* I, 87; Mme. de Staël, *Oeuvres complètes,* II, 221.

36. Mme. de Staël, *Oeuvres complètes,* I, 1–2.

37. Ibid., I, 49–50.

38. Ibid., I, 237.

39. Ibid., I, 313.

40. Ibid., I, 239. On cosmopolitanism, see J.-J. Texte, *Jean-Jacques Rousseau and the Cosmopolitan Spirit in Literature*, trans. J. W. Matthew (London, 1899); A. D. McKillop, "Local Attachment and Cosmopolitanism—The Eighteenth-Century Pattern," in *From Sensibility to Romanticism*, ed. F. W. Hilles and H. Bloom (New York, 1965), pp. 191–218.

41. Mme. de Staël, *Oeuvres complètes*, I, 243.

42. Ibid., I, 267 (my translation).

43. Cf. D. Stewart, *Philosophical Essays* (Edinburgh, 1810), pp. 10–12; M. J. de Chénier, *Fragmens du cours de littérature fait à l'Athénée de Paris, en 1806 et 1807* (Paris, 1818). The reviews in England were of one mind on this. See S. Deane, "The Reputation of the French 'Philosophes' in the Whig Reviews between 1802 and 1824," *Modern Language Review* 70, no. 2 (April 1975), 271–290.

44. *Eclectic Review* 8 (March 1812), 310; 11, n. ser. (March 1819), 203.

45. *Blackwood's Magazine* 3 (September 1818), 633; but not all the reviews were favorable. Sydney Smith gave *Delphine* a venomous review in *Edinburgh Review* 2 (April 1803), 172–177; and *Dix années d'exil* was harshly reviewed in John Scott's *London Magazine* 4 (October 1821) 394–400. See also R. Whitford, *Mme. de Staël's Literary Reputation in England* (Chicago, 1918); R. C. Escarpit, *L'Angleterre dans l'oeuvre de Mme. de Staël* (Paris, 1959).

46. *A Charge Delivered to the Clergy of the Diocese of London at the Visitation of That Diocese in the Year MDCCXCIV* (London, 1795); cf. R. Valpy, *Two Assize Sermons* (London, 1793), pp. 47–49, 50n.

47. *Philosophical Reflections on the Late Revolution in France and Conduct of the Dissenters in England, in a Letter to the Rev. Dr. Priestley* (London, 1790), pp. 17–18.

48. *View of the Causes and Progress of the French Revolution*, 2 vols. (London, 1795), I, 22, 24. On the correspondence of Frederick II with Voltaire and D'Alembert, see *Anti-Jacobin Review and Magazine* 10 (1802), 498; *The British Critic* 29 (1799), 508–509; Stephen Jones in *Monthly Review* 52 (April 1807), foreign appendix, p. 481; and Robert Bland in *Monthly Review* 74 (August 1814), foreign appendix, p. 526.

49. *Reflections on the Political and Moral State of Society at the Close of the Eighteenth Century* (London, 1800–1801), p. 126n.

50. *The Gentleman's Magazine* 67 (October 1797), 820–822.

51. H. H. Jebb, *A Great Bishop of One Hundred Years Ago: Being a Sketch of the Life of Samuel Horsley, LL.D.* (London, 1909), pp. 84, 137–138.

52. *History the Interpreter of Prophecy*, 3 vols. (Oxford, 1799), III, 48; cf. p. 43.

53. See *The Gentleman's Magazine* 67 (December 1797), 1009–1010; 64 (March 1794), 250–251; 68 (July 1798), 606–607; *The British Critic* 5 (1795), 471–473; 10 (1798), 156–170, 407–410, where Barruel is reviewed next to Robinson so "that one may as much as possible, illustrate the other"; 11 (1798), 284–293; 13 (1799), 389–396; 19 (1802), 513–516; 20 (1802), 135–145; *Anti-Jacobin Review and Magazine* 1 (August 1798), 226–227; 1 (September 1798), 360; 10 (December 1801), appendix, p. 495. See J. A. R. Séguin, ed., *Voltaire and The Gentleman's Magazine, 1731–1868: An Index* (New York, 1962). Gratry's *Vie polémique de Voltaire* was favorably reviewed in *Monthly Review* 38 (June 1802) by the same reviewer, Christopher Moody, who had congratulated Bishop Horsley (see n. 51) for

his attack on the philosophes and for his advertising the Barruel conspiracy thesis in *Monthly Review* 26 (1801), 31.

54. As, for example, in L. Hughes, *Historical View of the Rise, Progress, and Tendency of the Principles of Jacobinism* (London, 1799); S. Payson, *Proofs of the Real Existence and Dangers of Illuminism* (London, 1802).

55. R. Watson, *Anecdotes of the Life of the Bishop of Llandaff* (London, 1817), p. 294; G. Gleig, *Sermons Preached Occasionally* (Edinburgh, 1803), p. 328n.

56. See Watson, *Anecdotes*, p. 285; W. Richards, *Reflections on French Atheism and on English Christianity* (London, 1794), pp. 23–24; B. Flower, *The French Constitution, with Remarks on Some of Its Principal Articles*, 2d ed. (London, 1792), pp. 366–367.

57. R. Bage, *Hermsprong; Or, Man as He Is Not* (London, 1796), p. 50; on the political novel at this time, see J. M. S. Tompkins, *The Popular Novel in England, 1770–1800* (London, 1932; reprint, 1961), pp. 296–328; H. Steeves, *Before Jane Austen* (London, 1966), pp. 272–314.

58. *Vaurien*, I, 289–290.

59. *Edmund Oliver*, 2 vols. (Bristol, 1798), p. viii.

60. *The Works of Hannah More*, 14 vols. (London, 1853), VII, 253.

61. *Memoirs of Modern Philosophers*, 3 vols. (Bath, 1800), II, 77.

62. *Letters of a Hindooh Rajah*, 2 vols. (London, 1796; 5th ed., 1811), II, 340.

63. *A Tale of the Times*, 3 vols. (London, 1799), II, 153.

64. E. Du Bois, *St. Godwin, a Tale of the Sixteenth, Seventeenth, and Eighteenth Centuries by Count Reginald de St. Leon* (London, 1799; reprint Dublin, 1800), p. 192.

65. The most important of these were translated; all were widely reviewed. See especially *The Unpublished Correspondence of Mme. du Deffand*, trans. Mrs. Meeke, 2 vols. (London, 1810); *Letters of the Marquise du Deffand to the Hon. Horace Walpole . . . to Which Are Added Letters of Madame du Deffand to Voltaire from 1759 to 1775*, ed. M. Berry, 4 vols. (London, 1810); *Historical and Literary Memoirs and Anecdotes, Selected from the Correspondence of Baron de Grimm and Diderot* (London, 1814); *Original Correspondence of Jean-Jacques Rousseau with Madame La Tour de Franqueville, and M. du Peyrou, Late Burgher of Neufchâtel*, 2 vols. (London, 1804); J. de La Harpe, *Correspondence littéraire*, 6 vols. (Paris, 1801–1807); L. F. P. de La Live d'Epinay, *Mémoires et correspondence de Madame d'Epinay*, 3 vols. (Paris, 1818); *Mémoirs inédits de l'Abbé Morellet*, 4 vols. (Paris, 1822); Mme. de Genlis, *Précis de la conduite de Madame de Genlis depuis la révolution* (Hamburg, 1796); *Les diners du Baron d'Holbach* (Paris, 1822); *Mémoires inédits de Madame la Comtesse de Genlis sur le dix-huitième siècle*, 8 vols. (Paris, 1825); and as a culmination to the spate of works on Rousseau, primarily by Dussaulx, Corancez, and others, V. D. Musset-Pathay, *Histoire de la vie et des ouvrages de J.-J. Rousseau* (London, 1821). See also H. Roddier, *Jean-Jacques Rousseau en Angleterre au XVIIIe siècle* (Paris, 1947); and J. Voisine, *Jean-Jacques Rousseau en Angleterre à l'epoque romantique* (Paris, 1956).

66. *Sir Thomas More; or, Colloquies on the Progress and Prospects of Society*, 2 vols. (London, 1829), II, 43.

67. A. Cobban, *Edmund Burke and the Revolt against the Eighteenth Century*, 2d ed. (London, 1960), pp. 198–203.

68. *Colloquies*, I, 18.

69. R. Southey, *Essays Moral and Political*, 2 vols. (London, 1832), I, 369. Cf. Macaulay's remark: "He [Southey] would have tyranny and purity together; though the most superficial observation might have shown him that there can be no tyranny without corruption." Quoted from an *Edinburgh Review* article of January 1830 on Southey's *Colloquies*, in *Robert Southey: The Critical Heritage*, ed. L. Madden (London, 1972), p. 347.

70. Southey, *Essays*, I, 415.

71. Ibid., I, 126.

72. M. F. Brightfield, *John Wilson Croker* (Berkeley, 1940), pp. 261–262.

73. Cf. K. G. Feiling, *Sketches in Nineteenth-Century Biography* (London, 1930), pp. 58–62; H. Ben-Israel, *English Historians of the French Revolution* (Cambridge, 1968), pp. 175–202.

74. *Quarterly Review* 61 (April 1836), 66–71.

75. Ibid., 17 (April 1817), 282.

76. On Croker and Burke and 1688, see Croker's *Essays on the Early Period of the French Revolution* (London, 1857), p. v; and *The Correspondence and Diaries of the Late Right Honourable John Wilson Croker*, ed. L. J. Jennings, 3 vols. (London, 1889), II, 83.

77. *British Review* 2 (December 1811), 287–288.

78. Ibid., 5 (February 1814), 344.

79. *A Visit to Paris in 1814, Being a Review of the Moral, Political, Intellectual, and Social Conditions of the French Capital* (London, 1815), pp. 171–172.

80. J. Scott, *Sketches of Manners, Scenery, &c. in the French Provinces, Switzerland, and Italy, with an Essay on French Literature* (London, 1821), p. 36.

81. *Paris Revisited in 1815 by Way of Brussels, Including a Walk over the Field of Battle at Waterloo* (London, 1816), p. 195. D. Low, in "A Biographical and Critical Study of John Scott (1784–1821)" (Diss., Cambridge University, 1967), p. 184, says, "Scott had two main objects in writing *Paris Revisited*: to describe the scene of Waterloo, and to give an account of the stripping of the Louvre that followed the conquest of Paris."

82. *Sketches of Manners*, p. 81.

83. *Quarterly Review* 9 (March 1813), 93–94.

84. *Edinburgh Review* 21 (July 1813), 284.

85. *The Convention of Cintra*, in *The Prose Works of William Wordsworth*, ed. A. B. Grosart, 3 vols. (London, 1876), I, 164.

86. G. Carnall, *Robert Southey and His Age: The Development of a Conservative Mind* (Oxford, 1960); F. M. Todd, *Politics and the Poet: A Study of Wordsworth* (London, 1957).

87. *New Letters of Robert Southey*, ed. K. Curry, 2 vols. (London, 1965), I, 215.

88. Ibid., II, 231.

89. Southey, *Essays*, I, 14–15.

90. Ibid., I, 126.

91. Ibid., I, 127.

92. His references to the prospect of bloody revolution in England are numerous. See *The Life and Correspondence of Robert Southey*, ed. C. C. Southey, 6 vols. (London, 1849–50), III, 342–343, and VI, 175, 179. See also J. Simmons, *Southey* (London, 1945), p. 183; W. Haller, "Southey's Later Radicalism," *PMLA* 38 (June 1922), 288–289.

93. W. Wordsworth, *The Excursion, Being a Portion of The Recluse* (London, 1814), bk. 4, ll. 1004–1005.
94. Wordsworth, *Prose Works,* I, 42.
95. Ibid., I, 161–162.
96. *The French Revolution,* in *The Works of Thomas Carlyle,* 30 vols. (London, 1898), II, 281; III, 2.
97. Ibid., XXVIII, 204–205.
98. Madden, *Robert Southey,* p. 464.
99. *A Visit to Paris,* pp. xxv–xxvi. Cf. "French Pretensions," *London Magazine* 6 (October 1822), 293–304.

3. Mackintosh and France

1. For Coleridge, see *Collected Letters of Samuel Taylor Coleridge,* ed. E. L. Griggs, 6 vols. (Oxford, 1956–1962), I, 588, 633–636; II, 770, 931; III, 315–317; IV, 713; *The Notebooks of Samuel Taylor Coleridge,* ed. K. Coburn, vol. I, *1794–1804* (New York, 1957), pp. 634, 949; vol. II, *1804–1808* (London, 1962), pp. 2468, 2509, 2618. See also *Biographia Literaria,* ed. J. Shawcross, 2 vols. (Oxford, 1907), I, 67; and the poem "Two Round Faces on the Tombstone," in *The Complete Poetical Works of Samuel Taylor Coleridge,* ed. E. H. Coleridge, 2 vols. (Oxford, 1962), I, 157. A manuscript version of this poem is entitled "Epitaph on Sir James Mackintosh," British Library Additional Manuscripts, 28, 322 fol. 89 (hereafter cited as Add. Mss.); see C. R. Woodring, *Politics in the Poetry of Coleridge* (Madison, Wisc., 1961), pp. 151–153. For Hazlitt, see *The Complete Works of William Hazlitt,* ed. P. P. Howe, 21 vols. (London, 1930–1934), I, 63–64, 67–68n.; XI, 98–101.
2. In April 1820, while trying to persuade Mackintosh to take the professorship of moral philosophy at Edinburgh, Jeffrey wrote to say how much he admired him "and have ever looked upon you and spoken of you as the wisest and most accomplished person I have ever seen or heard of." Add. Mss. 52453.
3. See L. Sanders, *The Holland House Circle* (London, n.d.), pp. 257–263.
4. T. B. Macaulay, *Critical and Historical Essays,* 2 vols. (London, 1883), I, 320; R. P. Ward, *An Historical Essay on the Real Character and Amount of Precedent of the Revolution of 1688 . . .,* 2 vols. (London, 1838), I, 5–6. *A Notice of the Life, Writings, and Speeches of Sir James Mackintosh* was prefixed to Mackintosh's *History of the Revolution in England in 1688* (London, 1834), pp. v–clxxvi. The author was probably an Irishman, W. Wallace.
5. *Memoirs of the Life of the Right Honourable Sir James Mackintosh,* ed. R. J. Mackintosh, 2 vols. (London, 1835), I, 129–130. This passage, slightly emended and inaccurately dated, is from Add. Mss. 52451. Generally I have quoted from the Mackintosh Papers in the British Library rather than the *Memoirs,* which are not entirely accurate or reliable.
6. The history of this episode can be studied in the Mackintosh Papers, Add. Mss. 52453. According to Jeffrey, Macvey Napier was willing to withdraw his candidacy if Mackintosh went forward.
7. Add. Mss. 52451; Mackintosh, *Memoirs,* I, 88.
8. Mackintosh's *Memoirs,* I, 91, reproduce parts of the account by T. Green, *Diary of a Lover of Literature* (Ipswich, 1810), pp. 139–140, 234–235. Mackintosh

refers to it in his journal, November 14, 1811, Add. Mss. 52440: "Returning back to 1798 & 1800 seems like coming back to a preexistent State." J. W. Croker, in *Quarterly Review* 54 (July 1835), 267, quotes Addington (later Lord Sidmouth) as saying that at Beaconsfield on this occasion Mackintosh "renounced his early errors and *received absolution*." In the same review Croker also claims (p. 268) that Mackintosh asked Addington for the recordership of Bombay and was given it. Burke was less sanguine about Mackintosh's conversion: "This conversion is none at all." *The Correspondence of Edmund Burke*, ed. T. Copeland et al., 10 vols. (Cambridge, 1958–1978), IX, 204–205. The main sources for the facts of Mackintosh's life are *The Notice of the Life*; the *Memoirs*; a series of *Quarterly Review* articles by Croker, 51 (June 1834), 493–535; 54 (July 1835), 250–294; 74 (March 1849), 549–630; 88 (December 1850), 492–528; 91 (June 1852), 217–268; the account given in the DNB by Sir Leslie Stephen; the Mackintosh Papers in the British Library, Add. Mss. 52436–52453; 34487–34526; 51651–51657; 34613 fol. 450; 34614 fol. 1; 35344 fol. 186; 30115 fols. 26, 28; 27925 fol. 188. The bulk of these papers is not foliated in any consistent manner, so only the volume number is given in most cases.

9. The Benchers of the Inn surrendered the hall for the lectures only after pressure from Pitt, Canning, and Lord Loughborough.

10. W. Godwin, *Uncollected Writings (1785–1822)* (Gainesville, Fla., 1968), pp. 302–304.

11. Parr is especially guilty in this respect. His attacks on the spirit of "universal philanthropy" in his *Spital Sermon* (1800) are almost identical to Mackintosh's in *The Law of Nature and Nations*. See *The Works of Samuel Parr, LL.D.*, ed. J. Johnstone, 8 vols. (London, 1832), I, 397–399. Parr and Mackintosh quarreled; the issues are unclear. See W. Derry, *Dr. Parr: A Portrait of the Whig Dr. Johnson* (Oxford, 1966), pp. 155–157, 235–237, 251–254, 325; see also the Mackintosh Papers, Add. Mss. 52451, 52436, 52453, 52445. Since Parr burned all the papers relating to their quarrel, the full facts cannot be known. Cf. M. R. Adams, *Studies in the Backgrounds of English Radicalism* (Lancaster Pa., 1947), pp. 155–190, 303–304. On Coleridge, see *Collected Letters*, I, 359n; Coleridge, *Notebooks*, II, 2468. For further detail on the whole nexus of relationships, see H. E. Littlefield, *Emma Darwin: A Century of Family Letters*, 2 vols. (Cambridge, 1904), I, 25–40; and E. Meteyard, *A Group of Englishmen (1795 to 1815) Being Records of the Younger Wedgwoods and Their Friends* (London, 1871).

12. *British Review* 7, no. 14 (1816) 376–377; on gloomy and villainous heroes, see J. G. Lockhart in *Blackwoods Edinburgh Magazine* 2, no. 9 (December 1818), 270; reprinted in *The Edinburgh Magazine and Literary Miscellany* 2 (January 1818), 60; W. S. Ward, "Some Aspects of the Conservative Attitude towards Poetry in England, 1789–1820," *PMLA* 60 (1945), 397. Shelley made the point in the preface to *The Revolt of Islam*, in *The Complete Works of Percy Bysshe Shelley*, ed. R. Ingpen and W. E. Peck, 10 vols. (London, 1926; reprint, 1965), I, 241–242.

13. See Chapter 6 on Shelley and Chapter 7 on Hazlitt.

14. Cf. Littlefield, *Emma Darwin*, I, 343–344.

15. Sir H. Lytton Bulwer, Lord Dalling, *Historical Characters: Mackintosh, Canning, Talleyrand, Cobbett, Peel*, 5th ed. (London, 1876), p. 256.

16. Mackintosh, *Memoirs*, I, 137–138; see Sanders, *The Holland House Circle*, p. 257; E. Seymour, ed., *The Pope of Holland House* (London, 1906), pp. 19–37.
17. He sent his wife ahead of him to plead his cause in advance. He wrote to her on June 15, 1810, that he wished her "an opportunity of canvassing for me and keeping up my connection & reviving my popularity in every quarter." Add. Mss. 52437.
18. *Monthly Review* 19 (1796), 315–316. See L. A. McKenzie, "The French Revolution and English Parliamentary Reform: James Mackintosh and the *Vindiciae Gallicae*," *Eighteenth-Century Studies* 14 (1981), 264–282; J. T. Boulton, "James Mackintosh: *Vindiciae Gallicae*," "*Renaissance and Modern Studies* 21 (1977), 106–118; W. Christian, "James Mackintosh, Burke, and the Cause of Reform," *Eighteenth-Century Studies* 7 (1973–1974), 193–206.
19. *Monthly Review* 19 (1796), 315–316.
20. *Vindiciae Gallicae* (London, 1791), p. 17.
21. Ibid., p. 59.
22. Ibid., p. 139.
23. *Monthly Review* 20 (1796), 560. This is cited by Mackintosh from the book under review, De La Croix, *The French Spectator during the Revolutionary Government*.
24. See Add. Mss. 52436. On reading C. Butler, *A Connected Series of Notes on the Chief Revolutions of the Principal States Which Composed the Empire of Charlemagne* (London, 1807), in which Barruel is highly praised (p. 284), Mackintosh objected to this passage and denied that there was any support for Barruel's claims.
25. In the *Monthly Review* 19 (1796), 319–320: "Happy should we be if truth would permit us to say that advancing years, which have not repressed the fire of this great writer's genius, had added to his other excellencies that calm temper, that candid moderation, that mature prudence, and that sober dignity, which are so peculiarly becoming in the productions of age."
26. Mackintosh, *Memoirs*, I, 125.
27. Add. Mss. 52452, July 13, 1809.
28. The title is taken from Samuel Pufendorf's *De jure naturae et gentium*. There was a chair at Edinburgh named the Chair of the Law of Nature and Nations after the original chair created for Pufendorf at Heidelberg in 1661. See G. Bryson, *Man and Society: The Scottish Inquiry of the Eighteenth Century* (Princeton, 1945), esp. pp. 2–9, 21. F. Venturi gives a brief description of the differences between the Scottish and English Enlightenments in *Europe des lumières* (Paris, 1971). See also, for the Scottish achievement and background, J. Ramsay, *Scotland and Scotsmen in the Eighteenth Century*, ed. A. Allardyce, 2 vols. (Edinburgh, 1888); A. C. Chitnis, *The Scottish Enlightenment: A Social History* (London, 1976); J. Rendall, *The Origins of the Scottish Enlightenment* (London, 1978).
29. Mackintosh, *Memoirs*, I, 108.
30. *The Complete Works of William Hazlitt*, ed. P. P. Howe, 21 vols. (London, 1930–1934), I, 108.
31. Mackintosh, *Memoirs*, I, 110.
32. Coleridge, *Notebooks*, I, 949.
33. Cf. L. Whitney, *Primitivism and the Idea of Progress* (Baltimore, 1934), pp. 225–226.

34. *A Discourse on the Law of Nature and Nations* (London, 1799), in *The Miscellaneous Works of the Right Honourable James Mackintosh*, 3 vols. (London, 1846), I, 353–354.
35. Add. Mss. 52436, August 16, 1804. Cf. Mackintosh, *Miscellaneous Works*, I, 378.
36. Add. Mss. 52437, September 12, 1810.
37. See Add. Mss. 52452, October 11, 1809; 52452, December 3, 1812; July 1, 1813.
38. Add. Mss. 51653 fols. 5, 6.
39. Mackintosh, *Miscellaneous Works*, II, 638.
40. Add. Mss. 524561. See also Mackintosh, *Memoirs*, I, 335–336, 339–340.
41. Add. Mss. 52436; Mackintosh, *Memoirs*, I, 352.
42. Add. Mss. 52453.
43. Add. Mss. 52440, February 20, 1812. There is a truncated version in Mackintosh, *Memoirs*, II, 204.
44. Ibid., February 21, 1812.
45. *Notice of the Life*, p. xxv.
46. Cf. B. Groethuysen, *The Bourgeois: Catholicism versus Capitalism in Eighteenth-Century France*, trans. M. Ilford (London, 1968), p. 24.
47. Add. Mss. 52440, February 29, 1812.
48. Add. Mss. 52436, June 11, 1807.
49. *A Fragment on Mackintosh* (London, 1835), p. 38.
50. *Dissertation Second: Exhibiting a General View of Ethical Philosophy, Chiefly during the Seventeenth and Eighteenth Centuries*, in *Encyclopedia Britannica*, 7th ed. (Edinburgh, 1842), I, 297.
51. Ibid., I, 403.
52. Ibid., I, 404.
53. Ibid., I, 410.
54. *Fragment on Mackintosh*, p. 35.
55. Various avowals of his enthusiasm for penal reform are in Mackintosh, *Memoirs*, I, 342–343, and II, 43; Add. Mss. 52437, 52444.
56. *Anima poetae*, ed. E. H. Coleridge (London, 1895), p. 198.
57. Mackintosh, *Memoirs*, II, 148.
58. J. B. Hay, *Inaugural Addresses by Lords Rectors of the University of Glasgow* (Glasgow, 1839), p. 28.

4. Coleridge and Rousseau

1. *Collected Letters of Samuel Taylor Coleridge*, ed. E. L. Griggs, 6 vols. (Oxford, 1956–1971), I, 397.
2. Ibid., p. 397.
3. Quoted in K. Everest, *Coleridge's Secret Ministry: The Context of the Conversation: Poems 1795–1798* (Sussex, 1979), p. 140.
4. "Modern Patriotism," in *The Collected Works of Samuel Taylor Coleridge*, vol. II, *The Watchman*, ed. L. Patton (London, 1970), p. 99.
5. *Conciones ad populum; or, Addresses to the People*, in Coleridge, *Collected Works*, vol. I, *Lectures 1795 on Politics and Religion*, ed. L. Patton and P. Mann (London, 1971), p. 49; cf. L. Werkmeister, "Some Whys and Wherefore of Coleridge's

'Lines Composed in a Concert Room,' " *Modern Philology* 60 (February 1963), 203–204.

6. Coleridge, *Collected Works*, I, 46.

7. Ibid., II, 30.

8. Ibid., II, 374.

9. Everest, *Coleridge's Secret Ministry*, pp. 97–145. See also E. P. Thompson, *The Making of the English Working Class* (London, 1963); M. Butler, *Romantics, Rebels, and Reactionaries: English Literature and Its Background* (Oxford, 1981).

10. Coleridge, *Collected Letters*, I, 145–146.

11. Coleridge, *Collected Works*, I, 33.

12. Coleridge, *Collected Letters*, I, 279.

13. Coleridge, *Collected Works*, III, *The Friend*, ed. B. Rooke, 2 vols. (1969), i, 105; ii, 178–179. See J. Colmer, *Coleridge as Critic of Society* (Oxford, 1959), p. 100; on the general reconciliation between Rousseau and Burke, see J. Muirhead, *Coleridge as Philosopher* (London, 1930), p. 185.

14. *The Friend*, i, 159; ii, 195–196.

15. Cf. S. Gingerich, "From Necessity to Transcendentalism in Coleridge," *PMLA* 35 (1920), 38.

16. *The Friend*, i, 256.

17. Ibid., i, 178; cf. ii, 105.

18. Ibid., i, 189; ii, 124.

19. Ibid., i, 192; cf. ii, 126.

20. Ibid., i, 132; ii, 113.

21. Ibid., i, 192; ii, 126.

22. Ibid., i, 196; ii, 129.

23. Ibid., i, 201; ii, 132.

24. Ibid., i, 152.

25. *Coleridge on Logic and Learning*, ed. A. D. Snyder (New Haven, 1929), pp. 132–133.

26. Coleridge brought back a copy of Kant's *Die Metaphysik der Sitten*, which included the treatise on *Rechtslehre*, British Library Catalogue no. 43.b.5; *Zum Ewigen Frieden* was translated in *Essays and Treatises on Moral, Political, and Various Philosophical Subjects by Emanuel Kant*, 2 vols. (London, 1798), I, 244–314, under the title *Eternal Peace*. On Coleridge and Kant, see R. Wellek, *Immanuel Kant in England, 1793–1838* (Princeton, 1931); T. McFarland, *Coleridge and the Pantheist Tradition* (Oxford, 1969); J. A. Appleyard, *Coleridge's Philosophy of Literature* (Cambridge, Mass., 1965); N. Fruman, *Coleridge, The Damaged Archangel* (London, 1971); R. D. Ashton, *The German Idea in Four English Writers and the Reception of German Thought, 1800–1860* (Cambridge, 1980); J. Engell, *The Creative Imagination: Enlightenment to Romanticism* (Cambridge, Mass., 1981).

27. R. Derathé, *Le rationalisme de J.-J. Rousseau* (Paris, 1948), p. 177; E. Boutroux, "Remarques sur la philosophie de Rousseau," *Revue de métaphysique et de morale* 20 (1912), 273.

28. *Lettre à M. D'Alembert sur les spectacles*, ed. M. Fuchs (Lille, 1948), p. 22; cf. *Emile*, ed. F. and P. Richard (Paris, 1939), bk. 4, p. 298.

29. *Emile*, bk. 4, p. 353.

30. Among discussions of Rousseau's theory of natural goodness are A. Schinz, "La théorie de la bonté naturelle de l'homme chez Rousseau," *Revue de XVIII siècle* 1 (1913), 434–447; "La notion de vertu dans le Premier Discours de J.-J. Rousseau," *Mercure de France* 97 (June 1912), 532–555; G. R. Havens, "La théorie de la bonté naturelle de l'homme chez J.-J. Rousseau," *Revue d'histoire littéraire de la France* 31 (1924), 629–642, and 32 (1924), 212–225; J. Tresnon, "The Paradox of Rousseau," *PMLA* 43 (1928), 1010–1025; E. Cassirer, *The Question of Jean-Jacques Rousseau*, trans. and ed. P. Gay (New York, 1954), p. 104.

31. See M. B. Ellis, *Julie, or La nouvelle Héloïse: A Synthesis of Rousseau's Thought* (Toronto, 1949), p. 144.

32. *The Political Writings of Jean-Jacques Rousseau*, 2 vols. (Cambridge, 1962), I, 230; cf. J. H. Broome, *Rousseau: A Study of His Thought* (London, 1963), pp. 121–122; C. W. Hendel, *Jean-Jacques Rousseau, Moralist*, 2 vols. (London, 1934), I, 120; J. Maritain, *Trois réformateurs* (Paris, 1925); M. Bourguin, "Les deux tendances de Rousseau," *Revue d'histoire littéraire de la France* 49 (1949), 367.

33. N. Wilde, "The Development of Coleridge's Thought," *Philosophical Review* 28 (1919), 148; McFarland, *Coleridge and the Pantheist Tradition*, p. xxvi.

34. Cf. R. Grimsley, *Jean-Jacques Rousseau: A Study in Self-Awareness* (Cardiff, 1961), pp. 116–151; D. Mornet, *La nouvelle Héloïse de J.-J. Rousseau: Etude et analyse* (Paris, 1929); J. N. Shklar, *Men and Citizens: A Study of Rousseau's Social Theory* (Cambridge, 1969), pp. 57–74.

35. J. Starobinski, *Jean-Jacques Rousseau: La transparence et l'obstacle* (Paris, 1957).

36. H. C. Payne, *The Philosophes and the People* (New Haven, 1976), pp. 173–174.

37. Cf. marginalia on J. H. Green's copy of Kant's *Sammlung einiger* (British Library, C.45.a.9), p. 354: "This page is worth noticing as an instance of the false conclusions inevitable on the Logic of dichotomy: to the exchange of which for that of Trichotomy Kant owed his after-greatness."

38. *The Science of Right*, trans. W. Hastie (London, 1887), p. 118.

39. *The Friend*, i, 194.

40. On Kant and Rousseau, see G. Fester, *Rousseau und die Deutsche Geschichtsphilosophie* (Gottingen, 1927); E. Cassirer, *Rousseau, Kant, Goethe: Two Essays* (Princeton, 1945); M. J. Temmer, *Time in Rousseau and Kant* (Geneva, 1958); L. Duguit, *Jean Jacques Rousseau, Kant, and Hegel* (Paris, 1914); V. Delbos, "Rousseau et Kant," *Revue de métaphysique et de morale* 20 (1912), 429–439; L. Lévy-Bruhl, "De l'influence de J.-J. Rousseau en Allemagne," *Annales de l'Ecole Libre des Sciences Politiques* 2 (1887), 325–358.

41. *Science of Right*, p. 46.

42. Ibid., p. 47.

43. *Du contrat social*, bk. 1, chap. 2, in J.-J. Rousseau, *Oeuvre complètes*, ed. B. Gagnebin and M. Raymond, 3 vols. (Paris, 1959), III, 364.

44. *Kant's Perpetual Peace*, trans. H. O'Brien (London, 1927), p. 44. See C. E. Merriam, *History of the Theory of Sovereignty since Rousseau* (New York, 1900), pp. 47–48.

45. *Science of Right*, p. 257.

46. A. D. Snyder, "The Critical Principle of the Reconciliation of Opposites as Employed by Coleridge," in *Contributions to Rhetorical Theory*, ed. F. N. Scott,

(Ann Arbor, 1918), IX, 14; S. T. *Coleridge's Treatise on Method as Published in the Encyclopaedia Metropolitana,* ed. A. D. Snyder (London, 1934); see also C. Howard, *Coleridge's Idealism: A Study of Its Relationship to Kant and to the Cambridge Platonists* (Boston, 1924); H. L. Stewart, "The Place of Coleridge in English Theology," *Harvard Theological Review* 11 (January 1918), 27; H. P. Owen, "The Theology of Coleridge," *Critical Quarterly* (Spring 1962), 62; D. McKinnon, "Coleridge and Kant" in *Coleridge's Variety: Bicentenary Studies* ed. J. Beer (Cambridge, 1974).

47. *Coleridge on the Seventeenth Century,* ed. F. Brinkley (Durham, N.C., 1955), p. 197.

48. *The Life of John Sterling* (London, 1851), p. 60.

49. *The Philosophical Lectures of Samuel Taylor Coleridge,* ed. K. Coburn (London, 1949), pp. 245–246; cf. p. 264. Cf. H. Beeley, "The Political Thought of Coleridge," in *Coleridge Studies by Several Hands,* ed. E. Blunden and E. L. Griggs (London, 1934), pp. 169–172; Coleridge, *Collected Letters,* IV, 759.

50. Coleridge, *Philosophical Lectures,* lecture X, p. 306.

51. Ibid., lecture IX, p. 318.

52. Ibid., lecture VII, p. 245; cf. L. Werkmeister, "Coleridge on Science, Philosophy, and Poetry: Their Relation to Religion," *Harvard Theological Review* 52 (April 1959), 96.

53. Coleridge, *Philosophical Lectures,* lecture IX; cf. *Specimens of the Table Talk of the Late Samuel Taylor Coleridge,* ed. H. N. Coleridge, 2 vols. (London, 1835), II, 36–37; cf. *Confessions of an Inquiring Spirit,* ed. H. St. John Hart (London, 1956), esp. pp. 40–41, 79.

54. J. D. Boulger, *Coleridge as Religious Thinker* (New Haven, 1961), p. 105; A. O. Lovejoy, "Coleridge and Kant's Two Worlds," in *Essays in the History of Ideas,* 3d ed. (Baltimore, 1961), p. 271.

55. As in his recommendation that Shakespeare's history plays should be performed annually at Christmas to counteract "mock cosmopolitism"; *Shakespearean Criticism,* ed. T. Raysor, 2 vols. (Cambridge, Mass., 1930), I, 89. See also R. O. Preyer, "Bentham, Coleridge, and the Science of History," *Beitrage zur englischen Philologie* (Bochum-Langendreer, 1958), p. 19.

56. F. Schiller, *On the Aesthetic Education of Man: In a Series of Letters,* ed. E. M. Wilkinson and L. A. Willoughby (Oxford, 1967), pp. cliii–clvi.

57. The best discussion of the general issues here is in D. P. Calleo, *Coleridge and the Idea of the Modern State* (New Haven, 1966); see also J. Barrell, ed. *On The Constitution of the Church and State According to the Idea of Each* (London, 1972), pp. viii–xxxii.

5. Godwin, Helvétius, and Holbach

1. *A Picture of Christian Philosophy* (London, 1798), p.v.

2. See T. Green, *An Examination of the Leading Principle of the New System of Morals as That Principle Is Stated and Applied in Mr. Godwin's Enquiry Concerning Political Justice,* 2d ed. (London, 1799), p. 9; B. S. Allen, "The Reaction against William Godwin," *Modern Philology* 16 (1918), 225–243; P. H. Marshall, *William Godwin* (New Haven, 1984), pp. 98–103.

3. Cf. B. R. Pollin, *Education and Enlightenment in the Works of William Godwin* (New York, 1962), pp. 153–200, 200–221.

4. F. K. Brown, *The Life of William Godwin* (London, 1926), pp. 35–38; Marshall, *William Godwin*, pp. 195–205.

5. The influence of Helvétius and Holbach was recognized by contemporaries. See *The Monthly Magazine* 11 (January 20, 1802), 578; *The British Review* 7, no. 14 (1816), 376. Holbach was often confused with either Diderot or Mirabeau, both of whom had *Système de la nature* attributed to them. See also L. I. Bredvold, *The Brave New World of the Enlightenment* (Ann Arbor, 1961), p. 115; A. E. Hancock, *The French Revolution and the English Poets* (New York, 1899), p. 32; B. S. Allen, "Minor Disciples of Radicalism in the Revolutionary Era," *Modern Philosophy* 21 (1924), 278; C. K. Paul, *William Godwin: His Friends and His Contemporaries*, 2 vols. (London, 1876), I, 61.

6. Cf. E. J. Morley, ed., *H. C. Robinson on Books and Their Writers*, 3 vols. (London, 1938), I, 29.

7. W. Godwin, *Enquiry Concerning Political Justice and Its Influence on Morals and Happiness*, ed. F. E. L. Priestly, 3 vols. (Toronto, 1964), I, 228 (facsimile of 1798 edition).

8. *Political Justice*, I, 133.

9. Ibid., I, 81. Godwin's concept of virtue stressed motive as well as consequence. See I, 149, 309. On the relation between knowledge and feeling in Godwin's thought, see D. H. Monro, *Godwin's Moral Philosophy: An Interpretation of William Godwin* (Oxford, 1953), pp. 181–182.

10. *Political Justice*, II, 146.

11. Ibid., I, 400n.

12. Ibid., I, 386.

13. Ibid., I, 344.

14. *The Enquirer: Reflections on Education, Manners, and Literature* (London, 1797), essay 7, sec. 3, p. 281.

15. *Political Justice*, I, 433.

16. L. de la Roche, ed., *Oeuvres complètes d'Helvétius*, 14 vols. (Paris, 1795), vol. IV *De l'esprit* (1758; translated into English 1759), pp. 152–153. All passages quoted from this source are my own translation.

17. Cf. I. Cumming, *Helvétius: His Life and Place in the History of Educational Thought* (London, 1955), pp. 164–166; I. L. Horowitz, *Claude Helvétius: Philosopher of Democracy and Enlightenment* (New York, 1954), pp. 79–80; K. N. Momdjian, *La philosophie d'Helvétius* (Moscow, 1959); G. Richard, "Helvétius, précurseur de Marx," *Revue internationale de sociologie* nos. 7 and 8 (1927); on the question of the legislator, see J. Morley, *Diderot and the Encyclopaedists*, 2 vols. (London, 1878), I, 163; J. L. Talmon, *The Origins of Totalitarian Democracy* (London, 1952), pp. 28–37. On the issue of crime and penal reform and the links between Helvétius and Beccaria, see F. Venturi, *Utopia and Reform in the Enlightenment* (Cambridge, 1971), pp. 95–116; and *Italy and the Enlightenment: Studies in a Cosmopolitan Century*, trans. S. Corsi (London, 1972), pp. 23–24.

18. *Oeuvres complètes d'Helvétius*, XI, 110. From *De l'homme, de ses facultés intellectuelles, et de son éducation* (1772; translated into English 1777). Cf. *Pensées et réflexions*, CXII, vol. XIV, p. 152.

19. *Oeuvres complètes d'Helvétius*, III, 263.
20. Ibid., III, 134–136; cf. A. Keim, *Helvétius: Sa vie et son oeuvre* (Paris, 1907), p. 147.
21. *Oeuvres complètes d'Helvétius*, IV, 122–123; see also XIV, 130.
22. Ibid., IX, 64–65 *(De l'homme)*.
23. Ibid., II, 144–145 *(De l'esprit)*.
24. Ibid., II, 145–146.
25. D. W. Smith, *Helvétius: A Study in Persecution* (Oxford, 1965), p. 117.
26. Cf. E. C. Ladd, "Helvétius and Holbach," *Journal of the History of Ideas* 23 (April–June 1962), 222; L. Limentani, *La teorie psicologiche di Claudio Adriano Helvétius* (Verona, 1902), p. 126; see also E. Halévy, *The Growth of Philosophic Radicalism*, trans. M. Morris (London, 1949), pp. 192–242; J. B. Bury, *The Idea of Progress: An Inquiry into Its Origins and Growth* (London, 1932), pp. 165–170.
27. L. G. Crocker, *An Age of Crisis: Man and World in Eighteenth-Century French Thought* (Baltimore, 1959), p. 314.
28. N. S. Bergier, *Examen du matérialisme*, 2 vols. (Paris, 1771), II, 329–331; see R. R. Palmer, *Catholics and Unbelievers in Eighteenth-Century France* (Princeton, 1939), pp. 188–191; 214–218.
29. Cf. A. Lalande, "Quelques idées du Baron d'Holbach," *Revue philosophique de la France et de l'étranger* 33 (1892), 661.
30. K. Martin, *French Liberal Thought in the Eighteenth Century* (London, 1929; reprint, 1962), p. 174n. See also A. Kors, *D'Holbach's Coterie: An Enlightenment in Paris,* (Princeton, 1976).
31. V. W. Topazio, *D'Holbach's Moral Philosophy: Its Background and Development* (Geneva, 1956), p. 137.
32. *Système de la nature; ou, Les loix du monde physique et du monde moral*, 2 vols. (London, 1770), I, 69.
33. Ibid., I, 69.
34. Ibid., I, 82–83; see also p. 81.
35. Ibid., I, 185.
36. Ibid., I, 133.
37. *Système social; ou, Principes naturels de la morale et de la politique,* 3 vols. (London, 1773), I, 85.
38. *La morale universelle; ou, Le devoir de l'homme fondés sur sa nature,* 3 vols. (Paris, 1798; 1st ed., 1776), pp. 59–60. See Topazio, *D'Holbach's Moral Philosophy,* p. 138.
39. Although Holbach advocated sociability, he also emphasized the need for solitude and meditation. See H. Lion, "*La morale universelle* de d'Holbach," *Annales historiques de la révolution française* 1 (1924), 51.
40. *Système social*, II, 152.
41. Ibid., I, 175. Ambition is the active aspect of reputation; it mobilizes it within the calculus of private and public interests. See *Ethocratie; ou, Le gouvernement fondé sur la morale,* 3 vols. (Amsterdam, 1776), III, 133.
42. *Système social*, I, 152. This idea of a moral and material unity or coherence occurs frequently in Holbach. See P. Naville, *Paul Thiry d'Holbach et la philosophie scientifique au XVIIIe siècle* (Paris, 1943), p. 224.
43. *La morale universelle*, III, 236–237.

44. *Oeuvres complètes d'Helvétius*, II, 144–145.
45. There is, along with this, a primitivistic tendency in Holbach, most apparent in his *Politique naturelle*. See J. Delvaille, *Essai sur l'histoire de l'idée de progrès jusqu'à la fin de XVIIIe siècle* (Paris, 1910), p. 667. This conflicts, however, with his hatred of asceticism. Cf. *La morale universelle*, I, 243.
46. *Système social*, I, 150.
47. Ibid., I, 118.
48. Ibid., I, 119. Cf. also p. 211.
49. Ibid., I, 72–73.
50. *La morale universelle*, I, 61.
51. Ibid., I, 61.
52 *Système social*, I, 213.
53. Ibid., I, 157.
54. *Knave or Not? A Comedy in Five Acts* (London, 1798), advertisement.
55. See Sir W. Scott, *Edinburgh Review* 11 (April 1805), 182; J. Mackintosh, *Edinburgh Review* 25 (October 1815), 486.
56. *British Review* 11, no. 21, article 5 (1818), 378.
57. *The Edinburgh Magazine and Literary Miscellany* 2 (January 1818), 60; see also *The London Magazine* 2, no. 8 (August 1820), 163–169.
58. *Caleb Williams*, ed. D. McCracken (London, 1970), pp. vii–xxii; J. M. S. Tompkins, *The Popular Novel in England, 1770–1800* (London, 1932), p. 309; J. Meyer, *William Godwins Romane* (Leipzig, 1906); H. N. Brailsford, *Shelley, Godwin, and Their Circle* (Oxford, 1954); Marshall, *William Godwin*, pp. 144–154; P. Cruttwell, "On Caleb Williams," *Hudson Review* 11 (1958), XX, 87–95; J. T. Boulton, *The Language of Politics in the Age of Wilkes and Burke* (London, 1963), pp. 207–249; H. R. Steeves, *Before Jane Austen* (London, 1966), pp. 292–314.
59. W. Godwin, *Things as They Are; or, The Adventures of Caleb Williams*, 3d ed., 3 vols. (London, 1797), p.v.; *Caleb Williams*, ed. McCracken, p. 1.
60. The novel can be seen in contemporary political terms with Falkland as Burke, Tyrrel as Paine, and Williams as Holcroft. This was a common practice. See I. Ousby, " 'My Servant Caleb': Godwin's *Caleb Williams* and the Political Trials of the 1790s," *University of Toronto Quarterly* 44 (Fall 1974), 47–55.
61. See W. Hazlitt, *Complete Works*, ed. P. P. Howe, 21 vols. (London, 1930–1934), XVI, 404; and L. Stephen, *Studies of a Biographer*, 2d ser., 3 vols. (London, 1902), III, 147.
62. Godwin, *Caleb Williams*, I, 18–21; *Caleb Williams*, ed. McCracken, pp. 10–11. See E. Dowden, *The French Revolution and English Literature* (London, 1897), pp. 70–71.
63. Godwin, *Caleb Williams*, I, 36–37; *Caleb Williams*, ed. McCracken, pp. 15–16.
64. Godwin, *Caleb Williams*, I, 296–297; *Caleb Williams*, ed. McCracken, pp. 97–98.
65. Godwin, *Caleb Williams*, II, 94; *Caleb Williams*, ed. McCracken, p. 138.
66. H. Gross, "The Pursuer and the Pursued: A Study of *Caleb Williams*," *Texas Studies in Literature and Language* 1 (1959), 401–411; A. Wilson, "The Novels of William Godwin," *World Review* (June 1951), 37–40; D. Gilbert, "Things as They Were: The Original Ending of *Caleb Williams*," *Studies in English Literature* 6 (Summer 1966), 575–597; R. Storch, "Metaphors of Private Guilt and Social Rebellion in Godwin's *Caleb Williams*," *English Literary History* 34 (June

1967), 188–207; D. McCracken, "Godwin's Literary Theory: The Alliance between Fiction and Political Philosophy," *Philological Quarterly* 49 (January 1970), 113–133; R. Uphaus, "*Caleb Williams*: Godwin's Epoch of Mind," *Studies in the Novel* 9 (Fall 1977), 279–296; M. Butler, "Godwin, Burke, and *Caleb Williams*," *Essays in Criticism* 32 (1982), 237–257; R. Cronin, "Carps and *Caleb Williams*," *The Keats-Shelley Review* 1 (1986), 35–48. For general studies, see A. Gregory, *The French Revolution and the English Novel* (New York, 1915); D. Fleisher, *William Godwin; A Study in Liberalism* (London, 1951); A. E. Rodway, ed., *Godwin and the Age of Transition* (London, 1952); M. Butler, *Jane Austen and the War of Ideas* (Oxford, 1975); R. Kiely, *The Romantic Novel in England* (Cambridge, Mass., 1972); J. Clark, *The Philosophical Anarchism of William Godwin* (Princeton, 1977); D. Locke, *A Fantasy of Reason: The Life and Thought of William Godwin* (London, 1980); E. Rothstein, *Systems of Order and Inquiry in Later Eighteenth-Century Fiction* (Berkeley, 1975); J. de Palacio, *William Godwin et son monde intérieur* (Lille, 1980); W. Tysdahl, *William Godwin as Novelist* (London, 1981).

67. Godwin, *Caleb Williams*, II, 238; *Caleb Williams*, ed. McCracken, p. 187.

68. *The Theological and Miscellaneous Works of Joseph Priestley*, ed. J. T. Rutt, 25 vols. (London, 1817–1831), XXII, 386.

69. M. R. Adams, *Studies in the Literary Backgrounds of English Radicalism with Special Reference to the French Revolution* (Lancaster, Pa., 1947), p. 19; "William Godwin, Apostle of Universal Benevolence," *Times Literary Supplement* (April 4, 1936), 286; D. Bogue and J. Bennett, *History of the Protestant Dissenters*, 4 vols. (London, 1808), IV, 109–110; L. Whitney, *Primitivism and the Idea of Progress* (Baltimore, 1934), pp. 207–219. For further light on the Sandemanian sect, see *The Work of Mr. John Glas*, 2d ed., 5 vols. (Perth, 1782); Marshall, *William Godwin*, pp. 23–29; A. H. Lincoln, *Some Political and Social Ideas of English Dissent, 1763–1800* (London, 1938).

70. T. Holcroft, *Anna St. Ives*, ed. P. Faulkner (London, 1970), p. 30. On Holcroft, see also *The Adventures of Hugh Trevor*, ed. S. Deane (London, 1973), pp. vii–xiii; E. Colby, ed., *Life of Thomas Holcroft*, 2 vols. (London, 1925); C. B. A. Proper, *Social Elements in English Prose Fiction between 1700 and 1832* (Amsterdam, 1929), pp. 92–118; R. M. Baine, *Thomas Holcroft and the Revolutionary Novel* (Athens, Ga., 1965); V. R. Stallbaumer, "Holcroft's Influence on Political Justice," *Modern Language Quarterly* 14 (1953), 21–30.

71. *St. Leon: A Tale of the Sixteenth Century*, 4 vols. (Dublin, 1800), IV, 107.

72. *St. Leon*, preface, p. vii.

73. *Fleetwood; or, The New Man of Feeling*, rev. ed., 3 vols. (London, 1832), II, 141.

74. *Mandeville: A Tale of the Seventeenth Century in England*, 3 vols. (Edinburgh, 1817), II, 151.

75. Ibid., II, 143.

76. Ibid., I, 220; cf. I, 163.

77. Ibid., I, 288; cf. III, 18.

78. Ibid., I, 210–211.

79. See F. E. L. Priestley, "Platonism in William Godwin's *Political Justice*," *Modern Language Quarterly* 4 (1943), 63–69.

80. *Cloudesley: A Tale*, 3 vols. (London, 1833), pp. ix–x.

81. Ibid., pp. 208–209.

82. Ibid., pp. 210–211.
83. Ibid., p. 344.
84. *Deloraine*, 3 vols. (London, 1833), III, 216.
85. Ibid., III, 303. Cf. G. Sherburn, "Godwin's Later Novels," *Studies in Romanticism* 1 (Winter 1962), 71: "In only one of the novels after 1794 is the crucial act murder. In the others, errors so extremely cruel as to rival felonious crimes, induce agonies of remorse and expiation. In all five novels, there is much of what we may now call 'crime and punishment.' " See also A. Harvey, "The Nightmare of *Caleb Williams*," *Essays in Criticism* 26 (July 1976), 236–249.
86. *Thoughts on Man, His Nature, Productions, and Discoveries* (London, 1831), p. 224.
87. Ibid., p. 219.
88. Ibid., pp. 220–221.
89. Ibid., pp. 224–225.

6. Shelley, La Mettrie, and Cabanis

1. *The Complete Works of Percy Bysshe Shelley*, ed. R. Ingpen and W. E. Peck, 10 vols. (London, 1926; reprint 1965), V, 225–226, 264.
2. Cf. C. Woodring, *Politics in English Romantic Poetry* (Cambridge, Mass., 1970), pp. 33–47, 325; G. MacNeice, *Shelley and the Revolutionary Idea* (Cambridge, Mass., 1969), pp. 6–21; K. N. Cameron, *The Young Shelley* (London, 1951), pp. 150–151; A. M. D. Hughes, *The Nascent Mind of Shelley* (Oxford, 1947), pp. 221–230; P. M. S. Dawson, *The Unacknowledged Legislator: Shelley and Politics* (London, 1980). See also *The Letters of Percy Bysshe Shelley*, ed. F. L. Jones, 2 vols. (London, 1964), I, 504, in which he refers to "the master theme of the epoch in which we live—the French Revolution."
3. Preface to *Laon and Cythna*, later retitled *The Revolt of Islam*, in Shelley, *Complete Works*, I, 240–241; *The Complete Poetical Works of Percy Bysshe Shelley*, ed. N. Rogers, 4 vols. (Oxford, 1972–), II, 101–102.
4. Shelley, *Complete Works*, V, 12–13.
5. *The Poetical Works of Robert Southey*, 10 vols. (London, 1837–38), IV, bks. 10–12, esp. pp. 367, 392, 403.
6. C. Grabo, *The Magic Plant* (Chapel Hill, N.C., 1936), p. 166.
7. J. Barrell, *Shelley and the Thought of His Time: A Study in the History of Ideas* (New Haven, 1947), pp. 13–19; E. Barnard, *Shelley's Religion* (Minneapolis, 1937), pp. 15–16; J. Notopoulos, *The Platonism of Shelley* (Durham, N.C., 1947); N. Rogers, *Shelley at Work: A Critical Inquiry* (Oxford, 1956), pp. 27–33.
8. See L. Kellner, "Shelley's *Queen Mab* and Volney's *Les Ruines*," *Englische Studien* 22 (1896), 9–40; K. N. Cameron, "A Major Source of *The Revolt of Islam*," *PMLA* 56 (March 1941), 175–206; A. E. Hancock, *The French Revolution and the English Poets* (New York, 1899), pp. 55–56, and on Rousseau and Shelley, pp. 68–77. C. Frankel, in *The Faith of Reason: The Idea of Progress in the French Enlightenment* (New York, 1948), pp. 71–72, affirms the connection between Holbach and Volney.
9. Cameron, *The Young Shelley*, pp. 233–274; C. Grabo, *A Newton among Poets* (Chapel Hill, N.C., 1930), pp. 20–28; C. Baker, *Shelley's Major Poetry: The Fabric of a Vision* (Princeton, 1948), pp. 29, 273–274.

10. On Shelley and Godwin, see H. N. Brailsford, *Shelley, Godwin, and Their Circle*, 2d ed. (Oxford, 1954); A. E. Rodway, ed., *Godwin and the Age of Transition* (London, 1952); R. Holmes, *Shelley: The Pursuit* (London, 1974); *Shelley and His Circle, 1773–1822*, ed. K. N. Cameron and D. H. Reiman, 6 vols. (Cambridge, Mass., 1963–1973); K. N. Cameron, *Shelley: The Golden Years* (Cambridge, Mass., 1974); L. Stephen, "Godwin and Shelley," *Cornhill Magazine* 39 (March 1879), 281–302; P. Elsner, *Percy Bysshe Shelleys Abhangigkeit von William Godwins* Political Justice (Berlin, 1906); F. B. Evans III, "Shelley, Godwin, Hume, and the Doctrine of Necessity," *Studies in Philology* 37, no. 4. (October 1940), 632–640.

11. See I. J. Kapstein, "Shelley and Cabanis," *PMLA* 52 (1937), 238–243.

12. Although E. Wasserman, in *Shelley: A Critical Reading* (Baltimore, 1971), p. 261, seems to assume he had.

13. F. A. Lange, *The History of Materialism*, trans. E. C. Thomas, 3d ed. (London, 1925), pp. 49–123; J. L. Talmon, *The Origins of Totalitarian Democracy* (London, 1952), pp. 28–37. E. Halévy, in *The Growth of Philosophic Radicalism* (London, 1928), pp. 17–22, emphasizes the deep influence of Helvétius in England, while K. Martin, *French Liberal Thought in the Eighteenth Century*, ed. J. P. Mayer (London, 1962), pp. 172–174, stresses that of Holbach.

14. C. F. Volney, *The Ruins*, 2d ed. (London, 1795), p. 35.

15. Ibid., p. 16.

16. Ibid., p. 23.

17. See F. Venturi, *Europe des lumières* (Paris, 1971), pp. 131–142.

18. Sir W. Drummond, *Academical Questions* (London, 1805), p. 348.

19. Ibid., pp. 409–411.

20. "Immaturity," in *Prefaces by Bernard Shaw* (London, 1938), p. 664; cf. J. P. Guinn, *Shelley's Political Thought* (The Hague, 1969), pp. 120–125.

21. A. Vartanian, *La Mettrie's L'Homme Machine: A Study in the Origins of an Idea* (Princeton, 1960), pp. 14–15; and *Diderot and Descartes: A Study of Scientific Naturalism in the Enlightenment* (Princeton, 1953), pp. 214–215; L. C. Rosenfeld, *From Beast-Machine to Man-Machine: The Theme of Animal Soul in French Letters from Descartes to La Mettrie* (New York, 1941), pp. 141–146; A. Thomson, *Materialism and Society in the Mid-Eighteenth Century: La Mettrie's Discours préliminaire* (Geneva, 1981).

22. A. Cobban, *In Search of Humanity* (London, 1961), p. 117, describes the *De l'esprit* of Helvétius as "in effect La Mettrie's short pamphlets blown out to the size of three volumes and written in pompous turgidities, instead of the pithy epigrams of La Mettrie."

23. H. Dieckmann, *Le Philosophe: Texts and Interpretations* (St. Louis, 1948), pp. 68–103.

24. *Oeuvres philosophiques de La Mettrie*, 3 vols. (Berlin, 1796), II, 151.

25. Ibid., II, 151.

26. Ibid., II, 162.

27. Ibid., II, 164–165.

28. Ibid., II, 172.

29. Ibid., II, 174.

30. Ibid., II, 176.

31. Ibid., III, 172.

32. Ibid., II, 215.
33. Ibid., II, 181.
34. Ibid., III, 157–158.
35. *Letters of Percy Bysshe Shelley*, I, 342, 348n.
36. *Oeuvres philosophiques de Cabanis*, ed. C. Lehec and J. Cazeneuve (Paris, 1956), p. viii; see also A. Guillois, *Le salon de Madame Helvétius* (Paris, 1894), esp. the section beginning on p. 46.
37. Quoted in E. Cailliet, *La tradition littéraire des idéologues* (Philadelphia, 1943), p. 130.
38. *Théorie des sentimens agréables* (Geneva, 1747), p. 17.
39. Cabanis, *Oeuvres philosophiques*, Mémoires 1 and 8, pp. 160, 416. Unlike Shelley in this, he regards carnivores as superior to vegetarians.
40. Cabanis, *Oeuvres philosophiques*, Mémoire 10, p. 568; see also Mémoire I, p. 159. The existence of sympathy was believed to be borne out by medical theory and practice. See R. R. Male, Jr., "Shelley and the Doctrine of Sympathy," *University of Texas Studies in English* 29 (1950), 184. Adam Smith's *Theory of Moral Sentiments* (1759), translated into French in 1764 and 1774, is another possible source for Cabanis's ideas on sympathy. A later translation, by Mme. de Condorcet, the mistress of Fauriel, was published in 1798, followed by *Huit lettres sur la sympathie*. Cabanis refers to Smith's posthumous *Essays on Philosophical Subjects* (1795) in *La décade philosophique* of 30 Germinal, an VII (April 19, 1799). Shelley, however, shows no knowledge of Smith's writings. See also M. S. Staum, *Cabanis: Enlightenment and Medical Philosophy in the French Revolution* (Princeton, 1980).
41. On Shelley and Spinoza, see Hughes, *The Nascent Mind of Shelley*, pp. 241–243.
42. Cabanis, *Ouevres philosophiques*, Mémoire 6, p. 358.
43. All in *The Esdaile Notebook*, ed. K. N. Cameron (London, 1964), and Shelley, *Complete Poetical Works*, vol. 1.
44. Cf. E. Railo, *The Haunted Castle* (London, 1957), pp. 151–155, 191–217; E. Birkhead, *The Tale of Terror: A Study of the Gothic Romance* (New York, 1921); D. Punter *The Literature of Terror: A History of Gothic Fictions from 1765 to the Present Day* (London, 1980), pp. 61–130. See also the frequency of the incest theme in Shelley's reading, cited in D. King-Hele, *Shelley: His Thought and Work* (London, 1960), p. 136.
45. *The Esdaile Notebook*, p. 154; Shelley, *Complete Poetical Works*, I, 168.
46. Shelley, *Complete Works*, VI, 10.
47. Ibid., V, 20.
48. Ibid., V, 109, 130.
49. The most complete account of this aspect of Shelley is in J. Rieger, *The Mutiny Within: The Heresies of Percy Bysshe Shelley* (New York, 1967); for a general account, see M. Jacob, *The Radical Enlightenment: Pantheists, Freemasons, and Republicans* (London, 1981).
50. Shelley, *Complete Works*, V, 267.
51. Ibid., V, 263.
52. Ibid., V, 264.
53. Ibid., V, 264.
54. Ibid., VI, 295 *(Fragments on Reform)*.

55. Ibid., VI, 290.
56. Ibid., VI, 291.
57. *Laon and Cythna,* canto 11, p. viii, in Shelley, *Complete Works,* I, 391; Shelley, *Complete Poetical Works,* II, 247.
58. *Queen Mab,* VI, ll. 34–38, in Shelley, *Complete Works,* I, 106; Shelley, *Complete Poetical Works,* I, 269.
59. Shelley, *Complete Works,* I, 142; Shelley, *Complete Poetical Works,* I, 303.
60. *Queen Mab,* 9, l. 5, in Shelley, *Complete Works,* I, 127; Shelley, *Complete Poetical Works,* I, 288.
61. *Queen Mab,* 5, l. 147; ll. 161–166, in Shelley, *Complete Works,* I, 102; Shelley, *Complete Poetical Works,* I, 265.
62. *A Philosophical View of Reform,* in Shelley, *Complete Works,* VII, 43.
63. Shelley, *Complete Works,* VII, 42–43.
64. Cf. *Letters of Percy Bysshe Shelley,* I, 82 (to James Hogg, May 9, 1811): ". . . & I now *most perfectly* agree with you that political affairs are quite distinct from morality, that they cannot be united."
65. Shelley, *Complete Works,* VII, 75–76.
66. Ibid., VII, 64.
67. Ibid., VI, 196.
68. Ibid., VI, 194.
69. Drummond, *Academical Questions,* p. 20.
70. Shelley, *Complete Works,* VI, 201–202.
71. Cf. Wasserman, *Shelley,* pp. 131–153; S. Curran, *Shelley's Annus Mirabilis: The Maturing of an Epic Vision* (Princeton, 1975).
72. Shelley, *Complete Works,* VI, 163.
73. Ibid., II, 5.
74. Ibid., II, 14.
75. *Note on Prometheus Unbound,* in Shelley, *Complete Works,* II, 269.
76. *Speculations on Metaphysics,* in Shelley, *Complete Works,* VII, 65.
77. Shelley, *Complete Works,* VII, 118. Cf. the more typically Godwinian notion of disinterestedness expressed in *Proposals for an Association,* in Shelley, *Complete Works,* V, 263.
78. Shelley, *Complete Works,* II, 79 (I, ii, ll. 83–86).
79. Ibid., II, 71.
80. Rieger, *The Mutiny Within,* p. 125; Wasserman, *Shelley,* pp. 293–294.
81. Wasserman, *Shelley,* pp. 115–116.
82. Shelley, *Complete Works,* II, 148 (V, ii, l. 90).
83. Ibid., II, 147 (V, iii, ll. 78–86).
84. Ibid., II, 108 (III, i, ll. 207–210).
85. Ibid., II, 115 (III, ii, ll. 42–49).
86. Ibid., II, 135 (V, i, ll. 1–11).
87. Ibid., II, 138 (V, i, ll. 97–98; 101–103).
88. Ibid., II, 146 (V, ii, l. 32).
89. Ibid., II, 136 (V, i, ll. 30–33).
90. Ibid., II, 130 (IV, iv, ll. 46–52).
91. Ibid., I, 145.
92. Rieger, *The Mutiny Within,* p. 121, describes them as "halves of a single religious poem."

93. *Oeuvres posthumes de Fréderic II, roi de Prusse*, 15 vols. (Berlin, 1789), V, 111.
94. Shelley, *Complete Works*, III, 183.
95. Ibid., II, 221 (II, iv, l. 101).
96. Ibid., l. 110.
97. Ibid., ll. 119–120.
98. Ibid., II, 180 (I, i, ll. 34–36). Cf. L. J. Zillmann, ed., *Prometheus Unbound: A Variorum Edition* (Seattle, 1959), p. 99, where he acknowledges that morally based interpretations of the poem are the "most meaningful."
99. Shelley, *Complete Works*, II, 229 (III, ii, l. 73).
100. Ibid., II, 188 (I, i, ll. 286–291).
101. Ibid., l. 295.
102. Ibid., ll. 401–405.
103. Cf. C. E. Pulos, *The Deep Truth: A Study of Shelley's Scepticism*, 2d ed. (Lincoln, Neb., 1962); D. H. Rieman, *"The Triumph of Life": A Critical Study* (Urbana, Ill., 1965), p. 47; T. Webb, *Shelley: A Voice Not Understood* (London, 1977); L. Abbey, *Destroyer and Preserver: Shelley's Poetic Skepticism* (New York, 1979).

7. Hazlitt and the French

1. *The Complete Works of William Hazlitt*, ed. P. P. Howe, 21 vols. (London, 1930–1934), I, 24n.
2. See especially E. W. Schneider, *The Aesthetics of William Hazlitt: A Study of the Philosophical Basis of His Criticism* (Philadelphia, 1933, 1952); R. Park, *Hazlitt and the Spirit of the Age* (Oxford, 1971); D. Bromwich, *Hazlitt: The Mind of a Critic* (New York, 1983).
3. Although there is an important account of Hazlitt's political ideas in J. Kinnaird, *William Hazlitt: Critic of Power* (New York, 1978), see also W. P. Albrecht, *Hazlitt and the Creative Imagination* (Lawrence, Kans., 1965), pp. 29–62.
4. H. Baker, *William Hazlitt* (Cambridge, Mass., 1962), pp. 53–54. See also Hazlitt on the Dissenters in his essay 'On The Tendency of Sects,' in *The Round Table*, in Hazlitt, *Complete Works*, IV, 48–49n., and VII, 239–240.
5. Cf. Sir A. H. Lincoln, *Some Political and Social Ideas of English Dissent, 1763–1800* (Cambridge, 1938), pp. 18–30; F. Mineka, *The Dissidence of Dissent: The Monthly Repository, 1806–1838* (Durham, N.C., 1944), pp. 23–24; Bromwich, *Hazlitt*, pp. 5–8; A. Goodwin, *The Friends of Liberty: The English Democratic Movement in the Age of the French Revolution* (London, 1979), pp. 65–98.
6. P. Brown, *The French Revolution in English History* (London, 1918), pp. 22–27; S. Maccoby, *English Radicalism, 1786–1832* (London, 1955), pp. 22–27; E. Robinson, "The English 'Philosophes' and the French Revolution," *History Today* (February 1956), 117; "New Light on the Priestley Riots," *The Historical Journal* 3 (1960), 73–75; W. H. Chaloner, "Priestley, Wilkinson, and the French Revolution, 1789–1802," *Transactions of the Royal Historical Society* 8, 5th ser. (1959), 21–40.
7. See C. B. Cone, *The English Jacobins: Reformers in Late Eighteenth-Century England* (New York, 1968), p. 13. For a wider treatment of the general background, see E. Halévy, *History of the English People in the Nineteenth Century*, vol. I, *England in 1815* (London, 1924); E. P. Thompson, *The Making of the English*

Working-Class (London, 1964); G. S. Veitch, *The Genesis of Parliamentary Reform* (London, 1913; reprint 1965).

8. R. W. Davis, *Dissent in Politics, 1780–1813: The Political Life of William Smith, M. P.* (London, 1971), pp. 53–88.

9. On the combination of Utility with Dissent, see E. Halévy, *The Growth of Philosophic Radicalism* (London, 19   ), pp. 22–30. C. B. R. Kent, *The English Radicals: An Historical Sketch* (London, 1899), pp. 130–131; Park, *Hazlitt and the Spirit of the Age*, p. 74.

10. Henry Crabb Robinson was a hostile witness to Hazlitt's Jacobin reputation. See *On Books and Their Writers*, ed. E. J. Morley, 3 vols. (London, 1938), I, 386. On hearing of Hazlitt's death he wrote, "He was precisely the Jacobin so admirably described by Burke in his *Reflections*." Again, in 1854, "He, Hazlitt, is more truly described without a name by Burke as the literary Jacobin at the beginning of the *Reflections*" (II, 744). On Robinson and Hazlitt, see Bromwich, *Hazlitt*, pp. 263–264.

11. Hazlitt, *Complete Works*, IV, 379n.

12. Among many possibilities for comparison, see two articles in John Scott's *London Magazine*: "The Spirit of French Criticism and Voltaire's Notice of Shakespeare," 1 (January 1820), 126–129; and "French Pretensions," 6 (October 1822), 293–304.

13. Hazlitt, *Complete Works*, IV, 88.

14. Ibid., IV, 92–93.

15. Ibid., IV, 89n.

16. Ibid., IV, 91.

17. Ibid., I, 91.

18. Ibid., I, 127.

19. Cf. ibid., II, 123–254.

20. See Chapter 2.

21. Hazlitt, *Complete Works*, I, 147.

22. Ibid., I, 220, 229.

23. Ibid.

24. Hazlitt, *Complete Works*, II, 158–159.

25. See ibid., IV, 105n.; VII, 146; XIII, 50–52.

26. Ibid., IV, 24n.

27. Ibid.

28. Ibid., IV, 92.

29. Cf. ibid., XIII, 40: "Books alone teach us to judge of truth and good in the abstract: without a knowledge of things at a distance from us, we judge like savages or animals from our senses and appetites only; but by the aid of books and of an intercourse with the world of ideas, we are purified, raised, ennobled from savages into intellectual and rational beings."

30. Ibid., I, 24, 25n.; II, 158–159.

31. Cf. ibid., VII, 9: "Ah, John Bull! John Bull! thou are not what thou wert in the days of thy friend, Arbuthnot! Thou wert an honest fellow then: now thou are turned bully and coward." See also ibid., XIII, 49; compare these passages with William Cobbett's attack on the British government's war policy in *Eleven Lectures on the French and Belgian Revolutions and English Borough-mongering* (London, 1830), pp. 3–4.

32. Cf. H. Ben-Israel, *English Historians on the French Revolution* (Cambridge, 1968), pp. 7–10.
33. Hazlitt, *Complete Works*, XII, 193: "I place the heart in the centre of my moral system, and the senses and the understanding are its two extremities."
34. Cf. G. Schnockelborg, *Schlegels Einfluss auf Hazlitt als Shakespeare-Kritiker* (Münster, 1931).
35. Hazlitt, *Complete Works*, V, 161.
36. Ibid., VII, 181; cf. VII, 144.
37. Ibid., VII, 186–208.
38. Ibid., VII, 151.
39. Ibid., X, 281.
40. Ibid., X, 182.
41. J. Voisine, *J.-J. Rousseau en Angleterre à l'époque romantique: Les écrits autobiographiques et la légende* (Paris, 1956), pp. 345–424. See also the important articles in *Blackwood's Magazine*: 11 (February 1822), 138–139; 4 (November 1818), 156–157, 584; 5 (April 1819), 9, 13. The most important early works of travel literature of this kind were W. Coxe, *Sketches of the National, Civil, and Political State of Swisserland* (London, 1799); and J. E. Smith, *Sketch of a Tour on the Continent in the Years 1786 and 1787* (London, 1793).
42. Hazlitt, *Complete Works*, XI, 37.
43. Ibid., XIII, 92.
44. Ibid., XIV, 185.
45. Ibid., XI, 37.
46. Ibid., XVI, 121; cf. XVI, 138.
47. Ibid., XI, 68.
48. Ibid., XI, 71.
49. Ibid., XIII, 50.
50. Ibid., XX, 171.
51. Ibid., XVI, 89.
52. Ibid., VII, 319; XIII, 56.
53. Ibid., XIV, 197.
54. Ibid., VIII, 85.
55. Ibid., XIII, 55.
56. Ibid., XIII, x.
57. Ibid., I, 105–107.
58. Ibid., VII, 12; see also XIII, ix.
59. Although Hazlitt does see a similarity between the political philosophies of Hobbes and Rousseau; see ibid., II, 145.
60. Ibid., XIII, ix.
61. Ibid., XIII, 49.
62. Ibid., VII, 74.
63. Like Mme. de Staël, Hazlitt associated Protestantism with the rise of liberty in Europe (ibid., VII, 240) and admired Sismondi's ability, in his *Littérature du midi*, "to connect, in glowing terms, the rise or fall of letters with the political independence or debasement of the states in which they flourished or decayed" (ibid., XVI, 24).
64. Ibid., XI, 37. See J. J. Texte, *Jean-Jacques Rousseau and the Cosmopolitan Spirit in Literature*, trans. J. W. Matthews (London, 1899); T. J. Schlereth, *The Cos-*

mopolitan Ideal in Enlightenment Thought (South Bend, Ind., 1977); F. Venturi, *Italy and the Enlightenment: Studies in a Cosmopolitan Century*, trans. S. Corsi (London, 1972), pp. xix–xx.

65. Hazlitt, *Complete Works*, VII, 12.
66. See A. D. McKillop, "Local Attachment and Cosmopolitanism: The Eighteenth-Century Pattern," in *From Sensibility to Romanticism*, ed. F. W. Hilles and Harold Bloom (New York, 1965), pp. 191–218.
67. Hazlitt, *Complete Works*, VII, 67.
68. Ibid., IV, 67.
69. Ibid., XX, 167.
70. Ibid., XX, 317.
71. Ibid., XX, 324.
72. Cf. Woodring, *Politics in English Romantic Poetry* (Cambridge, Mass., 1969), pp. 42–43.
73. Cf. Hazlitt, *Complete Works*, XX, 162.
74. Ibid., I, 147–148.
75. Ibid., I, 128n.
76. Cf. R. Price, *A Review of the Principal Questions in Morals*, ed. D. D. Raphael (Oxford, 1968), pp. 40–56.
77. Hazlitt, *Complete Works*, XX, 61–62.
78. Cf. ibid., I, 23, 27. See also J. M. Bullitt, "Hazlitt and the Romantic Conception of the Imagination," *Philological Quarterly* 24 (1945), 343–361; J. D. O'Hara, "Hazlitt and the Functions of the Imagination," *PMLA* 81 (1966), 552–562; J.-C. Salle, "Hazlitt the Associationist," *Review of English Studies* 15 (1964), 38–51.
79. Hazlitt, *Complete Works*, I, 69, 70n.
80. Ibid., XX, 169.
81. On Hazlitt and Kant, see R. Wellek, *Immanuel Kant in England, 1793–1838* (Princeton, 1931), pp. 164–171; on Hazlitt's moral theory, see Park, *Hazlitt and the Spirit of the Age*, pp. 43–91.
82. Hazlitt, *Complete Works*, I, 50n.
83. Cf. ibid., II, 160, in which he describes Condillac's *Logic* "as the quintessence of slender thought and of the art of substituting words for things." See also I, 25–26n.
84. Ibid., X, 99.
85. Ibid., X, 166.
86. Ibid., XIII, 56.
87. Ibid., X, 138; see also X, 99.
88. Ibid., XIV, 316.
89. On Tracy, see ibid., XX, 170–171; on the Westminster Reformers, see XII, 183.
90. Ibid., XI, 47.
91. Ibid., XI, 100.
92. Cf. ibid., II, 197.
93. Ibid., IV, 120.
94. Ibid., XIX, 222.
95. Ibid., XIX, 302–320.
96. Ibid., XI, 11.

97. Ibid., XI, 13.
98. Ibid., XI, 16.
99. Ibid., XI, 24.
100. Ibid., XX, 343.

8. *English Dissent and the Philosophes*

1. See H. Perkins, *Origins of Modern English Society, 1780–1880* (London, 1969).
2. I. Parker, *Dissenting Academies in England* (Cambridge, 1914), pp. 103–108. Cf. R. Southey, *Essays, Moral and Political*, 2 vols. (London, 1832), II, 78–79: "It is well-known that the Socinian academy at Hackney was given up, notwithstanding the high character and learning of some of its conductors, because almost all the students pushed the principles in which they were educated further than their tutors. The dry-rot was in the foundation and the walls, as well as in the beams and rafters, and the unfortunate pupils came away believers in blind necessity and gross materialism—and in nothing else. The literary journals, at the commencement of the French Revolution, were in the hands of those dissenters, among whom this change during half a century had been taking place. The writers therefore were men in all stages of disbelief,—for everything was tolerated except orthodoxy."
3. A. H. Lincoln, *Some Political and Social Ideas of English Dissent, 1763–1800* (Cambridge, 1938), esp. the section beginning on p. 74.
4. *Memoirs of the Life of the Right Honourable Sir James Mackintosh*, ed. R. J. Mackintosh, 2 vols. (London, 1835), I, 350.
5. *The Theological and Miscellaneous Works of Joseph Priestley*, ed. J. T. Rutt, 25 vols. (London, 1817–1831), XXIV, 266–267; see F. T. H. Fletcher, "*L'Esprit des Lois* before Early British Opinion," *Revue de littérature comparée* 14 (1934), 538.
6. *Letters to the Inhabitants of Northumberland* (Philadelphia, 1801), in Priestley, *Works*, XXV, 107n., 131.
7. *An Essay on the First Principles of Government*, in Priestley, *Works*, XXII, 11.
8. Priestley, *Works*, XXII, 226; see also XXV, 131: "Mr. Stone is a person who, together with myself, earnestly wished for a reformation of abuses in English government, in order to prevent an entire revolution, which we did not think was wanted there. He now sees, or thinks he sees, that no such reformation is to be expected, and therefore wishes a revolution to take place, thinking it to be absolutely for the good of the people. I own that I am now inclined to his opinion."
9. Ibid., XXII, 237.
10. Cf. *Sermon Preached to Protestant Dissenters at Leeds* (1773), in Priestley, *Works*, XV, 26: "I trust, however, from a view of the present state of things, compared with the writings of the prophets . . . that the time is fast approaching when an end will be put to all antichristian tyranny."
11. *Letters to a Philosophical Unbeliever*, in Priestley, *Works*, IV, 336–423n.
12. Priestley, *Works*, XXI, 87–127.
13. Ibid., XXI, 133–134.
14. Cf. *Letters to Burke*, in Priestley, *Works*, XXIII, 152–153. Other Dissenters said the same sort of thing. See F. Stone, *An Examination of Burke's Reflections*

(London, 1792), p. 88; R. Woolsey, *Reflections upon Reflections* (London, 1790), pp. 3–4.

15. *The Present State of Europe Compared with Ancient Prophecies*, in Priestley, *Works*, XXV, 551.

16. R. Hall, *Modern Infidelity Considered with Respect to Its Influence on Society* (1799), in *Miscellaneous Works*, 6 vols. 2d ed. (London, 1832), IV, 25; see also his *Apology for the Freedom of the Press, and for General Liberty* (1793), in *Miscellaneous Works*, III, 172–173.

17. *The Interest of Great Britain Respecting the French War*, 5th ed. (London, 1793), p. 7; cf. W. Belsham, *Essays, Philosophical and Historical and Literary*, 2 vols. (London, 1789), I, 78.

18. W. Richards, *Reflections on French Atheism and on English Christianity* (London, 1794), pp. 23–24.

19. *Thoughts on the Impending Invasion of England* (London, 1794), p. 14.

20. *The Eclectic Review* 2, pt. 2 (July 1806), preface, p. iv.

21. G. Carnall, "The Monthly Magazine," *Review of English Studies* 5, new ser. (1954), 158–164.

22. *The Anti-Jacobin Review and Magazine* 1 (July 1798), 4; cf. W. Graham, *English Literary Periodicals* (London, 1955), p. 189.

23. J. W. Robberds, *A Memoir of the Life and Writings of the Late William Taylor of Norwich*, 2 vols. (London, 1843), I, 171. See Taylor's attack on the historian John Adolphus in *The Critical Review* 25 (1799), 368–369; he is also possibly the reviewer of Adolphus's *History of France* in *The Critical Review* 2, 3d ser., no. 4 (August 1804), 238. In his *Biographical Memoirs of the French Revolution*, 2 vols. (London, 1799), Adolphus quotes Barruel's *Memoirs* eight times, his *History of the Clergy* twice, and Robison's *Proofs of a Conspiracy* twice in the first volume. He attacks the philosophes directly in *Biographical Memoirs*, I, 296–309, and Paine in II, 288–327. Taylor is credited in the Robberds *Memoir* with two hundred articles for *The Monthly Review* between 1793 and 1799 and with sixty-one for *The Critical Review* between 1803 and 1804.

24. *The Monthly Review* 5 (1791), 93.

25. J. S. Harford, *Some Account of the Life, Death, and Principles of Thomas Paine*, 3d ed. (Bristol, 1820), p. 15.

26. B. Boothby, *Observations on the Appeal from the New to the Old Whigs and on Mr. Paine's Rights of Man* (London, 1792), pp. 273–274; *An Examination of Mr. Paine's Writings* (London, 1793), pt. 2, p. 131; J. P. Estlin, *Evidences of Revealed Religion* (Bristol, 1796), p. 10; C. E. Harrington, *The Republican Refuted* (London, 1791), p. 50. By contrast, some radical writers praised Paine's eloquence and attacked Burke's windy rhetoric. See J. Thelwall, *The Rights of Nature against the Usurpation of Establishments* (London, 1796), p. 99; J. Towers, *Thoughts on the Commencement of a New Parliament* (Dublin, 1791), p. 87; C. Macaulay, *Observations on the Reflections of the Right Honourable Edmund Burke* (Dublin, 1791), p. 60; W. Currie, *Memoirs of Dr. Currie*, 2 vols. (London, 1831), I, 523.

27. See Publicola [J. Q. Adams], *Observations on Paine's Rights of Man in a Series of Letters*, 3d ed. (Edinburgh, 1792), pp. 17–18; S. Drew, *Remarks on . . . the Age of Reason*, 2d ed. (St. Austle, 1820), p. x; J. St. John, *A Letter from a Magistrate to W. Rose on Mr. Paine's Rights of Man* (London, 1791), pp. 9, 14–15; J. Tytler, *An Answer to the Second Part of Paine's Age of Reason* (Edinburgh,

1797), pp. 2–3; F. Oldys [G. Chalmers], *The Life of Thomas Pain* [sic] . . . *with a Defence of His Writings*, 3d ed. (London, 1791), pp. 43, 125.

28. *The Autobiography of William Cobbett*, ed. W. Reitzel (London, 1947), p. 130.

29. H. H. Clark, "An Historical Interpretation of Thomas Paine's Religion," *University of California Chronicle* 25 (January 1933), 74; C. E. Merriam, Jr., "The Political Theories of Thomas Paine," *Political Science Quarterly* 14 (1899), 402; H. J. Laski, "A Valiant Pamphleteer," *Manchester Guardian Weekly* (February 5, 1937), 116.

30. For general accounts, see A. Aspinall, *Politics and the Press, 1780–1850* (London, 1949), pp. 1–35; R. K. Webb, *The British Working-Class Reader, 1790–1848* (London, 1955), pp. 14–47.

31. *The Complete Writings of Thomas Paine*, ed. P. S. Foner, 2 vols. (New York, 1945), I, 351, 358.

32. Ibid., I, 4.

33. Ibid., I, 357.

34. Ibid., I, 494.

35. Ibid., I, 600.

36. Ibid., I, 5; II, 603.

37. Ibid., I, 289, 291, 341, 364–365; II, 572.

38. Ibid., I, 6, 361, 506.

39. Cf. R. R. Palmer, "Tom Paine: Victim of the Rights of Man," *Pennsylvania Magazine of History and Biography* 66 (April 1942), 162.

40. Paine, *Complete Writings*, II, 241, 256.

41. Ibid., I, 299.

42. See A. O. Aldridge, *Man of Reason: The Life of Thomas Paine* (Philadelphia, 1959); H. H. Clark, "Thomas Paine's Relation to Voltaire and Rousseau," *Revue anglo-américaine* (April 1932), 305–318, and (June 1932), 393–405; V. E. Gibbens, "Tom Paine and the Idea of Progress," *Pennsylvania Magazine of History and Biography* 66 (April 1942), 204.

43. Cf. T. Crawford, *The Edinburgh Review and Romantic Poetry* (Wellington, New Zealand, 1955), p. 26; J. O. Hayden, *The Romantic Reviewers, 1802–1824* (London, 1969); on the *Edinburgh Review* and the philosophes, see especially J. Clive, *Scotch Reviewers: The Edinburgh Review, 1802–1815* (London, 1957), p. 97.

44. *Westminster Review* 1 (January 1824), 225.

45. Ibid., 2 (April 1824), 521–522; cf. 6 (July 1826), 67–68.

46. Ibid., 6 (July 1826), 251.

47. Ibid., 9 (April 1828), 263–264.

48. Ibid., 12 (January 1830), 262.

49. On Ireland, see M. Elliott, *Partners in Revolution: The United Irishmen and France* (New Haven, 1982).

50. See *The Complete Works of William Hazlitt*, ed. P. P. Howe, 21 vols. (London, 1930–1934), XIX, 302–320; XI, 11–16.

51. Ibid., XI, 24.

52. *The Prose Works of William Wordsworth*, ed. A. B. Grosart, 3 vols. (London, 1876), I, 12–13.

Index